MW00676553

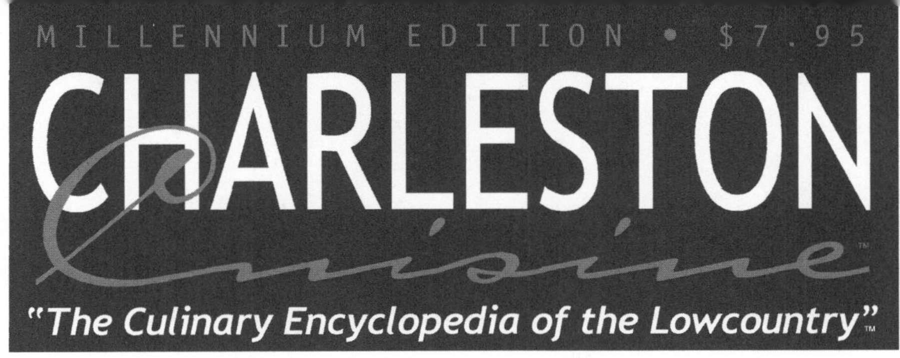

Cards

American Express® is a proud corporate sponsor of Charleston Cuisine

Member of the Greater Charleston Restaurant Association

This Book is Dedicated in the Memory of:
Richard A. Turley

Cover Photo
Photo by Ron Blunt, Courtesy of Drayton Hall/National Trust for Historic Preservation.

An accredited museum, Drayton Hall is nationally known for its exceptional guided house tour of the authentic plantation house. Built between 1738 and 1742. Drayton Hall is one of the finest examples of Georgian Palladian architecture in American and is the only plantation house on the Ashley River to survive the Revolutionary and Civil Wars. Admission includes the guided house tour, self-guided walks of the marsh and river, and an African American focus program. A National Trust historic site, Drayton Hall is open daily from 9:30 am until 4:00 pm, March to October, and until 3:00 pm, November to February. Museum Gift Shop. Handicapped accessible. Nine miles NW of downtown Charleston, 843-769-2600. www.draytonhall.org

READERS NOTE: All information is current at the time of publication. Restaurants reserve the right to change menus and prices. Participating restaurants encourage telephone inquiries to confirm information published in Charleston Cuisine.

PUBLISHED BY FEEDING FRENZY INC.
DBA CHARLESTON CUISINE
320 CLUB VIEW ROAD
SUMMERVILLE, SC 29485
(843) 851-1380

Publisher
Thomas A. Stumph

Graphic Design, Art Direction, and Production
Davis Designs

Cover Design
Rhino Design Group, Inc.

Cover Photography
John Ormond

Website Design
Quinn Shamblin and Shane Richard

Support Staff
Pam Stumph

Distribution
Feeding Frenzy, Inc.

Accounting
Daniel Murrill, Inc.

Legal Council
H.C. Prettyman, Jr.
Thomas L. Landwerlen

Special Thanks To
Diane Forrest, American Express Company; John Keener, Missy Walker and Kathy Britzius, The Greater Charleston Restaurant Association; Madison Toms, Jonathan Kenin, David Tosh of Charleston Place Hotel and Chef Bob Waggoner and his staff of Charleston Grill for a wonderful Chef's Party.

Special thanks to Ben-Arnold-Sunbelt Beverage Company for the beverages that were donated for the chefs party.

Cover Chefs:

Bottom Row, left to right: Massimiliano Sarrocchi (Il Cortile del Re), Philip Corr (Atlanticville), Kenny Pohlman (Maybanks Restaurant), Aimee R. Barrera and Keith Chinn (Woodlands Resort & Inn), Kerri McGill (Gilligan's Steamer & Raw Bar), Scott Kinney (Colony South Corporation), Wayne Simms (Gilligan's Steamer & Raw Bar), Arthur Godinez (Charleston Crab House), Mark Gibson (Barbadoes Room) **Second Row:** Enzo Steffenelli, Simon Andrews (Elliott's on the Square), Jason Scholz (High Cotton), Frank Lee (Slightly North of Broad), William Ratley (Poogan's Porch), Ginny Regopoulos (Reminisce), John Cuff (Rosebank Farms Café), Andrew Cook (Idlewild), Vito Palmietto (Portside Grille) **Third Row:** Trace Paradise (Privateer), Peter Stone (Ellis Creek Bistro), Rose Durden (Carolina's), Douglas Hepburn (Library at Vendue), Gay Slough (Gibson Cafe Restaurant), Mae Roberts (LaTasha's), Koji Kuzuhara (Sushi Kanpai). **Fourth Row:** Steve Stone (82 Queen), Jack Bogan (Blossom Cafe), Stephen Kish (82 Queen), Jeff Lanzaro (The Boathouse Restaurant), Robert Pinkney (LaTasha's). **Fifth Row:** Brian Dunn (A.W. Shucks), Billy Noisette (Bocci's), Stephanie Dean-Carr (Kaminsky's), Jeffery Mair (Starfish Grille), Molly Anderson (Kaminsky's), Herman McNeill (McNeill's of Summerville), Syd Stephens (McNeill's of Summerville), Kimberly Brock Brown (Charleston Place Hotel). **Sixth Row:** Robert Short and Dwayne Kieber (SpiritLine Dinner Cruise), Peter Thomason (Maybank's), Robert Dickson (Robert's of Charleston), John Hewson (Jasmine), Douglas Blair (Beaumont's). **Seventh Row:** John Olsson (Meritäge), Lance Howard (Locklear's), Jeffery Maddox and Edmond Floyd (Hyman's Seafood), George Odachowski and William Kistler (Red Sky Grill), Brian Hallam and Jeffery Gibbs (Charleston Chops). **Eighth Row:** Stephan Jordan and Brett McKee (Brett's Restaurant), Don Drake and Donald Barickman (Magnolias), Chad Campbell and Jassen Campbell (Geralyn's), Louis Osteen (Louis's Restaurant). **Ninth Row:** Bill Brodsky (Palmetto Cafe), Bob Waggoner (Charleston Grill), Kenneth Vedrinski (Woodlands Resort & Inn). **Top Row:** Bob Carter (Peninsula Grill).

Welcome to Charleston Cuisine, the Lowcountry's premiere dining guide.

I am delighted to bring to you the Millennium Edition of Charleston Cuisine. The enthusiasm for our publication in our city by the restaurants, the hotel industry and by you, our readers, has been extraordinary. It remains a thrill for this publisher to visit some of the finest restaurants in the Southeast and to sample first-hand the cuisine of the Lowcountry.

Charleston has become a dining destination unsurpassed by a city of its size in the United States. Having more restaurants per capita than any other city. Charleston certainly offers a variety of wonderful restaurants from which to choose. With our publishing partners, The American Express Company and The Greater Charleston Restaurant Association, we strive to provide you, the dining consumer, with every detail about each restaurant so that you may experience the culinary artistry Charleston has to offer.

New for 2000 is our website, Charlestoncuisine.com which will offer most of the information contained in our book in an electronic version. It will have features such as reservation capabilities, virtual restaurant tours, restaurant review feedback and an e-commerce section where the user can buy all types of food related items. Look for our national site which will feature top dining destinations in other cities at nationalcuisine.com.

The staff and I would like to thank the owners and chefs of Charleston's finest restaurants for making this an exciting city in which to dine. Thank you for allowing me to assist in your dining decisions and I wish you many enjoyable dining experiences.

Sincerely,

Tom Stumph

Thomas A. Stumph
Publisher

My most sincere gratitude to my wife Pam and my children, Nicole, Josh, Logan, and Nolan for allowing me more time away than the average husband and dad dares to steal. Also a special thanks to my parents, my sister, and my brother-in-law for being my guiding light.

Introduction

Restaurant Indexes 6

View Charleston's gourmet offerings at a glance. Our comprehensive Index section presents each restaurant's features according to area, types of cuisine, dining options, entertainment, special services, attire guidelines, reservation suggestions, payment options and more.

Area Maps 12

Restaurant Gallery 17

This special section presents beautiful photographs and illustrations highlighting the ambiance and cuisine of many of our fine dining establishments. Restaurants appearing in this section are also cross-referenced in the Menu section. Look for this symbol RG 16 in the upper corners of the Menu Listing section. It indicates the restaurant's presence and page number in the Restaurant Gallery.

Menu Listings 58

Our Menu Listing section provides useful insights into each restaurant's variety of dishes and their prices, availability of vegetarian and heart-smart meals, and late night dining. You will also find information regarding hours of operation, attire suggestions, entertainment options and more.

Recipes 145

Re-create your favorites at home! We have specialties from the Lowcountry's top chefs broken down into Appetizers, Soups, Salads, Vegetable Dishes, Pastas, Meat and Poultry Entrees, Seafood Entrees and Desserts.

Recipe Index 144

Glossary 172

From abalone to zuppa inglese, definitions of culinary terms to enhance your knowledge of the universal language of Fine Dining.

Wine Glossary 179

As an additional interest, we've added this resource to help you better understand the terminology of wines.

Restaurant Indexes

			PAGE #'S		MEALS SERVED						DINING INFO.								ENT.		
RESTAURANT	**LOCATION**	**PHONE**	Menu Listing	Restaurant Gallery	Breakfast	Lunch	Dinner	Sunday Brunch	Twilight Dinner	Late Night Dining	Terrace/Patio Dining	Heart Smart Meals	Vegetarian Meals	Take Out Meals	Seasonal Menus	Children's Menu	Extensive Wine Menu	Other	Lounge/Bar	Live Entertainment	Dancing
82 Queen	Charleston	(843) 723–7591	58	18		•	•	•	•		•	•					•		•		
Anson	Charleston	(843) 577-0551	60	19			•				•		•	•	•	•	•				
Atlanticville Restaurant & Cafe	Sullivan's Island	(843) 883-9452	61			•	•	•	•	•	•		•	•	•	•	•			•	
A.W. Shuck's Restaurant & Bar	Charleston	(843) 723-1151	62	20		•	•				•					•				•	
Barbadoes Room Restaurant	Charleston	(843) 577-2400	63		•	•	•	•			•	•	•	•	•	•			•	•	
Beaumont's Cafe & Bar	Charleston	(843) 577-5500	64	21		•	•	•			•				•		•			•	
Blossom Cafe	Charleston	(843) 722-9200	65	22		•	•	•		•	•		•				•		•		
Boathouse Restaurants	Mult. Locations	see menu page	66	23			•				•	•	•	•	•	•	•		•	•	
Bocci's Italian Restaurant	Charleston	(843) 720-2121	68	24		•	•					•	•	•		•	•				
Brett's Restaurant	Charleston	(843) 795-9964	69	IBC		•	•	•				•	•	•	•		•				
Bull & Finch Restaurant & Pub	Mt. Pleasant	(843) 884-6455	70			•	•			•	•								•		
Café St. Tropez	Seabrook Island	(843) 768-1500	71	25			•				•		•		•		•		•		
California Dreaming	Charleston	(843) 766-1644	72	26		•	•							•		•			•		
Carolina's	Charleston	(843) 724-3800	73	IFC			•					•	•	•		•	•				
Charleston Chops	Charleston	(843) 937-9300	74	27			•										•		•	•	
Charleston Crab House	Mult. Locations	see menu page	78	28		•	•				•	•	•	•		•					
Charleston Grill	Charleston	(843) 577-4522	76	29			•						•		•		•		•	•	
Easterby's Family Grille	Mult. Locations	see menu page	79			•	•												•		
Elliott's on the Square	Charleston	(843) 724-8888	80		•	•	•								•						
Ellis Creek Bistro	Charleston	(843) 795-3838	81				•						•	•	•		•		•		
Garibaldi Cafe	Charleston	(843) 723-7153	82				•				•		•	•	•	•	•				
Gennaro's Italian Ristorante	North Charleston	(843) 760-9875	83				•									•	•		•	•	
Geralyn's	Mt. Pleasant	(843) 881-8981	84	30		•	•			•	•			•	•	•				•	
Gibson Cafe Restaurant	Sullivan's Island	(843) 883-3536	85			•	•				•		•	•	•				•		
Gilligan's Steamer & Raw Bar	Mult. Locations	see menu page	86	31		•	•				•	•		•		•			•	•	
Hank's Seafood Restaurant	Charleston	(843) 723-3474	92	32			•								•	•	•				
High Cotton	Charleston	(843) 724-3815	88				•										•		•		
Hyman's Seafood Co.	Charleston	(843) 723-6000	90			•	•		•			•		•	•	•	•		•		
Idlewild	Mt. Pleasant	(843) 881-4511	93	33		•	•						•	•	•	•	•				
Il Cortile del Re	Charleston	(843) 853-1888	94				•				•		•		•		•				
Il Pescatore	Mt. Pleasant	(843) 971-3931	95				•					•	•			•	•		•		
J. Bistro	Mt. Pleasant	(843) 971-7778	96	34			•	•					•	•	•	•	•				
Jasmine Restaurant	Charleston	(843) 853-0006	97			•	•										•				
John's On The Market	Charleston	(843) 534-1234	98	35	•	•	•	•		•	•	•	•	•	•	•	•		•	•	

ADD. SERVICES						ATTIRE					RESERVATIONS					SMOKING				PAYMENT							
Full Service Catering	Private Parties	Private Rooms	Banquet Facilities	Meeting Facilities	Lodging	Casual	Resort Casual	Jacket Required	Semi Formal	Formal	Not Taken	Not Required	Suggested	Required	Valet Parking	Not Permitted	Smoking Section/Area	Cigar or Pipe Friendly	Handicap Facilities	**American Express**	Visa	Master Card	Discover Card	Diners Club Card	Carte Blanche	Checks Accepted	**CUISINE**
	•	•	•				•						•				•	•	•	•	•	•	•				Lowcountry
	•	•					•						•			•			•	•	•	•	•	•			Lowcountry, Seafood, Southern
•	•	•		•		•						•					•	•	•	•	•	•				•	Thai, Continental, Seafood
	•					•	•				•	•					•		•	•	•	•	•	•		•	Seafood
•	•	•	•	•	•	•							•				•	•	•	•	•	•	•				Continental
	•					•							•				•	•	•	•	•	•	•	•		•	Classic, French, Mediterranean
		•				•							•				•			•	•	•		•		•	Contemporary American
						•	•						•		•		•		•	•	•	•				•	Lowcountry, Seafood, Steak
						•						•	•				•	•	•	•	•	•	•	•		•	Italian
•	•	•					•						•				•		•	•	•	•				•	Northern Italian, American
	•	•	•				•					•					•		•	•	•	•	•				English Pub
	•					•							•				•		•	•	•	•		•			Contemp., Continental, Mediter.
						•						•					•			•	•	•	•				American
•	•						•						•				•		•	•	•	•	•	•			Contemporary, Eclectic
	•						•						•				•		•	•	•	•	•	•			American, Steak House, Eclectic
	•	•	•	•		•											•		•	•	•	•	•				Lowcountry, Seafood, Southern
	•	•			•				•					•	•		•		•	•	•	•	•	•	•		Contemporary Lowcountry
•	•	•		•		•						•					•		•	•	•	•	•	•		•	American, BBQ, Seafood/Steak
•	•					•						•	•		•		•		•	•	•	•	•	•			American, Contemporary
	•					•						•	•			•			•	•	•	•				•	American, Contemporary
	•					•											•			•	•	•					Italian, Seafood
			•			•							•						•	•	•	•		•		•	Continental, Italian
	•					•						•					•		•	•	•	•				•	American, Lowcountry, Southern
•	•					•							•				•		•		•	•	•			•	American, French, Seafood
•	•	•				•						•					•		•	•	•	•	•				Seafood, American
							•							•			•		•	•	•	•	•	•			American Seafood
•	•		•			•							•		•		•		•	•	•	•	•	•			American
			•			•					•						•		•	•	•	•	•				Cajun, Deli, Seafood
						•						•					•		•	•	•	•	•			•	Southern, New American
	•	•				•							•								•	•				•	Italian
•	•						•						•			•				•	•	•	•			•	Southern/Northern Italian
•							•					•			•		•			•	•	•				•	New American
							•						•				•		•	•	•	•					Progressive American, Seafood
•	•	•	•				•					•					•			•	•	•	•	•			Lowcountry,Seafood Steakhouse

Restaurant Indexes

			PAGE #'S		MEALS SERVED						DINING INFO.								ENT.		
RESTAURANT	LOCATION	PHONE	Menu Listing	Restaurant Gallery	Breakfast	Lunch	Dinner	Sunday Brunch	Twilight Dinners	Late Night Dining	Terrace/Patio Dining	Heart Smart Meals	Vegetarian Meals	Take Out Meals	Seasonal Menus	Children's Menu	Extensive Wine Menu	Other	Lounge/Bar	Live Entertainment	Dancing
Kaminsky's Most Excellent Cafe	Charleston	(843) 853-8270	99	36		•	•		•	•	•			•		•	•	•		•	•
LaTasha's Taste of New Orleans	Charleston	(843) 723-3222	100			•	•						•			•					
Library at Vendue	Charleston	(843) 577-7970	101	37		•	•				•	•	•	•	•		•		•	•	
Locklear's	Mult. Location	see menu page	102	38		•	•					•		•		•					
Louis's Restaurant & Bar	Charleston	(843) 853-2550	104				•			•					•		•				
Magnolias Uptown/Down South	Charleston	(843) 577-7771	105	22		•	•			•			•				•		•		
Maybank's Restaurant	James Island	(843) 795-2125	106				•						•				•	•			
McNeill's of Summerville	Summerville	(843) 832-0912	107			•	•					•	•	•	•	•	•		•		
Meritäge	Charleston	(843) 723-8181	108	39			•				•	•	•	•	•		•	•	•	•	
North Towne/Old Towne	Mult. Locations	see menu page	110			•	•					•	•	•	•	•	•		•		
Palmetto Café	Charleston	(843) 722-4900	112	40	•	•	•	•			•		•	•	•	•	•		•	•	
Peninsula Grill	Charleston	(843) 723-0700	109				•				•						•		•		
Poogan's Porch	Charleston	(843) 577-2337	116	41		•	•	•			•		•		•	•	•				
Privateer Seafood Restaurant	Seabrook Island	(843) 768-1290	114				•		•			•	•	•	•	•	•		•		
Red Sky Grill	Seabrook Island	(843) 768-0183	117			•	•							•		•			•		
Reminisce	Summerville	(843) 821-4388	118	42		•	•	•			•	•	•	•	•	•	•				
Robert's of Charleston	Charleston	(843) 577-7565	119				•											•		•	
Rosebank Farms Café	Seabrook Island	(843) 768-1807	121			•	•				•		•		•		•		•		
Saracen	Charleston	(843) 723-6242	122	43			•								•		•		•		
Seafare Seafood Buffet	North Charleston	(843) 566-7840	123	44		•	•							•		•			•	•	
Sermet's Corner	Charleston	(843) 853-7775	124			•	•						•	•		•	•			•	
Slightly North of Broad	Charleston	(843) 723-3424	127			•	•								•						
Slightly Up The Creek	Mt. Pleasant	(843) 884-5005	125				•				•				•						
Southend Brewery	Charleston	(843) 853-4677	128	45		•	•							•		•			•		
SpiritLine Dinner Cruise	Charleston	(843) 722-2628	129	46			•						•		•				•		•
Starfish Grille	Folly Beach	(843) 588-2518	131			•	•	•			•	•	•	•		•			•		
Sticky Fingers Restaurant & Bar	Multi. Locations	see menu page	132	47		•	•				•			•	•	•			•		
Stono Cafe	James Island	(843) 762-4478	133	48		•	•	•			•		•	•	•	•	•		•		
Sushi Kanpai	Charleston	(843) 723-7800	134	49		•	•						•	•							
TBONZ Gill & Grill	Mult. Locations	see menu page	135	50		•	•			•	•		•	•		•					
Tommy Condon's	Charleston	(843) 577-3818	136	51		•	•				•			•		•				•	
Vickery's Bar & Grill	Mult. Locations	see menu page	138	52		•	•	•		•	•	•				•	•		•		
Wild Wing Cafe	Charleston	(843) 722-WING	139	53		•	•			•	•	•	•	•	•	•			•	•	
Woodlands Dining Room	Summerville	(843) 875-2600	141	BC	•	•	•				•		•		•		•		•	•	

ADD. SERVICES						ATTIRE					RESERVATIONS					SMOKING				PAYMENT							
Full Service Catering	Private Parties	Private Rooms	Banquet Facilities	Meeting Facilities	Lodging	Casual	Resort Casual	Jacket Required	Semi Formal	Formal	Not Taken	Not Required	Suggested	Required	Valet Parking	Not Permitted	Smoking Section/Area	Cigar or Pipe Friendly	Handicap Facilities	**American Express**	Visa	Master Card	Discover Card	Diners Club Card	Carte Blanche	Checks Accepted	**CUISINE**
	•					•						•					•	•	•	•	•	•				•	Dessert & Coffee
•						•															•	•	•	•	•	•	Cajun/Creole, Seafood
•	•	•	•	•	•		•		•				•		•	•			•	•	•	•	•	•			Eclectic, Lowcountry, Amer.
•	•					•							•				•		•	•	•	•	•				American, Lowcountry
	•	•		•		•							•		•		•	•	•	•	•	•	•	•			Southern
	•	•					•						•				•			•	•	•	•			•	New Southern, Contemporary
	•						•						•				•		•	•	•	•				•	American, French, Southern
•	•					•							•				•		•	•	•	•				•	American, Internat., Italian
	•	•				•					•						•		•	•	•	•		•			International Tapas
•	•	•	•	•		•						•					•			•	•	•	•	•		•	American, Greek, Seafood
	•					•							•		•		•		•	•	•	•	•				Contemporary, American
	•	•	•	•	•				•				•				•		•	•	•	•	•	•		•	American, Southern Regional
•	•	•	•			•	•						•							•	•	•					Lowcountry, Seafood, Southern
•	•	•	•	•			•						•				•	•	•	•	•	•	•	•			Seafood, Steak, Pasta
						•							•				•		•	•	•	•					American, Eclectic
•	•	•	•	•		•							•				•		•	•	•	•	•			•	Continental, French, Internat.
	•					•								•						•	•	•					Continental
							•				•						•		•	•	•	•	•	•		•	Lowcountry, Southern
	•	•				•							•				•			•	•	•		•			Contemporary, Eclectic
	•					•						•					•		•	•	•	•	•	•		•	American, Seafood, Lowcountry
						•						•					•		•	•	•	•				•	Eclectic
						•					•					•			•	•	•	•	•	•			Southern
•	•					•							•			•			•	•	•	•	•	•			Seafood
	•		•			•						•					•	•		•	•	•	•			•	American, Microbrewery
	•	•	•				•							•			•		•	•	•	•	•			•	American Southern, Lowcountry
						•						•					•		•	•	•	•	•	•		•	Eclectic, Seafood
•	•	•	•			•						•					•		•	•	•	•	•	•	•		Rib House
•	•					•						•					•		•	•	•	•				•	Lowcountry, Seafood, Southern
						•							•			•			•	•	•	•					Japanese, Seafood, Sushi
•	•		•	•		•						•					•		•	•	•	•				•	American, Steak House
•	•	•	•	•		•						•					•	•	•	•	•	•	•	•	•	•	Irish, Seafood
						•						•			•		•		•	•	•	•	•				American, Cuban
•						•					•				•		•		•	•	•	•	•				American, BBQ, Mexican
•	•	•	•	•	•								•		•		•	•	•	•	•	•	•	•	•	•	Amer., Contemporary, Asian

BY CUISINE

Southern

Sports Bar

Steak House

BY LOCATION

Charleston

Folly Beach

Isle of Palms

James Island

John's Island

Ladson

Mt. Pleasant

North Charleston

Seabrook Island

Sullivan's Island

Summerville

West Ashley

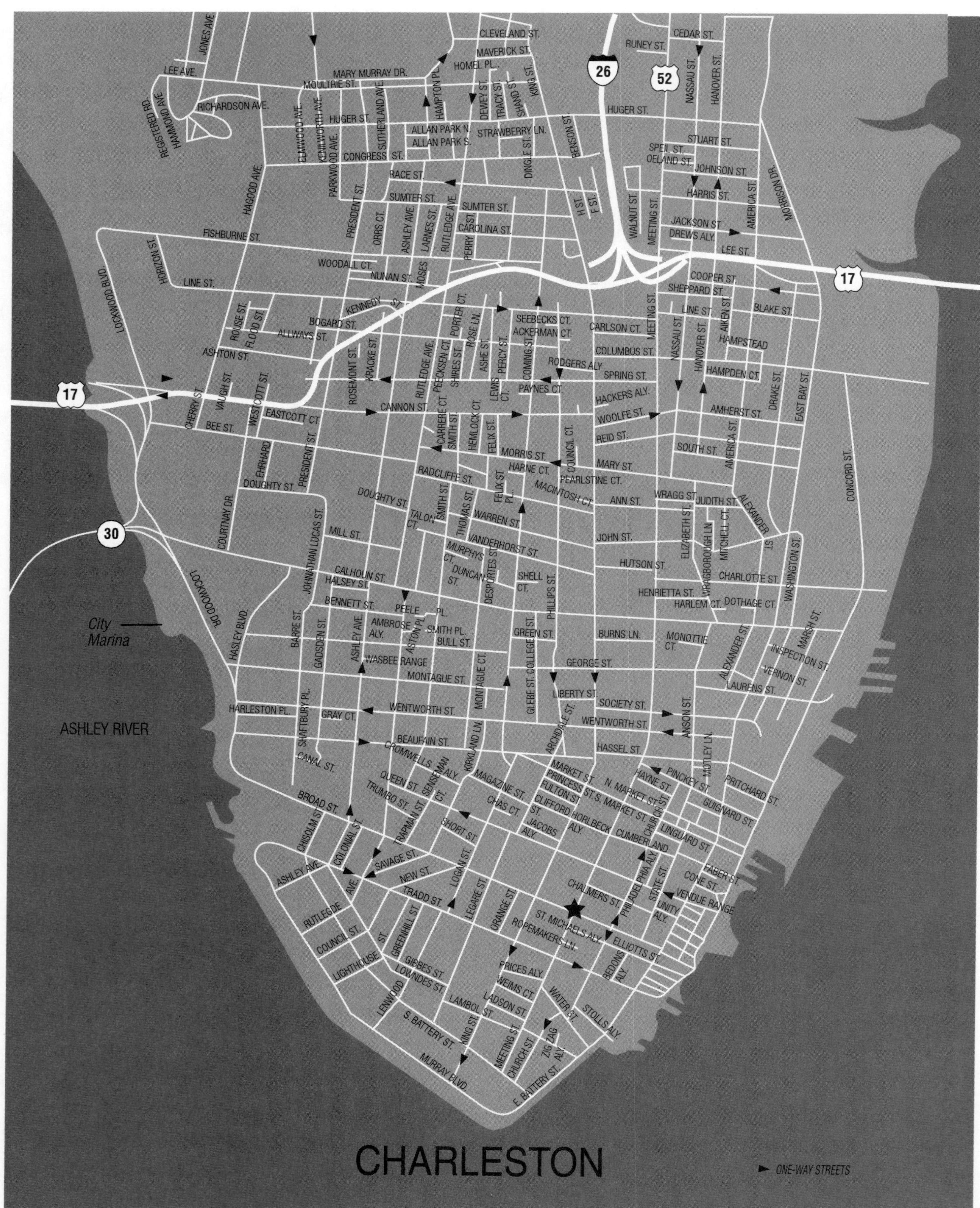
CLEVELAND ST.
CEDAR ST.
JONES AVE.
MAVERICK ST.
RUNEY ST.
HOMEL PL.
LEE AVE.
MARY MURRAY DR.
26
52
MOULTRIE ST.
NASSAU ST.
HANOVER ST.
KING ST.
SHAND ST.
TRACY ST.
DEWEY ST.
HAMPTON PL.
RICHARDSON AVE.
REGISTERED RD.
HAMMOND AVE.
ELMWOOD AVE.
KENILWORTH AVE.
SUTHERLAND AVE.
HUGER ST.
PARKWOOD AVE.
ALLAN PARK N.
ALLAN PARK S.
STRAWBERRY LN.
BENSON ST.
HUGER ST.
STUART ST.
SPEIL ST.
OELAND ST.
JOHNSON ST.
CONGRESS ST.
DINGLE ST.
HAGOOD AVE.
RACE ST.
PRESIDENT ST.
HARRIS ST.
AMERICA ST.
MORRISON DR.
SUMTER ST.
SUMTER ST.
H ST.
F ST.
WALNUT ST.
MEETING ST.
ORRS CT.
ASHLEY AVE.
LARNES ST.
RUTLEDGE AVE.
CAROLINA ST.
JACKSON ST.
DREWS ALY.
FISHBURNE ST.
PERRY ST.
LEE ST.
HORIZON ST.
WOODALL CT.
NUNAN ST.
MOSES
17
COOPER ST.
SHEPPARD ST.
LINE ST.
LOCKWOOD BLVD.
KENNEDY ST.
PORTER CT.
LINE ST.
AIKEN ST.
BLAKE ST.
ROUSE ST.
FLOOD ST.
BOGARD ST.
SEEBECKS CT.
ACKERMAN CT.
CARLSON CT.
MEETING ST.
NASSAU ST.
HANOVER ST.
HAMPSTEAD
ALLWAYS ST.
ROSE LN.
ASHE ST.
PERCY ST.
COLUMBUS ST.
ASHTON ST.
ROSEMONT ST.
KRACKE ST.
RUTLEDGE AVE.
PEECKSEN CT.
SHIRES ST.
COMING ST.
RODGERS ALY.
SPRING ST.
HAMPDEN CT.
DRAKE ST.
EAST BAY ST.
17
CHERRY ST.
VAUGH ST.
WESTCOTT ST.
LEWIS CT.
PAYNES CT.
HACKERS ALY.
CANNON ST.
AMHERST ST.
EASTCOTT CT.
CARRERE CT.
SMITH ST.
HEMLOCK CT.
WOOLFE ST.
BEE ST.
FELIX ST.
COUNCIL CT.
REID ST.
AMERICA ST.
SOUTH ST.
EHRHARD
PRESIDENT ST.
MORRIS ST.
MARY ST.
CONCORD ST.
HARNE CT.
PEARLSTINE CT.
RADCLIFFE ST.
DOUGHTY ST.
MACINTOSH CT.
FELIX ST. PL.
WRAGG ST.
JUDITH ST.
ALEXANDER ST.
ANN ST.
DOUGHTY ST.
SMITH ST.
THOMAS ST.
TALON CT.
WARREN ST.
30
COURTNAY DR.
JOHNATHAN LUCAS ST.
MILL ST.
ELIZABETH ST.
WRAGBOROUGH LN.
MITCHELL CT.
JOHN ST.
WASHINGTON ST.
VANDERHORST ST.
MURPHYS CT.
HUTSON ST.
LOCKWOOD DR.
CALHOUN ST.
DUNCAN ST.
DESPORTES ST.
SHELL CT.
CHARLOTTE ST.
HALSEY ST.
PHILLIPS ST.
HENRIETTA ST.
BENNETT ST.
HARLEM CT.
DOTHAGE CT.
PEELE PL.
City Marina
HASLEY BLVD.
BARRE ST.
GADSDEN ST.
ASHLEY AVE.
AMBROSE ALY.
ASTON PL.
SMITH PL.
BULL ST.
GREEN ST.
BURNS LN.
MONOTTIE CT.
MARSH ST.
INSPECTION ST.
WASBEE RANGE
COLLEGE ST.
GLEBE ST.
GEORGE ST.
ALEXANDER ST.
VERNON ST.
MONTAGUE ST.
MONTAGUE CT.
LAURENS ST.
LIBERTY ST.
SOCIETY ST.
HARLESTON PL.
SHAFTBURY PL.
GRAY CT.
WENTWORTH ST.
WENTWORTH ST.
ANSON ST.
ASHLEY RIVER
BEAUFAIN ST.
ARCHDALE ST.
HASSEL ST.
MOTLEY LN.
CANAL ST.
CROMWELLS ALY.
KIRKLAND LN.
SENSEMAN CT.
MARKET ST.
N. MARKET ST.
HAYNE ST.
PINCKNEY ST.
PRITCHARD ST.
QUEEN ST.
MAGAZINE ST.
PRINCESS ST.
S. MARKET ST.
TRUMBO ST.
FULTON ST.
CHURCH ST.
GUIGNARD ST.
BROAD ST.
CHAS CT.
CLIFFORD ST.
HORLBECK ALY.
TRAPMAN ST.
JACOBS ALY.
LINGUARD ST.
CHISOLM ST.
COLONIAL ST.
SHORT ST.
CUMBERLAND
PHILADELPHIA ALY.
FABER ST.
SAVAGE ST.
LOGAN ST.
ASHLEY AVE.
NEW ST.
COLONIAL AVE.
STATE ST.
CONE ST.
CHALMERS ST.
VENDUE RANGE
TRADD ST.
LEGARE ST.
ORANGE ST.
RUTLEGDE
UNITY ALY.
ST. MICHAELS ALY.
COUNCIL ST.
GREENHILL ST.
ROPEMAKERS LN.
ELLIOTTS ST.
LIGHTHOUSE ST.
GIBBES ST.
PRICES ALY.
BEDONS ALY.
LOWNDES ST.
WEIMS CT.
WATER ST.
LENWOOD
LADSON ST.
LAMBOL ST.
STOLLS ALY.
S. BATTERY ST.
KING ST.
MEETING ST.
CHURCH ST.
ZIG ZAG ALY.
MURRAY BLVD.
E. BATTERY ST.
CHARLESTON
ONE-WAY STREETS

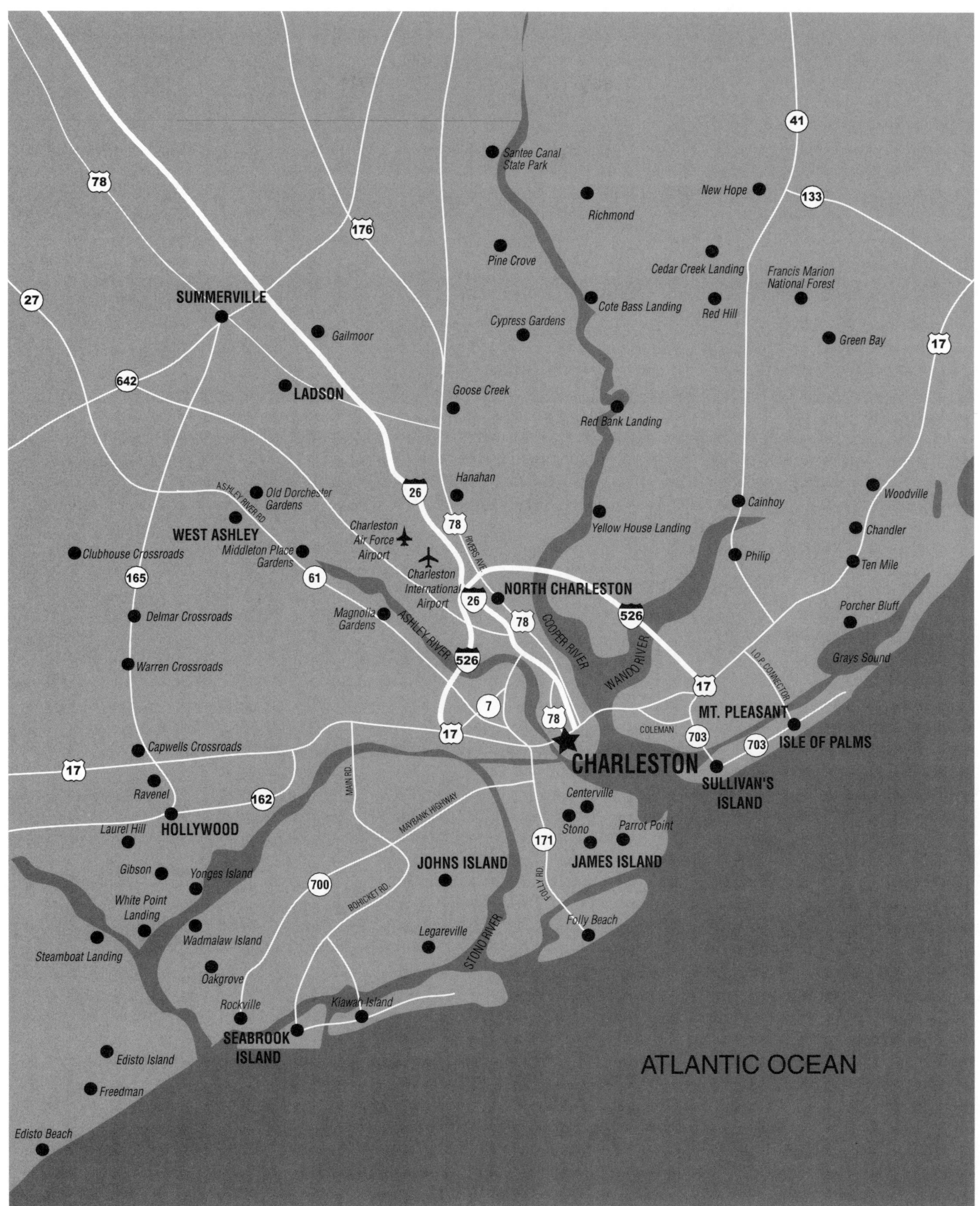

Santee Canal State Park
Richmond
New Hope
41
133
78
176
Pine Crove
Cedar Creek Landing
Francis Marion National Forest
27
SUMMERVILLE
Cote Bass Landing
Red Hill
Gailmoor
Cypress Gardens
Green Bay
17
642
LADSON
Goose Creek
Red Bank Landing
Hanahan
26
Old Dorchester Gardens
ASHLEY RIVER RD
Cainhoy
Woodville
78
Yellow House Landing
WEST ASHLEY
Charleston Air Force Airport
Chandler
Clubhouse Crossroads
Middleton Place Gardens
RIVERS AVE.
Philip
Ten Mile
165
61
Charleston International Airport
NORTH CHARLESTON
26
Magnolia Gardens
78
526
Porcher Bluff
Delmar Crossroads
ASHLEY RIVER
COOPER RIVER
Warren Crossroads
526
WANDO RIVER
Grays Sound
I.O.P. CONNECTOR
17
7
MT. PLEASANT
78
COLEMAN
17
Capwells Crossroads
703
703
ISLE OF PALMS
CHARLESTON
17
SULLIVAN'S ISLAND
Ravenel
162
MAIN RD.
MAYBANK HIGHWAY
Centerville
Laurel Hill
HOLLYWOOD
Stono
Parrot Point
171
JOHNS ISLAND
JAMES ISLAND
Gibson
Yonges Island
700
FOLLY RD.
White Point Landing
BOHICKET RD.
Folly Beach
Wadmalaw Island
Legareville
STONO RIVER
Steamboat Landing
Oakgrove
Rockville
Kiawah Island
SEABROOK ISLAND
Edisto Island
ATLANTIC OCEAN
Freedman
Edisto Beach

20th Annual
Taste of Charleston
October 8, 2000 • Boone Hall Plantation

IT IS WITH PLEASURE THAT THE GREATER CHARLESTON RESTAURANT ASSOCIATION IS PART OF CHARLESTON CUISINE MAGAZINE.

Charleston, world-renowned for its historic seaport, elegant mansions, and picturesque streets, has also become a dining destination for millions of visitors each year. The distinction and quality of our restaurants assures an experience that will delight even the most discriminating taste.

The Greater Charleston Restaurant Association is an active group which is involved in charity work throughout the Lowcountry. Through the "Taste of Charleston" and the "Lowcountry Oyster Festival" the Association has donated over $400,000 to local charities. The charities include the Ronald McDonald House, Hollings Cancer Center, Youth Service Charleston, Charleston County Science Materials Resource Center and the Travel Council. When dining in one of our restaurants, not only will you have a fine dining experience, but you will also be helping these worthwhile charities.

Please feel free to call the Greater Charleston Restaurant Association if you have any questions or need more information, the phone number is (843) 577-4030.

Bob Shipley,
President, Greater Charleston Restaurant Association
General Manager, Desperado Entertainment Complex

18th Annual
Lowcountry Oyster Festival
February, 2001 • Boone Hall Plantation

American Express Presents The

Millennium Edition

Charleston Cuisine Restaurant Gallery

These fine restaurants warmly welcome the American Express Card

AMERICAN EXPRESS

Cards

82 Queen

Specialties of the House

Appetizers

Award Winning
Charleston She Crab Soup

Charleston Spiced Oysters

Fried Green Tomatoes

Entrees

Shrimp & Crawfish Jambalaya

Pan Fried
McClellanville Crabcakes

Crisp Plantation Duck

Southern Comfort
BBQ Shrimp & Grits

Charleston Bouillabaisse

Mixed Grill of
Filet Mignon, Lamb Loin
& Carolina Quail

Desserts

Peach Praline Cobbler

Death By Chocolate

Bourbon Pecan Pie

Reservations Recommended

843•723•7591
1•800•849•0082

82 Queen Street
Charleston, SC 29401

Between Meeting & King Streets.
Short walk from most downtown hotels.

www.82queen.com

Chef Proprietor
Stephen G. Kish, C.E.C.

Serving the Lowcountry for 18 years

Best City Restaurant

"Readers' Choice Awards"
Southern Living Magazine

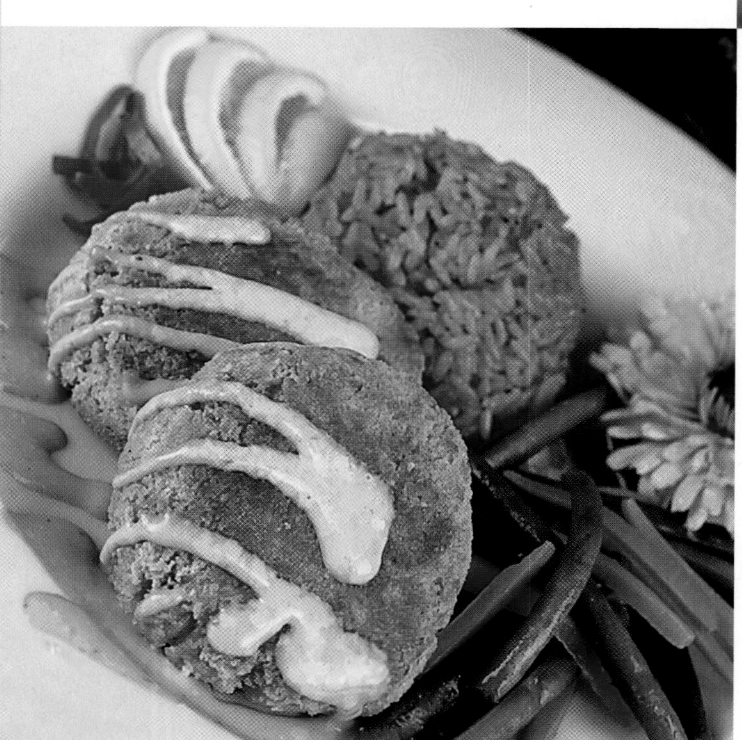

Offering eleven elegant dining rooms to accommodate individual groups from 10 to 40 guests.*

**Larger groups can be accommodated*

WHY *SOUTHERN LIVING* READERS VOTED 82 QUEEN "BEST CITY RESTAURANT" 2 YEARS IN A ROW

Outstanding Lowcountry cuisine... Desserts that make your mouth water...Charleston's Best She-Crab Soup... Great wines... Warm Southern Hospitality... Romantic Charleston captured in elegant dining rooms and a garden courtyard.

Open 365 Days A Year

Lunch Daily 11:30 am til 2:30 pm

Lite Menu 2:30 pm til 5:00 pm

Dinner 6:00 pm til 10:00 pm
Sunday thru Thursday

Dinner 6:00 pm til 10:30 pm
Friday & Saturday

Sunday Brunch 11:30 am til 2:30 pm

82 Queen Group Services

- Custom Menus & Group Prices
- Superb On & Off Site Catering
- Group Service Coordinator
- Meeting Planners Packet Available
- Meeting Planners Specs @ www.82queen.com

All Major Credit Cards Accepted

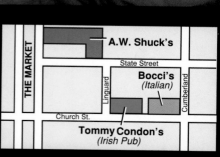

"The dinners could grace the cover of the finest food publication"

"It was so delicious that we couldn't leave a crumb"

★★★★- Jane Kronsberg, *The Charleston Post & Courier*, July 1999

You'd have to travel to Provence to find food as authentically French as Beaumont's.

Featured in Food & Wine, Southern Living and the Atlanta Journal, Chefs Christian Deslandes and Doug Blair offer a classic and innovative menu. Deliciously prepared and expertly presented as only the French can do.

The warm ambiance, attractive decor and courtyard view make for a truly memorable dining experience.

Just off East Bay, discover the flavors of France.

Beaumont's
CAFE & BAR

12 Cumberland Street
Charleston, South Carolina
(843) 577-5500

Open Nightly for Dinner 5:00 pm
Lunch Friday & Saturday 11:30 am
Brunch Sunday 11:00 am

Full Bar
Major Credit Cards Accepted

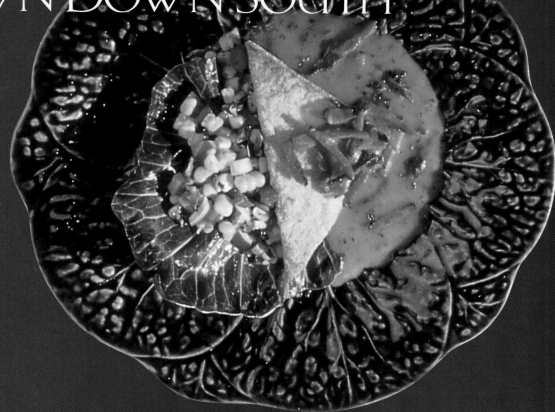

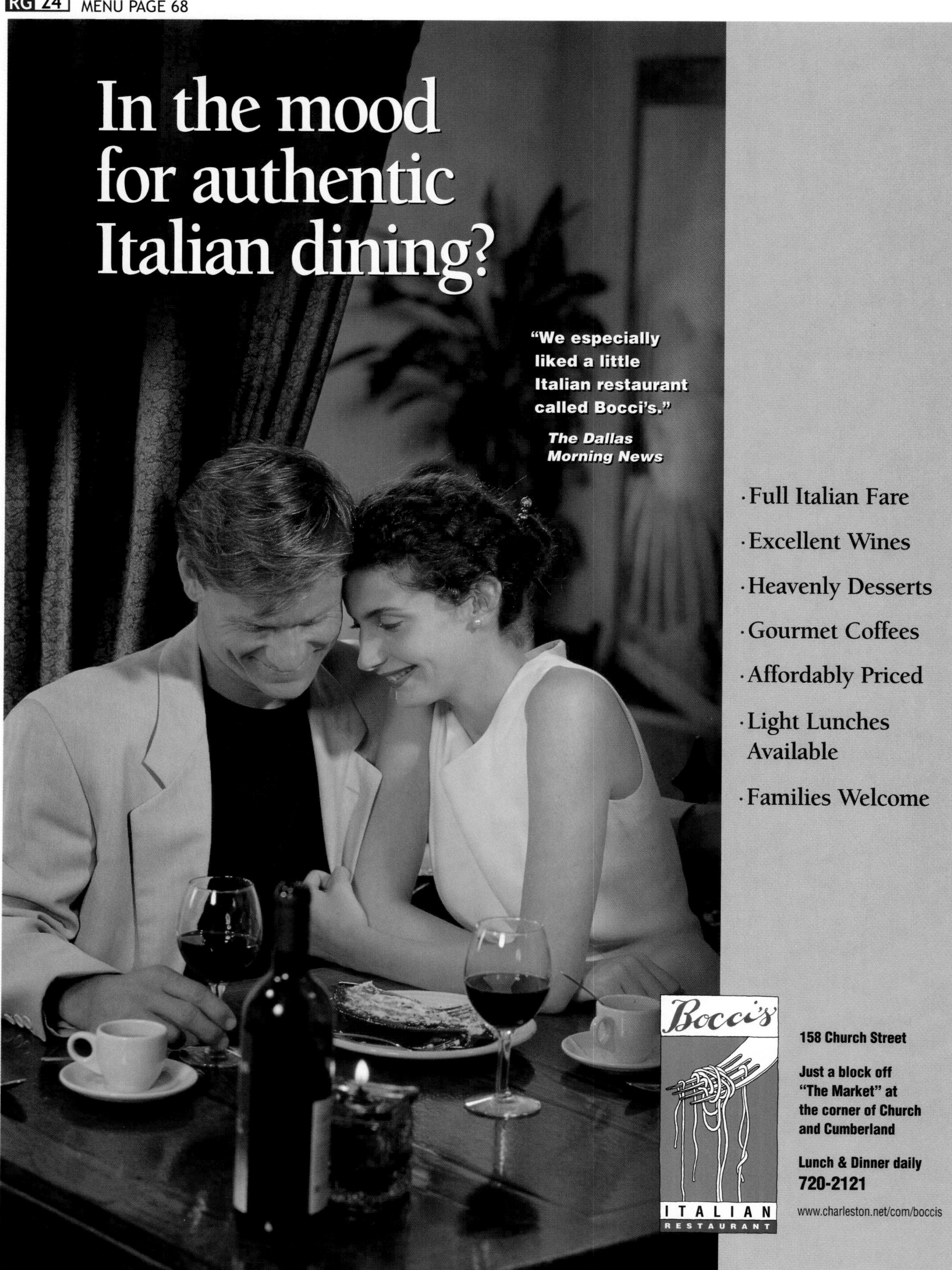
In the mood for authentic Italian dining?
"We especially liked a little Italian restaurant called Bocci's."
The Dallas Morning News
· Full Italian Fare
· Excellent Wines
· Heavenly Desserts
· Gourmet Coffees
· Affordably Priced
· Light Lunches Available
· Families Welcome
Bocci's
ITALIAN RESTAURANT
158 Church Street
Just a block off "The Market" at the corner of Church and Cumberland
Lunch & Dinner daily
720-2121
www.charleston.net/com/boccis

MENU PAGE 71

PRESENTED WITH THE GRACE & CHARM OF THE FRENCH RIVIERA & CHARLESTON'S SEA ISLANDS

SALADS & SOUPS THAT ARE FRESH AND EXCITING
APPETIZERS THAT ARE SIMPLY TANTALIZING
ENTREÉS FEATURING FRENCH PROVENCAL & AMERICAN CONTEMPORARY FARE
INCLUDING FRESH FISH, GAME, BEEF, LAMB AND PASTA
WITH EXCITING DAILY AND SEASONAL SPECIALS
AND SINFUL DESSERTS

OUR WINE CELLAR INCLUDES AN EXTENSIVE ARRAY OF THE BEST WINES FROM AROUND THE WORLD

EXCELLENCE IN DINING

OVERLOOKING BOHICKET MARINA BETWEEN KIAWAH & SEABROOK ISLANDS...PHONE (843) 768-1500...FROM 5PM DAILY
SUNSET VIEWS...CASUAL ATTIRE...RESERVATIONS SUGGESTED

A Great Meal With An Unmatched View Does Not Have To Be Expensive.

CALIFORNIA DREAMING
RESTAURANT AND BAR

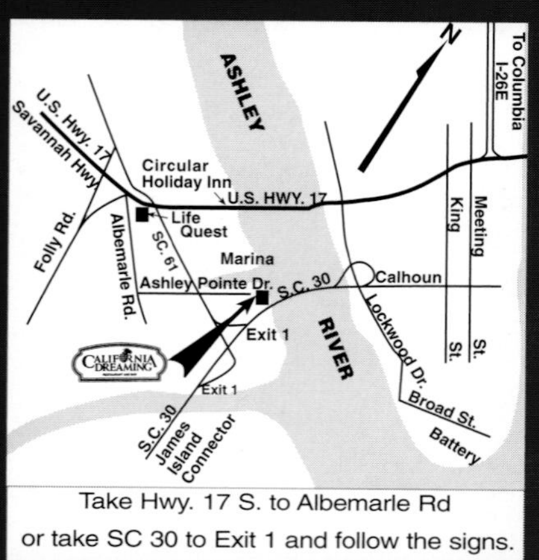

STEAKS • SEAFOOD • PRIME RIB
SALADS • CHICKEN • RIBS

Lunch & Dinner 7 Days
Reservations & phone ahead seating
766-1644

#1 ASHLEY POINTE DRIVE

Cards

We Warmly Welcome the American Express® Card

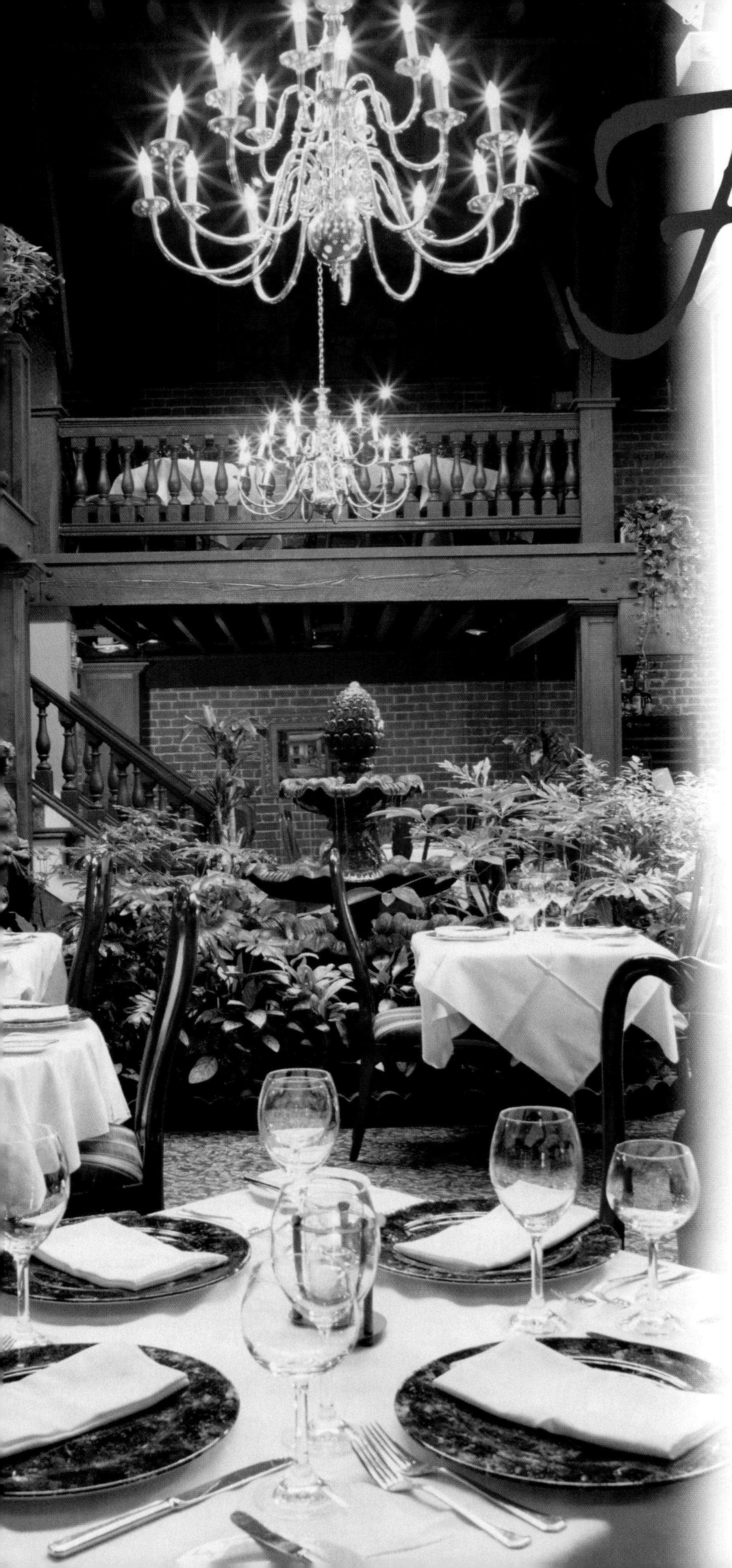

is the philosophy of Charleston Chops. We pride ourselves in great service, exquisite food, and the best piano entertainment. Corporate Chef Jeffery Gibbs serves only the finest ***Certified Angus Beef***™ and creates daily soups, housemade breads and other nightly features for an even greater dinner selection. Ostrich, Shepherd's Pie, and Mixed Grills of Wild Game are just a few of the unusual dishes we serve. Our culinary creations pair perfectly with over 220 wines from around the world as well as fine cognacs, small batch bourbons, and single malt scotches. The list could go on, but it's better if you visit. We invite you to experience an evening of "Friendly Fine Dining" at Charleston Chops.

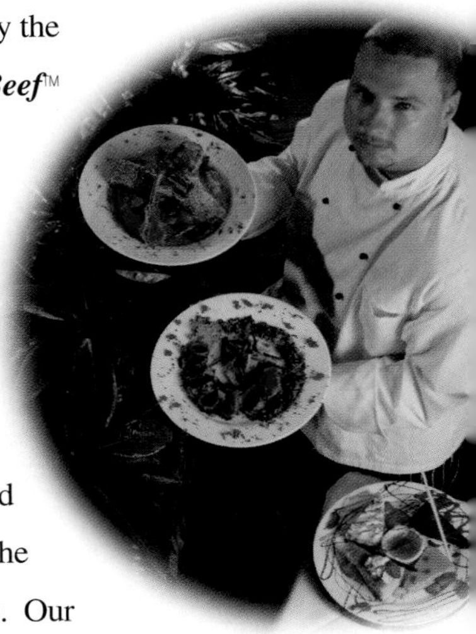

www.charlestonchops.com

In Charleston, South Carolina:
188 East Bay Street
Charleston, SC 29401
Phone: 843-937-9300
Fax: 843-937-9308

In Cornelius, North Carolina:
19918 North Cove Road
Cornelius, NC 28031
Phone: 704-896-5525
Fax: 704-896-5562

The Lowcountry's Best

Rare
Talent

Freshest
Ingredients

Vintage
Wine

Soulful
Jazz

charleston place • 224 king street • charleston, south carolina • tel. 843•577•4522

Dinner Sunday – Thursday 6 pm to 10 pm • Friday – Saturday 6 pm to 11 pm Plantation Supper Sundays 6 pm to 9 pm
Bar open Daily from 4 pm • Nightly Jazz from 7 pm

★ ★ ★ ★ *The only Mobil Four•Star restaurant in Charleston.* ★ ★ ★ ★

MENU SAMPLER

Starters

Southern Fried Green Tomatoes

Pecan Crusted Quail Legs
with a Jack Daniels Chutney

BBQ Duck Quesadilla
with Avacado-Tomato Salsa

Black Bean and Crawfish Cakes

Entrees

Pan Fried Carolina Crabcakes wtih a
Red Pepper Remoulade and Cilantro Oil

Cast Iron Seared Pork Tenderloin,
Sweet Potato-Andouille Hash

Lowcountry Shrimp and White Cheddar
Grits, Stewed Tomatoes,
Applewood Bacon

Opal Basil Marinated Ribeye,
BBQ Steak Butter and Fried Onions

Charleston Fishwater

Desserts

Peach-Passion Fruit Cheesecake

Deep Dish Bourbon Pecan Pie

Chocolate Truffle Souffle Tort

Located in the Heart of Mt. Pleasant, in Historic Shem Creek Village, Geralyn's Offers Contemporary Southern Regional Cuisine Using Ingredients Indigenous to the Lowcountry of South Carolina.

SHEM CREEK VILLAGE
202 Coleman Boulevard - Mt. Pleasant, South Carolina
843.881.8981
www.geralynsrest.com

Johns Island
160 Main Road
843-766-2244
Just off Hwy. 17 South

Mt. Pleasant
1475 Long Grove Dr.
843-849-2244
Seaside Farms

Lexington
938 Northlake Dr.
803-359-2244
1/4 Mile from Hwy. 378

Summerville
3852 Ladson Rd.
843-821-2244
2-1/2 Miles from Hwy. 78

Open Everyday For Lunch & Dinner

In Charleston, You Go to The Market for Great Seafood.

723-FISH

Corner of Church & Hayne
IN THE HEART OF THE OLD MARKET

IDLEWILD

CREATIVE COASTAL CUISINE

With the freshest local ingredients, talented Chef David Porter along with Chef/Owner Andrew Cook have designed Idlewild's four star menu, providing regional favorites that lowcountry residents have grown to love. Dine in the restaurant, or sit at the bar and experience Idlewild's extensive wine list, which offers over 25 wines by the glass.

Idlewild for a cheerful and cozy Atmosphere for lunch and dinner. Come see for yourself why Idlewild was given a ★★★★ review by the Post & Courier restaurant critic. The cuisine is fresh, diverse and wonderful.

Located on the corner of Coleman Boulevard and Houston Northcutt.

976 Houston Northcutt Boulevard • Mount Pleasant, SC 29464 • (843) 881-4511

Lunch • Monday-Saturday 11:30am-3:00pm

Dinner • Monday-Thursday 5:30pm-10:00pm, Friday & Saturday 5:30pm-11:00pm

Some wine with your sunset?

...A rooftop bar, with a
panoramic view of the city
and harbor you won't believe.

...An intimate restaurant, serving
progressive American cuisine
with a distinctly Charleston flair.

Come, be our guest...

23 Vendue Range • 723-0485

Reservations suggested

Located just off East Bay near the New Waterfront Park.

www.charlestonvendueinn.com

GREAT
CATCH.
Lance Howard
Executive Chef
Owner
-Winner-
CRITICS CHOICE
FOR BEST SHE CRAB SOUP
-Winner-
FIRST HEART CHOICE
COOKING COMPETITION
-Winner-
1999 CHARLESTON OYSTER COOKOFF
Locklear's
427 COLEMAN BLVD • MT. PLEASANT, SC 29464
843-884-3346
504 FOLLY ROAD • JAMES ISLAND, SC 29412
843-762-2549

Charleston's only all
appetizer restaurant!
Meritage is an Americanized tapas restaurant.
The concept that has been popular in Spain
for centuries, namely "Tapas" or small plates.
Meritäge
Chef John Olsson creates our selections
from only the freshest, and highest
quality products available.
235 E. Bay Street
hours: 5:00 pm-1:00 am
Charleston, SC 29401
843.723.8181
Late night & patio dining.
Enjoy great food and great wine
with great company.
Enjoy the experience!

Inside Charleston Place Hotel — *130 Market Street* — *843.722.4900 ext. 7951*

Photo by Pam Dullum, Charleston Click

Enjoy Fresh Seafood and Lowcountry Cuisine in an Old Charleston Home.
Dine Indoors or Outside on our Porches or Patio.

72 Queen Street ✦ (843) 577-2337

Our Garden Gazebo Offers a Romantic Setting For Weddings and Parties.

Southern Hospitality Atmosphere in a Historic Victorian Home.

Featuring Lowcountry Cuisine with French, Italian and American Influences.

North Cedar Street
Summerville, SC
843.821.4388

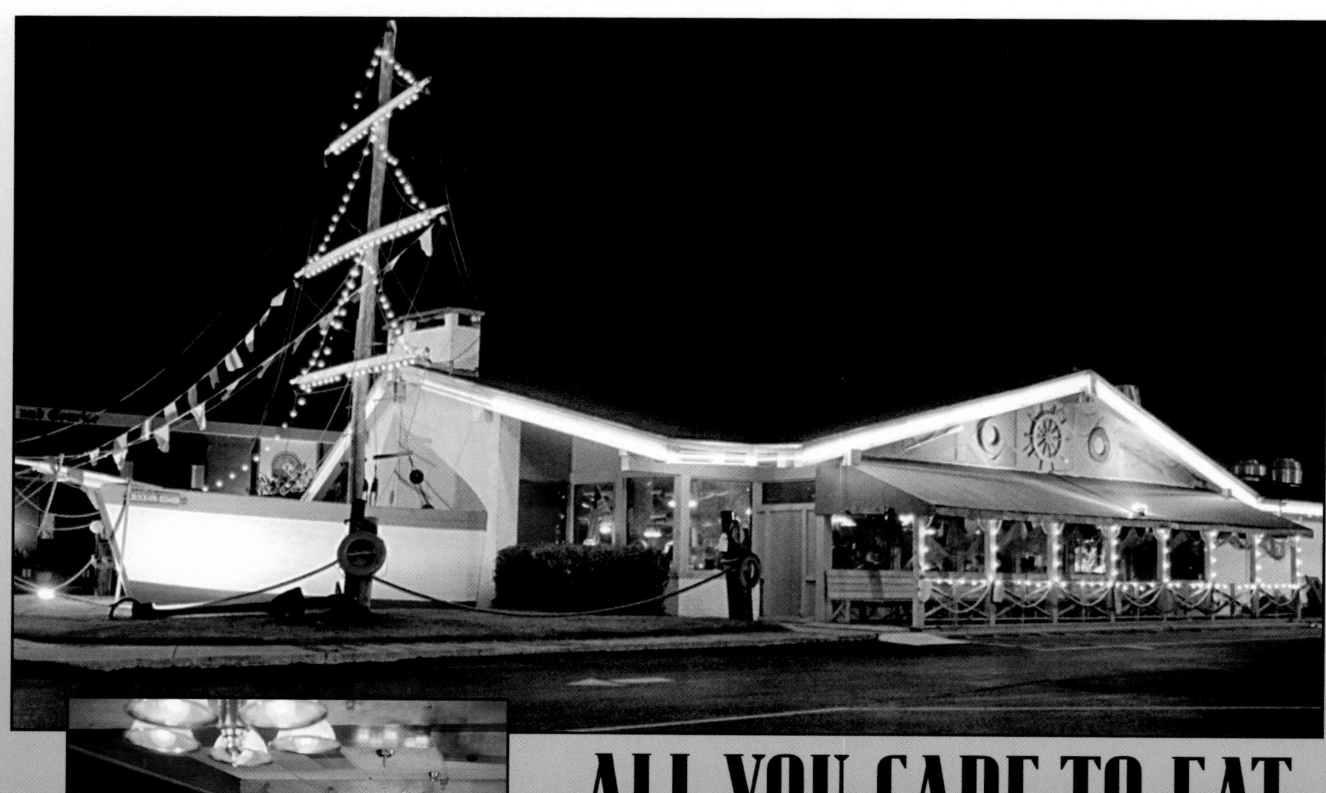

ALL-YOU-CARE-TO-EAT

70 Item Seafood Buffet
Including Alaskan Crab Legs

Come See Our New Mahogany Oyster Bar

Lunch Specials Start at 11:00 am

Happy Hour Monday-Saturday 4:00 pm - 7:00 pm

Also Featuring Live Local Blues Talent - Wednesday through Saturday

6258 Rivers Ave. in North Charleston

843-566-7840

Located in a historic downtown building on East Bay Street, **Southend Brewery** offers a diverse menu of **regional American cuisine** including pastas, pizzas, fresh fish, and our specialty in-house smoked items such as BBQ ribs, chicken and sausage.

THREE SPACIOUS FLOORS feature dining, live entertainment, and banquet facilities. Our **glass elevator** will take you up to our HARBORVIEW BAR overlooking Charleston Harbor. The atrium houses large copper and **stainless steel brew tanks** which enhance your dining experience as our brew-masters create the very ales and lagers you are about to enjoy! An **exhibition kitchen** runs the length of the restaurant extending into a large WOODBURNING OVEN.

Like a **fine handcrafted beer**, Southend Brewery and Smokehouse must be experienced to be fully appreciated.

161 East Bay St. Charleston, SC 803.853.4677
www.southend-brewery.com

FORT SUMTER TOURS  SPIRITLINE CRUISES

Charleston's Premier Cruise Fleet

SpiritLine
Dinner Cruise

Aboard the New *Spirit of Carolina*

Charleston's premier dining experience! Cruise by Charleston's beautiful and intriguing waterfront as you enjoy an exquisite meal prepared to order onboard. Enjoy live entertainment, dancing, and your favorite beverages on Charleston's largest, most elegant dining yacht. The 3-hour SpiritLine Dinner Cruise departs from Patriots Point. Reservations required.

SpiritLine Charters

Charleston's Largest Charter Fleet

SpiritLine Cruises boasts the finest charter fleet in South Carolina. Both of our elegant dining yachts – the *Spirit of Carolina* and the *Spirit of Charleston* – are just right for charters of 50 to over 400 people. For those special occasions – whether a corporate meeting, wedding reception, social event, or incentive group – our professional sales staff will assist you in planning a charter your guests will never forget.

FORT SUMTER TOURS, INC. & SPIRITLINE CRUISES, LLC
205 King Street, Suite 204 • Charleston, SC 29401-3145
1-800-789-3678 • 843-722-BOAT (722-2628) • Fax: 843-720-4263 • E-mail: sales@spiritlinecruises.com
Visit our Web site at: www.spiritlinecruises.com

The Stono Café has been creating fabulous meals for the past ten years. Originally starting in an unpretentious roadhouse and recently moving to its current quarters down the road, Chef Barry Waldrop is well known for his generous serving portions with great flavor. Come watch Barry and his staff, through the open kitchen and behind a very handsome bar, as they prepare their creations in the kitchen.

1956 Maybank Highway
James Island, SC
843.762.4478

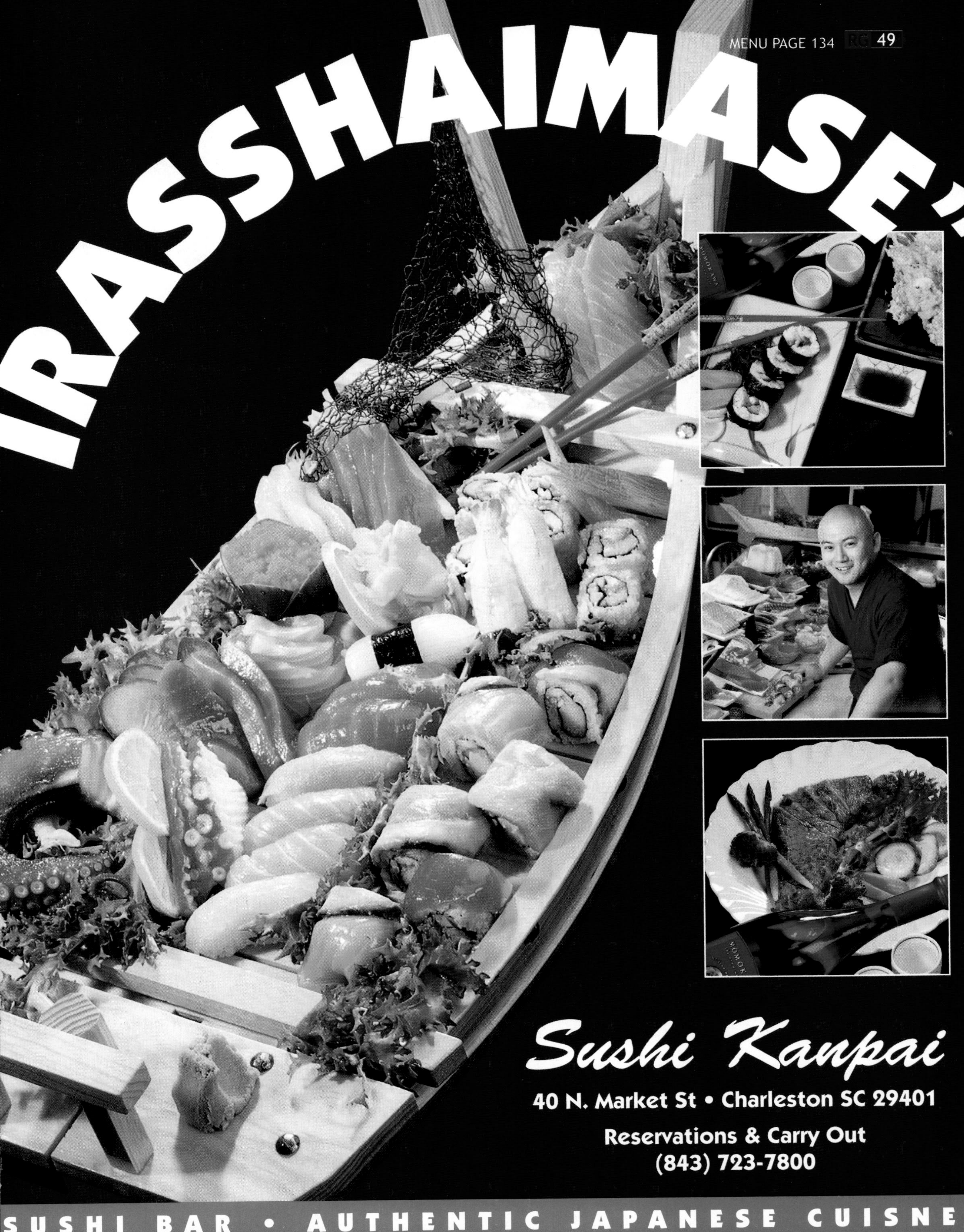
"IRASSHAIMASE"
Sushi Kanpai
40 N. Market St • Charleston SC 29401
Reservations & Carry Out
(843) 723-7800
SUSHI BAR • AUTHENTIC JAPANESE CUISNE

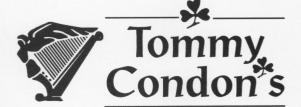

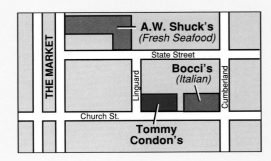

Fresh Not Frozen...
Charleston SC
VICKERY'S
Bar & Grill
Late Night Dining.
Bar open 'til 2:00am
15 Beaufain Street • 577-5300
1313 Shrimp Boat Lane • 884-4440

THE SHOPS
CHARLESTON PLACE
THE RIVIERA

Menu Listing

82 Queen

Voted Best City Restaurant
"Readers Choice Awards"
Southern Living Magazine

82 Queen Voted Best City Restaurant For 3 Years In A Row.

"Readers' Choice Awards"
Southern Living Magazine

"Outstanding Lowcountry cuisine - Desserts that make your mouth water and Charleston's Best She-Crab Soup," are only a few reasons why the readers of *Southern Living Magazine* voted 82 Queen "Best City Restaurant" for 3 years in a row. During the Spring, the most popular mealtime spot at 82 Queen is the open air courtyard, where dining is accentuated by warm southern breezes, blooming Azaleas and the shade of the stately Magnolia tree. 365 days a year, 82 Queen's gracious staff serves garden fresh cuisine reflecting it's rich southern history. In Charleston, more than any other restaurant, 82 Queen embodies the hospitality and tradition of the South."

DINNER APPETIZERS

She Crab Soup, Award Winning, $4.50
laced with Sherry

Chef's Soup du Jour $4.50
created from only the freshest of ingredients

Southern Comfort Barbeque Shrimp $7.95
served over Lowcountry Creamy Grits with Apple Smoked Bacon, Scallions and Cheddar Cheese

Fried Calamari in a Light Herb Breading $7.25
served with a Sweet & Spicy Red Pepper Marmalade

Grilled Venison & Wild Blueberry Sausage $7.95
with a Raspberry-Honey BBQ Sauce, Fresh Goat's Cheese, and Grilled Foccacia

Smoked Salmon & Dill Cream Cheese $7.95
served with Lowcountry Green Tomato Relish and French Bread

Baked Brie Cheese $6.95
glazed with Roasted Pecan Praline and served with French Bread

Fried Oysters $7.95
served over a Black Bean Sauce with Sour Cream and Chives

Deviled Crab Cakes $7.50
lightly fried and served with Red Pepper Cream Sauce

Fried Green Tomatoes $7.50
served over Creamy Grits with Lowcountry Pepper Sauce and Fresh Chives

SALADS

Crisp Mesclun Greens, Ripe Tomatoes, and Enoki Mushrooms $4.95
served with a Creamy Vidalia Onion Dressing

Fresh Younges Island Spinach Salad and French Brie $4.95
served with a Fresh Herb Vinaigrette

82 Queen House Salad $7.95
with Pickled Okra, Tomatoes, Apple Smoked Bacon and Brie Cheese, choice of dressings

"Nestled in the heart of the historic district, 82 Queen's beautiful buildings are situated on the site of the former Schencklingh's Square. Part of the original walled city of Charles Towne, the Square dates back to the 1600's when South Carolina was just a newly formed colony."

82 Queen

CHARLESTON
82 Queen Street
Charleston, SC 29401
PHONE
(843) 723-7591
1-800-849-0082
FAX
(843) 577-7463
WEBSITE
www.82queen.com
HOURS
11:30 am-10:30 pm
MEALS SERVED
Lunch
Dinner
Sunday Brunch
Twilight Dinners
CUISINE
Lowcountry Cuisine
DINING INFORMATION
Terrace/Patio Dining
Heart Smart Meals
Extensive Wine Menu
LOUNGE BAR
ADDITIONAL SERVICES
Private Parties
Banquet Facilities
Private Rooms

ATTIRE
Resort Casual
RESERVATIONS
Suggested
SMOKING
Smoking in Courtyard
Cigar & Pipe Friendly
HANDICAP FACILITIES
CREDIT CARDS
American Express
Visa
Master Card
Discover Card
CHECKS
Not Accepted

Reigning in Charleston Today - as it has for over fifty years - is a place renowned in the culinary world for its simplicity and complexity; its grace and casual air; its hearty tables, napery, crystal and decor, coupled with a presentation of food, wine and service so divine as to be, itself, a work of Southern Fiction."

Hospitality Today
November 19, 1998

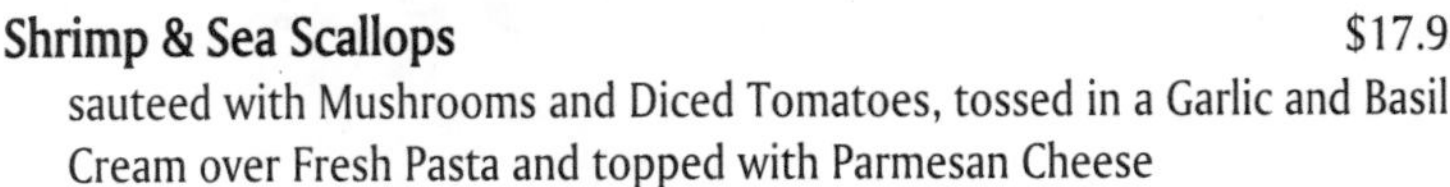

GRITS AND PASTA

Shrimp & Sea Scallops $17.95
sauteed with Mushrooms and Diced Tomatoes, tossed in a Garlic and Basil Cream over Fresh Pasta and topped with Parmesan Cheese

Pecan Fried Flounder $16.50
over Lowcountry Creamy Grits with a Spicy Orange Marmalade and Fresh Vegetables

Southern Comfort Barbecue Shrimp $15.95
served over Lowcountry Creamy Grits topped with Apple Smoked Bacon, Cheddar Cheese, & Scallions

Sauteed Lobster & Cheese Tortellini $20.95
with Mushrooms and Spinach tossed in a Chardonnay & Parmesan Cream

Grilled Carolina Quail $17.95
over Creamy Grits with Country Ham Gravy & Lowcountry Collard Greens

LOWCOUNTRY DINNERS

Grilled Chicken & Shrimp $16.50
simmered in a Tasso Cream

Pan Fried McClellanville Crab Cakes $19.95
over a Roasted Sweet Pepper Cream Sauce

Crisp Plantation Duck $17.75
topped with Sun Dried Cherry and Grand Marnier Glaze

Shrimp & Chicken Gumbo $17.95
served with Andouille Sausage, Stewed Tomatoes, and Okra

Shrimp & Crawfish Jambalaya $16.95
with Tasso Ham, Diced Tomatoes, Carolina Rice, and Lowcountry Seasonings

GRILLED DINNERS

Grilled Pork Tenderloin $16.75
with a Bourbon Brown Sugar Glaze and Roasted Pecans

Grilled Rosemary Marinated Lamb Loin $19.95
in a Roasted Garlic Merlot Sauce

Grilled Rib Eye $18.50
smothered in sauteed Mushrooms and Roasted Garlic Butter

Grilled Filet Mignon $19.95
topped with a Cabernet Sauce

Mixed Grill
Filet Mignon, Carolina Quail, and Venison Sausage $21.95

82 Queen Specialties served with served with fresh garden vegetables and parsley mashed potatoes.

Profiles of the restaurant and Chefs Steve Kish and Steve Stone - and some of their most innovative recipes - appear regularly in general circulation and restaurant industry publications like:

Nation's Restaurant News

Simply Seafood

House Calls Magazine

ANSON

CHARLESTON
12 Anson Street
Charleston, SC 29401
PHONE
(843) 577-0551
FAX
(843) 720-1955
E-MAIL
anson@charleston.net
HOURS
Open Every Night
@ 5:30 pm
MEALS SERVED
Dinner
CUISINE
Lowcountry
Seafood
Southern
DINING INFORMATION
Terrace/Patio Dining
Vegetarian Meals
Take Out Meals
Seasonal Menus
Childrens Menu
Extensive Wine Menu
ADDITIONAL SERVICES
Private Parties
Private Rooms

ATTIRE
Resort Casual
RESERVATIONS
Suggested
SMOKING
Smoking Not Permitted
HANDICAP FACILITIES
CREDIT CARDS
American Express
Visa
Master Card
Discover Card
Diners Club Card
CHECKS
Not Accepted

★★★★★
"Seafood Caught Daily in Charleston Waters"
"Lowcountry Cuisine"
"Big City Chops & Light Entrees"
Post & Courier

Anson

Anson receives ★★★★★ Five Stars from Charleston's *Post & Courier* for **Seafood Caught Daily in Charleston Waters, Lowountry Cuisine, Big City Chops and Light Entrees.** *The New York Times* writes that Anson has "choices ranging from pasta to She Crab soup prepared with finesse" and is "abuzz with a good-time crowd of residents and tourists." Located in the heart of the old city market, Anson's rich architectural details, cozy velvet booths, and antique oil paintings make it the perfect southern setting for intimate dining and large parties.

APPETIZERS

CRACKLING CALAMARI – APRICOT SAUCE	7.50
GORGONZOLA, PEAR & PISTACHIO PIZZA	8.95
LOCAL LUMP CRAB CAKES – ROASTED RED PEPPER SAUCE	9.95
GRILLED SHRIMP & SAUSAGE – CRACKED MUSTARD SEED BBQ	8.95
FRIED CORNBREAD OYSTERS & POTATO CAKE	6.95
SHRIMP COCKTAIL – COCKTAIL PARFAIT & ASHLEY CUCUMBER SALAD	7.95
ESCARGOT, WILD MUSHROOMS & LEEKS	8.50
PEPPERONI PIZZA	7.50
MUSSELS – GARLIC, WHITE WINE & PARSLEY	7.95
SHRIMP & CREAMY STONE GROUND GRITS – COUNTRY HAM GRAVY	7.50

SOUPS & SALADS

ICEBERG SALAD – TOMATOES & CLEMSON BLUE CHEESE DRESSING	4.95
BABY GREENS – CITRUS VINAIGRETTE	5.95
CHARLESTON SHE CRAB SOUP – LACED WITH SHERRY	CUP 5.25 BOWL 6.25
SOUP OF THE DAY	
CAESAR & CRISP CORNBREAD OYSTERS	8.95

SEAFOOD & CHOPS

CRISPY FRIED SHRIMP – REMOULADE SAUCE	17.95
LOWCOUNTRY BARBEQUE GROUPER – CREAMY CAROLINA GOLD RICE, FRESH PEAR & SUNDRIED APRICOT CHUTNEY	23.95
CRISPY DOUBLE CUT PORK CHOP – BRAISED SEASONAL GREENS, PENNE PASTA GRATIN & LIGHT MUSHROOM CREAM	18.95
CHARLESTON BOUILLABAISSE – CLAMS, DIVER SCALLOPS, SHRIMP, MUSSELS, CALAMARI, LOCAL FISH IN A SAFFRON NAGE	21.95
CASHEW CRUSTED GROUPER – CHAMPAGNE SAUCE	22.95
SAUTÉED LOCAL SHRIMP & ARUGULA – SEA ISLAND SWEET ONION BUTTER SAUCE & PENNE PASTA	17.95
CRISPY FLOUNDER	22.95
CHARLESTON DAY BOAT SEAFOOD SPECIALS	MARKET PRICE
CRISPY ROAST DUCK – VEGETABLE CREPES	18.95
PECAN CRUSTED CHICKEN – BLACKBERRY BOURBON SAUCE	15.95
GRILLED TENDERLOIN – DEMI GLACE	PETITE 19.95/23.95
12 OZ. AGED PRIME NEW YORK STRIP	24.95
CHOP OF THE DAY – CHEF'S CHOICE	MARKET PRICE

DESSERTS

CREME BRULEE	6.50
CHOCOLATE OBLIVION TORTE	5.95
BANANA CREME PIE	5.95
OLD FASHIONED CHOCOLATE LAYER CAKE – BENNE BASKET, MOCHA ALMOND ICE CREAM	6.95
LEMON SORBET – SEASONAL BERRIES	4.50
CRISP BENNE ALMOND BASKET – SEASONAL BERRIES & VANILLA BEAN ICE CREAM	7.50

Atlanticville Restaurant & Cafe

Great Food • Great Island

We invite you to join us for a unique dining experience. Just minutes from downtown Charleston on beautiful Sullivan's Island, Atlanticville Restaurant & Café offers contemporary American cuisine blending tastes and seasonings from around the world. Our eclectic menu features Lowcountry favorites, fresh local seafood and dishes influenced by Italy, the Pacific Rim, New England and the Southwest, just to name a few.

The Charleston area's only authentic Thai cuisine can be found at our Thai Tuesdays. Whether basking in the sunset on the deck or enjoying Brunch in the dining room, it is our pleasure to bring you one of Charleston's finest dining experiences in a delightful island setting.

Entrees

Fried Oysters with Sausage, Spinach & Garlic Mayonnaise 5.95

Grilled Halibut Served with Fried Scallops & Grilled Potato, Garlic Spinach & Artichoke Heart Sauté 16.75

Roasted Mahi-Mahi with Sausage, Saffron, Tiny Clams, Tomatoes & Paprika-Potato Casserole 14.50

Country-Fried Flounder with Lemon Butter & Cucumber Relish 14.75

Brace of Quail Stuffed with Cornbread, Bacon & Sage served with Collards & Sweet Potatoes 15.00

Braised Lamb Shank served with Sweet Italian Sausage & Fennel with Spinach Raviolis 15.95

Atlanticville Presents Thai Tuesday

Mussels Steamed with Green Curry, Peppers & Coconut Milk 6.50

Spicy Red Curry with Braised Beef, Fried Eggplant & Potatoes 11.95

Whole Fried Flounder with Sweet & Sour Dipping Sauce 14.95

B.B.Q. Pork Shoulder "Char Su" Style with Coriander Fried Rice 9.95

Thai B.B.Q. Glazed Salmon with Pancit Noodles, Lemongrass Broth & Shrimp Wontons 15.50

SULLIVANS ISLAND
2063 Middle Street
Sullivans Island, SC 29482

PHONE
(843) 883-9452

FAX/CATERING
(843) 883-9765

HOURS
Sunday-Thursday
5:30 pm-10:30 pm
Friday-Saturday
5:30 pm-10:30 pm
Sunday Brunch
10:00 pm-2:30 pm

MEALS SERVED
Lunch
Dinner
Sunday Brunch
Twilight Dinners
Late Night Dining

CUISINE
American
Continental
Seafood, Thai

DINING INFORMATION
Terrace/Patio Dining
Vegetarian Meals
Take Out Meals
Seasonal Menus
Childrens Menu
Extensive Wine Menu

LIVE MUSIC
Tuesdays & Fridays
8:30 pm-Till

ADDITIONAL SERVICES
Full Service Catering
Private Parties
Private Rooms
Meeting Facilities

ATTIRE
Casual

RESERVATIONS
Not Required

SMOKING
Section Available
Cigar & Pipe Smoking

HANDICAP FACILITIES

CREDIT CARDS
American Express
Visa
Master Card

CHECKS
Accepted

A.W. Shuck's Restaurant & Bar

CHARLESTON
70 State Street
Charleston, SC 29401

PHONE
(843) 723-1151

FAX
(843) 720-2114

HOURS
Sunday-Thursday
11:00 am-10:00 pm
Friday & Saturday
11:00 am-11:00 pm

MEALS SERVED
Lunch
Dinner

CUISINE
Seafood

DINING INFORMATION
Terrace/Patio Dining
Childrens Menu

ENTERTAINMENT
Spring & Fall on Patio
Tuesdays
6:00 pm-10:00 pm

ADDITIONAL SERVICES
Private Parties

ATTIRE
Casual
Resort Casual

RESERVATIONS
Not Required
Not Taken

SMOKING
Smoking Section

HANDICAP FACILITIES

CREDIT CARDS
American Express
Visa
Master Card
Discover Card
Diners Club Card

CHECKS
Accepted
(Local)

Located downtown in The Market, no one tops A. W. Shuck's for fresh seafood and fun. With both a vast indoor dining area and patio seating, A. W. Shuck's specializes in the food that made Charleston cuisine famous: fresh shrimp, scallops, and oysters, lightly fried or broiled to perfection . . . exquisite she-crab soup...fresh-off-the-boat fish specials...and a seafood casserole that's legendary among locals. Affordably priced, Shuck's offers a good-times atmosphere for everyone!

APPETIZERS

SHUCK'S "AWARD-WINNING STUFFED SHRIMP $5.95
Three plump shrimp, butterflied, stuffed with Carolina Deviled Crab, wrapped in bacon, and deep fried to perfection.

MARKET MIX SAMPLER $6.50
Our favorite sampler of hot'n spicy shrimp, stuffed shrimp, and fried green tomatoes.

BUFFALO OYSTERS $6.50
Plump oysters, deep fried to perfection and served with bleu cheese dressing, celery sticks and Shuck's own traditional Hot Sauce.

BOBBY'S BLUE CRAB DIP $5.95
A delicious creamy blend of choice crabmeat, cream cheese, cheddar cheese, and special seasonings, served with crackers.

RAW BAR

STEAMED SHRIMP $4.95 1/4 lb $8.95 1/2 lb
A lowcountry favorite, steamed in our own delicious blend of seafood seasonings, ready for you to peel, served on a bed of ice and accompanied by spicy cocktail sauce and crackers.

OYSTERS ON THE HALF SHELL $4.25 1/2 DOZ $8.50 DOZ $14.95 2 DOZ
Select, just opened fresh oysters served on a bed of ice and accompanied by spicy cocktail sauce and crackers.

STEAMED OYSTERS
$7.95 DOZ $13.95 2 DOZ
Dig in! A knife and a tray of steamers and you are the "shucker", complemented with our spicy cocktail sauce, drawn butter, and crackers.

FRESH FISH

GRILLED

Choose one of our homemade sauces:
Lemon Dill Cream, Roasted Red Pepper Cream, Honey Dijon Glaze, Mango Chutney, Jamaican Relish or Blackened

SALMON $14.95
MAHI-MAHI $14.95
CATFISH $14.95
SNAPPER $14.95
MAKO $14.95
TUNA $14.95
GROUPER $14.95
TROUT $14.95
TILAPIA $14.95

WAREHOUSE TRADITIONS

SHUCK'S AWARD WINNING STUFFED SHRIMP $12.95
Six plump shrimp butterflied, stuffed with Carolina deviled crab, wrapped in bacon and deep fried to perfection, served with Charleston red rice and steamed vegetables.

SEAFOOD JAMBALAYA $12.95
Chicken tenders, smoked sausage, fresh fish and creek shrimp simmered in a creole sauce served over red rice.

SHUCK'S "LEGENDARY" CASSEROLE $12.95
Baby creek shrimp and scallops, sautéed and layered over Carolina deviled crab, topped with a lobster cheese sauce and baked au gratin, served with your choice of a side.

SHRIMP AND GRITS $11.95
Fresh creek shrimp, sautéed in a sweet creamy sauce served over whole ground grits.

CRABCAKE DINNER $13.95
Two 5 oz. Carolina blue crabcakes, grilled to a golden brown and topped with your choice of any of our homemade sauces (listed under our fresh fish category). Served with your choice of a side item.

CRABCAKE AND STUFFED SHRIMP COMBO $14.95
A 5 oz. Carolina blue crabcake, grilled to a golden brown and topped with a roasted red pepper cream sauce. Accompanied with four of our award winning stuffed shrimp. Served with your choice of a side item.

SEAFOOD

FRIED or BROILED

SHRIMP $12.95
Fresh, succulent shrimp netted by our local shrimp boats, hand selected by our chef and prepared your way!

SCALLOPS $12.95
Tender and fresh from the cold waters of the Atlantic.

OYSTERS $12.95
Harvested from creek banks, plump, juicy and tempting, inspected daily for freshness so you can expect to eat the best oysters in town.

MARKET STREET PLATTER $15.95
Tender shrimp, select oysters, juicy scallops, and filet of flounder. It's a delectable combination of the best the ocean can offer from the cold waters of the Atlantic.

Mill House Hotel Barbadoes Room

Step through the distinctive arches and experience the famous Barbadoes Room restaurant. So named because of the extensive trading between Charleston and the West Indies in the 18th century, the Barbadoes Room restaurant provides an especially warm, intimate dining experience. An outstanding selection of Lowcountry specialities are featured in this elegant dining room. Enjoy daily breakfast buffet, lunch, dinner and the renowned Mills House Sunday Brunch Buffet, all enhanced by gracious Charleston service and hospitality.

Appetizers & Soups

SCALLOPS CEVICHE 6.95
Scallops, tomatoes, onions with sweet & hot peppers marinated in lime juice. Served in a tortilla shell.

OYSTERS ON THE HALF SHELL *(Steamed or Raw)*
Half Dozen 5.95
One Dozen 9.95

CHARLESTON STARTER 5.95
Crab & scallion dip, pimento cheese and shrimp paste served with toasted focaccia rounds and our red pepper onion marmalade.

STUFFED TOP NECK CLAMS 6.50
Clams topped with spinach and gorgonzola cream filling and baked.

BLACK BEAN CAKES 4.95
Spicy black bean cakes with chipotle salsa

CHARLESTON SHE CRAB 4.95
Topped with whipped cream and dry Sherry.

CONCH CHOWDER 3.95
Marinated conch, potatoes and a mirepoix of vegetables in a tomato broth

Salads

CAROLINA CAESAR 5.95
Traditional Caesar topped with tomato and bacon bits
With a grilled chicken breast 8.95

THE MILLS HOUSE SALAD 3.95
Tossed baby lettuce with fresh parmesan, croutons and roma tomatoes. Served with Aegean dressing.

CONCH SALAD 7.95
Lime marinated conch over mixed greens and vegetables. Served with tomato cilantro vinaigrette.

CALAMARI SALAD 7.95
Lightly fried calamari over tossed baby greens with feta cheese, tomatoes & ginger mango dressing.

TOSSED FRUIT AND BUTTER LETTUCE 5.95
Seasonal fresh fruit and berries tossed with butter lettuce & cantaloupe yogurt dressing and topped with Carolina pecans and shredded coconut.

MARINATED TOMATO & MONTRACHET ... 5.95
Sliced Wadamalaw tomatoes marinated in tomato cilantro vinaigrette served over butter lettuce and topped with montrachet cheese and calamata olives.

Pizza, Pasta & Grits

SEAFOOD BURRITO 13.95
Shrimp, scallops & local grouper in a sherry cream wrapped in a flour tortilla. Topped with red pepper coulis & sour cream.

SHRIMP & GRITS 9.95
Sautéed shrimp, tomatoes, scallions and bacon served over creamy stone ground grits with fresh sliced tomatoes.

SALMON FRITTERS & TOMATO BASIL PENNE PASTA 13.95
Crispy salmon fritters served over tomato basil penne pasta with a shiitake mushroom flavored cream sauce.

GRILLED VEGETABLES & PASTA 12.95
Grilled slices of zucchini, yellow squash & assorted vegetables served with tomato basil penne pasta and a shiitake cream sauce.

CUBAN SHRIMP PIZZA 10.95
Pineapple, mango, pepperoni, shrimp & mozzarella.

GREEK PIZZA 9.95
Calamata olives, sun dried tomatoes, sliced turkey, feta cheese, onion rings & fresh oregano.

Entrees

FRIED OYSTERS & SHRIMP 15.95
Lightly fried in our herb breading. Served with aioli & spicy cocktail dip.

SEARED GROUPER FILET 17.95
Served on a bed of mashed plantains and topped with a Thai compote.

GINGER ENCRUSTED TUNA 16.95
Cut thick and grilled to your specification. Topped with apple mango relish.

MOJO PORK TENDERLOIN 15.95
Marinated, then slow roasted and sliced. Topped with grapefruit, fresh rosemary and mojo sauce.

STUFFED FLOUNDER 17.95
Stuffed with shrimp and blue crab. Smothered in a citrus salsa.

FILET MIGNON 16.95
6 ounces of succulent Iowa-raised beef, wrapped in bacon & grilled to your liking.

This is a small selection of the fine cuisine available at The Barbadoes Room.

CHARLESTON
c/o Mill House Hotel
115 Meeting Street
Charleston, SC 29401

PHONE
(843) 577-2400 ext. 154

FAX
(843) 722-2112

HOURS
Daily
6:30 am-10:00 pn

MEALS SERVED
Breakfast
Lunch
Dinner
Sunday Brunch

CUISINE
Continental

DINING INFORMATION
Terrace/Patio Dining
Heart Smart Meals
Vegetarian Meals
Take Out Meals
Seasonal Menus
Childrens Menu

LOUNGE BAR

ENTERTAINMENT
Best Friend Lounge
Dale Kelly on guitar
First Shot Lounge
Dick Krauck on Piano
Monday-Thursday
5:00 pm-7:00 pm
Friday & Saturday
5:00 pm-10:00 pm

ADDITIONAL SERVICES
Full Service Catering
Private Parties
Banquet Facilities
Lodging
Private Rooms
Meeting Facilities

ATTIRE
Casual

RESERVATIONS
Suggested

SMOKING
Cigar & Pipe Friendly
in Courtyard and Lounge

HANDICAP FACILITIES

CREDIT CARDS
American Express
Visa
Master Card
Discover Card

CHECKS
Not Accepted

Beaumont's

CHARLESTON
12 Cumberland Street
Charleston, SC 29401
PHONE
(843) 577-5500
FAX
(843) 577-7413
HOURS
Lunch
Friday & Saturday
11:30 am-3:00 pm
Dinner
Monday-Sunday
5:00 pm-Closing
Sunday Brunch
11:00 am-3:00 pm
MEALS SERVED
Lunch
Dinner
Sunday Brunch
CUISINE
Classic
French
Mediterranean
DINING INFORMATION
Terrace/Patio Dining
Seasonal Menus
Extensive Wine Menu
ENTERTAINMENT
Thursday-Saturday
8:00 pm -
ADDITIONAL SERVICES
Private Parties

ATTIRE
Casual
RESERVATIONS
Suggested
SMOKING
Smoking Section
Cigar & Pipe Friendly
(Bar Only)
HANDICAP FACILITIES
CREDIT CARDS
American Express
Visa
Master Card
Discover Card
Diners Club Card
CHECKS
Accepted
(Local Only)

RESTAURANT CHARLESTON
Beaumont's
CAFE & BAR

You'd have to travel to provence to find food as authentically French as Beaumont's. Featured in Food & Wine, Southern Living and the Atlanta Journal, Chefs Christian Deslandes and Douglas Blair offer a classic and innovative menu. Deliciously prepared and expertly presented as only the French can do. The warm ambiance, attractive decor and courtyard view make for a truly memorable dining experience. Just off East Bay, discover the flavors of France.

SOUPS

ONION SOUP GRATINEE 5.25
hearty bouillon, croutons and swiss

BEAUMONT'S CRAB SOUP 5.95
our rendition of a Lowcountry favorite

MARSEILLE FISH SOUP 5.75
served with rouille and croutons

APPETIZERS, SALADS AND LIGHTER FARE

CAROLINA QUAIL 11.95
confit, with lentils and baby spinach

ESCARGOTS IN POTATO CRUST 9.75
garlic, light parsley cream and toasted almonds

MOUSSE DE CANARD 7.95
duck liver mousse with orange zest and toasted campagne

FROMAGERE OF MUSSELS AND SCALLOPS 8.75
oven baked with garlic and parmesan

HOUSE COLD SMOKED SALMON 9.25
cured and smoked served with capers, onions, and brioche toast

EGGPLANT GATEAU 8.25
oven baked smoked tomato and eggplant, pesto and regiano

BROCHETTE OF OYSTERS 9.95
wrapped in proscuitto, breaded and fried, with baby greens

PASTA AND RISOTTO

Can also be served as appetizer

SAFFRON RISOTTO WITH GRILLED CALAMARI 15.95

WILD MUSHROOM RISOTTO WITH SEARED SCALLOPS 17.95

SMOKED TOMATO RISOTTO WITH GRILLED, MARINATED SHRIMP 17.95

SEAFOOD PASTA 18.95
angel hair with extra virgin olive oil, lemon, garlic, and assorted seafood

ANGEL HAIR 'ADRIA II' 13.95
roma tomato, basil, garlic, olive oil and fresh mozzarella

CRISPY GNOCCHI 18.95
white truffle butter and shaved reggiano

ENTREES

GROUPER SUCCOTASH 19.95
sauteed with fava beans, corn, sweet pepper, chardonnay 'fumee' and cream

FLOUNDER MEUNIERE 17.00
lemon, parsley and butter served with saffron steamed potatoes and seasonal vegetables

SHRIMP PROVENCALE 21.00
sauteed with garlic, tomato, olive oil and served with reggiano risotto and seasonal vegetables

BOUILLABAISEE MARSEILLAISE 28.00
lobster, clams, mussels, scallops and fresh fish filet stewed in tomato-saffron-fennel broth served with rouille croutons and saffron potato.

CHARLESTON CRAB CAKES 19.00
lump crab served with onion contiture and remoulade, camargue rice or today's potato and seasonal vegetables

SALMON FILET 18.95
pan seared with belgian endive marmelade, lemon beurre blanc, carmargue rice or today's potato and seasonal vegetables

YELLOW FIN TUNA LOIN 19.95
sushi grade served rare with lentil mushroom mirepoix broth, carmargue rice or today's potato and seasonal vegetables

GRILLED LAMB CHOP AND BAKED CHARTREUSE 19.95
grilled and baked duo of lamb with herbs jus reduction served with today's potato and seasonal vegetables

GRILLED CHATEAUBRIAND mkt. price
for two people, bouquetiere of seasonal vegetables, today's potato, and bearnaise

FILET MIGNON 24.00
pan seared, with your choice of bearnaise, bordelaise demi or "au poivre" served with seasonal vegetables and today's potato

GRILLED ENTRECOTE PARISIENNE 18.00
grilled ribeye served with maitre d'hotel butter, gaufrette potato and salade verte

DOUBLE THICK CENTER CUT PORK CHOP 18.25
grilled and served with truffledemi, seasonal vegetables and today's potato

OSSO BUCCO 'CAMPAGNARD' 19.00
veal shank served with caramelized vegetables and pasta

Blossom Cafe

CHARLESTON
171 East Bay St.
Charleston, SC 29401
PHONE
(843) 722-9200
FAX
(843) 722-0035
E-MAIL
info@magnolias-blossom.com

HOURS
Monday-Thursday
11:30 am-11:00 pm
Friday & Saturday
11:30 am-12:00 am
Sunday
11:00 am-2:30 pm (Brunch)
5:00 pm-11:00 pm

MEALS SERVED
Lunch
Dinner
Sunday Brunch
Late Night Dining

CUISINE
Contemporary American with Italian Influences

DINING INFORMATION
Terrace/Patio Dining
Vegetarian Meals
Extensive Wine Menu

LOUNGE BAR
6:00 pm-Midnight

ADDITIONAL SERVICES
Semi-Private Dining
For Large Parties

ATTIRE
Casual

RESERVATIONS
Suggested

SMOKING
Section Available

CREDIT CARDS
American Express
Visa
Master Card
Diners Club Card

CHECKS
Accepted

BLOSSOM cafe®

Blossom Cafe is a high energy, contemporary restaurant located in downtown Charleston. Executive Chef/ Managing Partner, Donald Barickman and Chef Jack Bogan combine the finest imported ingredients with fresh seafood and regional produce to create an Italian influenced local cuisine. Dine in the charming courtyard or with a view of the exhibition kitchen and enjoy a fabulous meal. Blossom's menu features house-made pastas and breads, oak-roasted pizzas from the wood burning oven and a wide variety of appetizers, entrees and nightly specials.

Small Plates and Starters

Oven-Baked Carolina Goat Cheese 6.50
with Roasted Garlic, Tomato Basil Fondue and a Loaf of Housemade Bread

Potato Parmesan Gnocchi with 6.50
Brown Butter, Sage and Oregano

Poached Mussels with White Wine, ... 8.95
Garlic, Chervil, Tomatoes and Capers

Antipasta of Shrimp on Bruschetta, ... 9.25
with White Wine, Lemon, Parsley and Butter

Salads

Arugula Salad with Lemon 7.25
Olive Oil Dressing, Carolina Goat Cheese, Roasted Garlic and Red Peppers

Greek Spinach Salad with Feta Cheese 7.50
Red Onions, Calamata Olives, Pepperoncini, Roasted Peppers, and Oregano Vinaigrette

Fresh Mozzarella and Roma Tomatoes 6.95
with Basil Oil and Balsamic Vinegar

Pizzas from the Wood-Burning Oven

Oak-Roasted Chicken, Caramelized 9.25
Onions, Gorgonzola, Romano and Chervil

Spicy Lamb Sausage, Tomato Basil 9.50
Fondue, Carolina Goat Cheese and Oven-Dried Tomatoes

Pesto, Artichoke Hearts, Roma Tomatoes, ... 9.50
Calamata Olives, Red Onions, Parmesan and Mozzarella

Homemade Pastas & Risottos

Seasonal Vegetable Risotto 12.95
with Parmesan and Fresh Herbs

Carolina Crab Raviolis with 18.95
Yellow Corn, Spinach and a Porcini Mushroom Cream

Spinach Linguine with 15.95
Shrimp, Tomatoes, Capers, Roasted Garlic and Fresh Basil

Linguine with Oak-Roasted Chicken, ... 14.95
Prosciutto and a Porcini Mushroom Cream

Grill, Saute and Wood Oven Specialties

Oak-Roasted Eggplant Lasagna 11.95
with Spinach, Mushrooms, Tomato Basil Fondue and Three Cheeses

Fire-Roasted Salmon Filet with 17.25
Tomatoes, Calamatas, Garlic, Onions and Herbed Orzo

Scaloppine of Veal with Marsala 17.25
Wine Sauce, Mushrooms, Prosciutto, Dried Tomatoes and Herbed Angel Hair Pasta

Wasabi Rubbed Grilled Tuna Loin on 18.95
Wild Mushroom, Ginger and Soy Risotto with a Sesame Sweet Pepper Slaw and Scallions

Grilled Lamb Chops on a 23.95
Porcini Mushroom and Parmesan Risotto with Green Beans and Demiglace

Beef Tenderloin with White Beans 20.95
and a Portabello, Caramelized Onions, Spinach and Goat Cheese Ragout

Blossom Desserts

Chinese Firecracker with White Chocolate Mousse and Raspberry Coulis 5.75

Chocolate Raspberry Truffle Torte with White and Dark Chocolate Chunk Ice Cream, Creme Anglaise and Raspberry Coulis 5.75

Blossom Cafe Tiramisu with Marsala Sabayon 5.75

This is just a small sample of the fine cuisine available at Blossom Cafe

The Boathouse at Breach Inlet

ISLE OF PALMS
101 Palm Blvd.
Isle of Palms, SC 29451
PHONE
(843) 886-8000
FAX
(843) 886-0555
HOURS
Sunday-Thursday
5:00 pm-10:00 pm
Friday & Saturday
5:00 pm-11:00 pm
MEALS SERVED
Dinner
CUISINE
Lowcountry
Seafood
Steak
DINING INFORMATION
Terrace/Patio Dining
Heart Smart Meals
Vegetarian Meals
Take Out Meals
Seasonal Menus
Childrens Menu
Extensive Wine Menu
LOUNGE BAR
5:00 pm daily
ENTERTAINMENT
Sunday-Tuesday
6:30 pm-9:30 pm

ATTIRE
Casual
RESERVATIONS
Suggested
SMOKING
Smoking Section
HANDICAP FACILITIES
CREDIT CARDS
American Express
Visa
Master Card
CHECKS
Accepted

Voted
"BEST WATERFRONT DINING"
1999 Best of Charleston Readers Poll

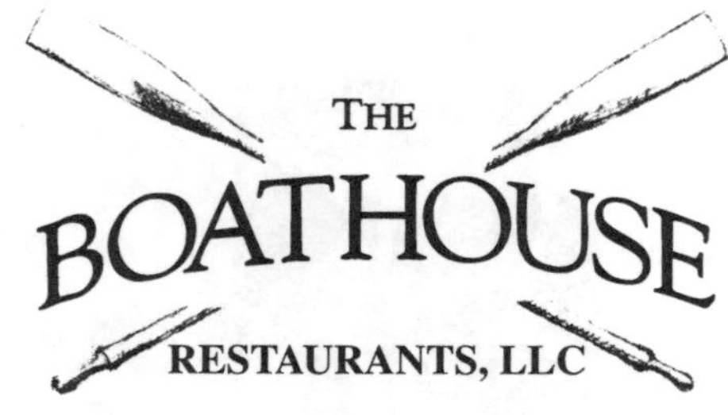

Poised between the Atlantic and the Intracoastal waterways, The Boathouse at Breach Inlet offers locals and travelers alike a seafood experience not to be missed! The concept is simple; abundant, creatively prepared fresh seafood, steaks & pasta served with impeccable service in a casual elegant setting. Choose to dine on the deck amid balmy breezes and unsurpassed sunset views of the ocean - or enjoy the comfortable, nautical theme of the polished mahogany & pine dining room.

Starters

House Salad with Marinated Tomatoes $2.95
Fried Green Tomatoes with Marinara $3.95
Steamed New Zealand Greenlip Mussels $6.95
Fried Oysters w/Smoked Jalapeno Mayo $5.95
Steamed Trio of Clams, Mussels & Shrimp $6.95
Fried Shrimp with Cocktail Sauce $5.95
Steamed Littleneck Clams $6.95
Seared Tuna with Green Tabasco Sauce $7.50
Roasted Corn & Crab Soup $3.95
Crab Fritters with Green Tabasco Sauce $7.50

Entree Salads

Entree size portions of our Caesar Salad with...

Grilled Chicken $7.95
Fried Sea Scallops $8.95
Fried Shrimp $9.95
Fried Oysters $8.95

Grilled Fresh Fish

Choose one of our homemade sauces:
Pesto, Tarragon, Butter, Dijon Mustard Glaze
or Blackened
(Served with your choice of two side items)

Mahi-Mahi $15.95
Yellowfin Tuna $16.95
Atlantic Salmon $14.95
Black Grouper $16.95

Fried Seafood

Shrimp $14.95
Scallops $12.95
Oysters $12.95
Combination $13.95

Specialties

SHRIMP & GRITS
Stone ground grits with sauteed shrimp, onions, mixed peppers, spicy andouille sausage, roma tomatoes & garlic drizzled with green tabasco sauce $13.95

CRAB CAKES
Two crab cakes with green tabasco sauce and fried red onions $17.95

FILET & CRAB CAKE
6 oz. filet and crab cake $18.95

FILET & LOBSTER
6 oz. filet & petite cold water lobster tails with drawn butter $20.95

LOBSTER TAILS
Broiled petite cold water lobster tails served with drawn butter $20.95

BAKED BLACK GROUPER
Romano & pinenut crusted with a marinara dipping sauce $16.95

Beef and Chicken

New York Strip - 14 oz. $17.95
Filet - 9 oz. $17.95
Grilled Chicken $10.95

Pastas

PENNE PRIMAVERA
Mixed peppers, onions, roma tomatoes, wild mushrooms, garlic & romano cheese in basil oil over penne pasta $9.95

PENNE PRIMAVERA WITH CHICKEN
Grilled chicken, mixed peppers, onions, roma tomatoes, wild mushrooms, garlic & tossed with penne pasta $10.95

PENNE PRIMAVERA WITH SHRIMP
Shrimp, mixed peppers, onions, roma tomatoes, wild mushrooms, romano cheese & garlic tossed with penne pasta $13.95

SEAFOOD LINGUINE
Shrimp, scallops, salmon, mahi-mahi, tuna and black grouper with garlic, wild mushrooms, romano cheese & fresh herbs in a chardonnay cream sauce over linguine $14.95

Responding to the demand for a second location in the heart of Charleston, a sister restaurant - The Boathouse on Easy Bay Street - was opened in 1999. With a slightly more sophisticated atmosphere, the Easy Bay location offers a similar menu and excellent wine list - with the popular addition of a raw bar. Architecturally, her spacious bi-level interior is fashioned to resemble the fine wooden boats that once graced Charleston's harbors - accentuated with Brazilian cherry, mahogany & teak and adorned throughout with newly restored authentic sailing vessels.

Raw Bar Selections

SPICED SHRIMP COCKTAIL
Served chilled and peeled with lemon & cocktail sauce
.... 1/4 lb. $7.50 1/2 lb. $13.95

BREACH INLET LITTLENECK CLAMS
(raw) .... $.95 each $4.95 1/2 Dozen

CHILLED PETITE LOBSTER TAILS
(Marinated and Chilled)
Served with a Hoisin-Ginger Sauce
.... 3 Tails $10.95 6 Tails $20.95

MUSSELS
New Zealand Greenlip Mussels
(Smoked and chilled) .... 1/2 doz. $6.95

Starters

Roasted Corn & Crab Soup $3.95
Fried Green Tomatoes with Marinara $3.95
Fried Shrimp with Cocktail Sauce $5.95
Steamed Littleneck Clams $6.95
Steamed Green Lip & P.E.I. Mussels $6.95
Side Ceasar Salad $3.95
Dry Cured in House Smoked Salmon with Wasbi Cream $6.95
House Salad with Marinated Tomatoes & Cukes $2.95
Pepper Seared Rare Tuna with Mild Green Tabasco $7.50
Fried Oysters with Smoked Jalapeno Mayo $5.95
Steamed Trio of Clams, Mussels & Shrimp $6.95
Crab Fritters with Mild Green Tabasco Sauce $7.50

Grilled Fresh Fish

Choose one of our homemade sauces:
Pesto, Tarragon, Butter, Dijon Mustard Glaze or Blackened
(Served with your choice of two side items)

Mahi-Mahi $15.95
Yellowfin Tuna $16.95
Atlantic Salmon $14.95
Black Grouper $16.95

Specialties

SHRIMP& GRITS $13.95
CRAB CAKES $17.95
FILET & CRAB CAKE $19.95
FILET & LOBSTER $21.95
BAKED BLACK GROUPER $16.95
LOBSTER TAILS $21.95

14 OZ. CENTER CUT PORK CHOP
Lightly smoked in-house, grilled and served with a Portabello demi-glace. $16.95

BAKED STUFFED MAHI-MAHI
Crabmeat stuffing with Lobster sauce $18.95

BRAISED SEA BASS
Served over a grit cake with roma tomatoes, wild mushroom, shallot & garlic broth $18.95

APPLEWOOD SMOKED SALMON
Atlantic salmon smoked in house with a roasted garlic sauce $15.95

MIXED BROILED SEAFOOD
Shrimp, clams, mussels, mahi, scallops, 1/2 Petite lobster tail with a roasted garlic cream sauce $19.95

Pastas

PENNE PRIMAVERA $9.95
PENNE PRIMAVERA w/CHICKEN ... $10.95
PENNE PRIMAVERA w/SHRIMP $13.95
SEAFOOD LINGUINE $14.95

SHELLFISH COMBINATION
Lobster, clams, mussels, scallops & andouille sausage, mixed pepper & garlic, sauteed then steamed in a marinara saffron broth $16.95

Fried Seafood

Fried Shrimp $14.95
Fried Scallops $12.95
Fried Oysters $12.95
Fried Combination (Choice of Two) ... $13.95

Beef & Chicken

New York Strip - 14 oz. $17.95
Filet - 9 oz. $17.95
Grilled Chicken $10.95

The Boathouse on East Bay Street

CHARLESTON
549 E. Bay St.
Charleston, SC 29403

PHONE
(843) 577-7171

FAX
(843) 577-7178

HOURS
Raw Bar, 4:00 pm Daily
Sunday-Thursday
5:00 pm-10:00 pm
Friday & Saturday
5:00 pm-11:00 pm

MEALS SERVED
Dinner

CUISINE
Lowcountry
Seafood
Steak

DINING INFORMATION
Terrace/Patio Dining
Heart Smart Meals
Vegetarian Meals
Take Out Meals
Seasonal Menus
Childrens Menu
Extensive Wine Menu

LOUNGE BAR
Sunday-Thursday
4:00 pm-10:00 pm
Saturday & Sunday
4:00 pm-11:00 pm

ADDITIONAL SERVICES
Private Luncheons
In-House Catering

ATTIRE
Resort Casual

RESERVATIONS
Suggested

SMOKING
Smoking Section

VALET PARKING

HANDICAP FACILITIES

CREDIT CARDS
American Express
Visa
Master Card

CHECKS
Accepted

Voted
"BEST SEAFOOD"
1999 Best of Charleston Readers Poll

Bocci's Italian Restaurant

CHARLESTON
158 Church Street
Charleston, SC 29401
PHONE
(843) 720-2121
FAX
(843) 720-2102
HOURS
Lunch
Daily
11:30 am-4:30 pm
Dinner
Sunday-Thursday
4:30 pm-10:00 pm
Friday & Saturday
4:30 pm-11:00 pm
MEALS SERVED
Lunch
Dinner
CUISINE
Italian
DINING INFORMATION
Heart Smart Meals
Vegetarian Meals
Take Out Meals
Childrens Menu
Extensive Wine Menu

ATTIRE
Casual
RESERVATIONS
Not Required
Suggested
SMOKING
Smoking Section
Cigar & Pipe Friendly
HANDICAP FACILITIES
CREDIT CARDS
American Express
Visa
Master Card
Discover Card
Diners Club Card
CHECKS
Accepted

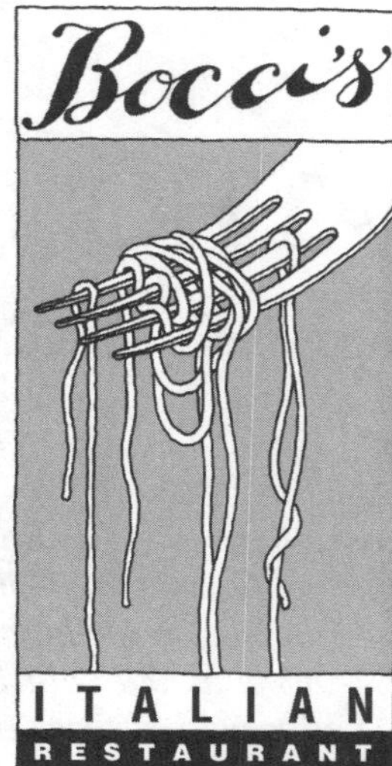

Located downtown just steps from The Market, Bocci's has been a favorite among locals for years; tucked away on the corner of Cumberland and Church, most visitors simply fail to notice it. If you're in the mood for some exquisite Italian, however, you'll want to make a point of finding Bocci's. You'll find full Italian fare, excellent wines, heavenly desserts, and affordable prices. Lunch & dinner. Families are welcome.

INSALATA

CAESAR SALAD
Romaine lettuce in a traditional caesar dressing tossed with fresh baked croutons. $3.25

ANTIPASTA SALAD
Lettuce wedge, prosciutto, salami, artichoke hearts, olives, marinated mushrooms, pepperoncini and provolone cheese...anchovies on request. $5.95

ANTIPASTI

MINESTRONE SOUP
A classic - a hearty broth with ham, beans, pasta, and fresh vegetables. Topped with fresh grated parmesan cheese. Cup $2.50 Bowl $3.50

FOCACCIA
Italian flatbread brushed with herbs and grilled; then served with our creamy artichoke dip. $4.25

CALAMARI
Tender fried calamari served with our spicy marinara sauce. $5.95

FRIED EGGPLANT
Tender eggplant round, lightly breaded and fried, topped with pesto, melted provolone, and tomato basil sauce, and served on a bed of fried angelhair pasta. $5.25

SPAGHETTI

MARINARA
A garden fresh all vegetable tomato sauce. $8.50

TOMATO BASIL
A traditional sauce of tomatoes, olive oil and fresh basil. $8.50

MEATSAUCE
A Bolognese with tomatoes, spicy Italian sausage, veal and beef. $8.95

LASAGNE VERDE
A rich combination of cheeses layered between our homemade spinach lasagne noodles, then oven baked and topped with two sauces. $11.95

BAKED ZITI
Fresh ziti, meat sauce, parmesan and cream baked in a casserole and topped with fresh grated provolone cheese. $9.95

FETTUCINI ALFREDO
Bocci's egg fettucini tossed in a light cream sauce and topped with fresh grated parmesan cheese. $9.50

PASTA

RAVIOLI ARRABIATA
Spinach ravioli topped with a spicy marinara, fresh spinach and Italian sausage. $12.95

PASTA WITH CHICKEN & LEMON BASIL SAUCE
Sauteed boneless breast of chicken atop our angelhair pasta in a delicate lemon basil cream sauce with mushrooms. $11.95

RISO WITH SHRIMP AND SCALLOPS
Shrimp and scallops sauteed with tomatoes, scallions, and white wine; then tossed with Bocci's Italian riso. $13.95

CARNE E PESCE

CHICKEN MARSALA
A boneless breast of chicken sauteed with mushrooms and onions in a marsala and veal sauce served over angel hair pasta. $12.95

CHICKEN FLORENTINO
A grilled boneless breast of chicken, stuffed with proscuitto ham, spinach and three cheeses, then baked. $12.95

VEAL SALTIMBOCCA
Veal scaloppine, fresh sage and proscuitto ham topped with a mushroom and marsala sauce served over linguini. $14.95

BEEF TENDERLOIN
A 8 oz. tenderloin filet grilled to perfection and topped with mushroom and red wine sauce. $16.95

SCALLOPS WRAPPED IN PROSCIUTTO
Large sea scallops wrapped with thinly sliced prosciutto, baked and served on a florentine cream sauce. $14.95

MIXED GRILL
Shrimp, beef tenderloin, and lamb, grilled and served on top of Bocci's Italian riso. $16.95

SPAGHETTI DELLA PINA FOR TWO
A traditional Italian Bouillabaisse. A bountiful array of sauteed clams, mussels, scallops, calamari and shrimp served atop Bocci's spaghetti. $26.95

Brett's Restaurant

Chef Brett McKee is the creative force behind Charleston's newest four star restaurant. Peter Herman, food critic for the Post & Courier, calls Brett's food "...sophisticated, complex and very tasty"; as well as, "a feast for the eyes and the senses." Brett's specialties include an array of veal, chicken, beef and fresh seafood. Additionally, prepare yourself for Italian flare of gnocchi, risotto and individually baked gourmet pizzas. Come experience a meal you won't soon forget in ambience created in either of their lovely dining rooms. Brett's also offers a variety of on and off premise catering options.

Salads

Beef Salad with Goat Cheese & Walnuts $6

Buffalo Mozzarella, Tomatoes & Basil with Seasoned Olive Oil & Balsamic Vinegar $9

Tuscan Style Tomato & Bread Salad $5

Spinach Salad with a Warm Balsamic Vinaigrette and Pancette Bacon $9

Appetizers

Filet Mignon Tartare with Toast Points $9

Prosciutto de Parma with fresh Melon & Shaved Parmesan $8

Grilled Marinated Portobello Mushroom with Arugula, Crumbled Gorgonzola, & Tomatoes $8

Grilled Asparagus with Shaved Parmesan & Sauce Beurre Blanc $8

Steamed Mussels or Clams in a Lemon White Wine or a Light Marinara Sauce' $11

Lobster, Shrimp, & Crab Cake with a Lobster Butter Sauce $9

Risotto

With Sausage, Tomato & Arugula $14

With Wild Mushrooms $14

Gnocchi

With Wild Mushrooms, Pancetta & Three Cheeses $14

With Marinara & Mozzarella $12

Fried with Brown Butter, Sage & Proscuitto $13

Pasta

Eggplant Parmesan with Spaghettini & Marinara $13

Four Cheese Lasagna $14

Penne Pasta & Pancetta with a Spicy Vodka Pepper Sauce $13

Spaghettini with Veal Meatballs & Marinara $14

Linguine Alla Carbonara $13

Chicken

Roasted Lemon Chicken, Sweet Potatoe Puree, Sausage-Yellow Squash Casserole & Grilled Asparagus $17

Cacciatore over Spaghettini $15

Marsala with Garlic Mashed Potatoes & Julienne Vegetables $15

Parmesan over Spaghettini with Marinara Sauce $15

Veal

Fresh Cut Veal Chop with Fresh Sage, Cannellini Bean Fricasee & a Wild Mushroom Demi-Glace $27

Picatta with Creany Parmesan Potatoes & Julienne Vegetables $18

Marsala with Garlic Mashed Potatoes & Julienne Vegetables $19

Saltimbocca with Garlic Mashed Potatoes & Julienne Vegetables $20

Beef & Sausage

Pan Seared Tenderloin of Beef with Gorgonzola Potatoes Gratin, Grilled Asparagus & a Wild Mushroom Demi-Glace $21

Grilled Italian Sausage, Cannellini Bean Fricasee, Garlic Mashed Potatoes & a Red Grape Demi-Glace $15

Italian Sausage with Peppers & Onions over Spaghettini & Marinara $15

Seafood

Potato Wrapped Grouper, Sauteed Spinach, Julienne Vegetables & Fried Leeks $19

Littleneck Clams or Mussels over Linguine in a Lemon White Wine or Marinara Sauce $15

Grilled Marinated Yellow-Fin Tuna, Spicy Ginger Asian Slaw & Wasabi Mashed Potatoes $20

Seafood Fra Diavlo, Shrimp, Mussels, Scallops, Clams & Calamari over Spaghettini in a Spicy Marinara Sauce $20

Shrimp Scampi over Linguini $19

Shrimp, Sausage Tomatoes & Leeks over Linguini $19

CHARLESTON
1970 Maybank Highway
Charleston, SC 29412

PHONE
(843) 795-9964

FAX
(843) 795-1416

HOURS
Lunch
Monday-Friday
11:30 am-2:30 pm
Dinner
Monday-Saturday
5:30 pm - until
Brunch
Sunday
10:30 am-2:30 pm

MEALS SERVED
Lunch
Dinner
Sunday Brunch

CUISINE
Northern Italian
American

DINING INFORMATION
Heart Smart Meals
Vegetarian Meals
Take Out Meals
Seasonal Menus
Extensive Wine Menu

ADDITIONAL SERVICES
Full Service Catering
Private Parties
Private Rooms

ATTIRE
Nice Casual

RESERVATIONS
Suggested

SMOKING
Smoking Section

HANDICAP FACILITIES

CREDIT CARDS
American Express
Visa
Master Card

CHECKS
Accepted
(Local)

Bull & Finch
Restaurant & Pub

MT. PLEASANT
1324 Theater Drive
Town Center
Mt. Pleasant, SC
PHONE
(843) 884-6455
HOURS
7 Days A Week
11:00 am-Until
MEALS SERVED
Lunch
Dinner
Late Night Dining
CUISINE
English Pub
DINING INFORMATION
Terrace/Patio Dining
LOUNGE BAR
SPORTS PROGRAMING
CIGAR LOUNGE &
BILLIARD PARLOR
ADDITIONAL SERVICES
Private Parties
Banquet Facilities
Private Rooms

ATTIRE
Resort Casual
RESERVATIONS
Not Required
SMOKING
Smoking Section
HANDICAP FACILITIES
CREDIT CARDS
American Express
Visa
Master Card
Discover Card
CHECKS
Not Accepted

God save the Queen...and her English folklore and food with the opening of the new Bull & Finch restaurant and pub in the Mt. Pleasant Town Center opening at 11:00 am, seven days a week. The Bull & Finch is your perfect meeting spot for lunch, dinner, happy hour or late night. The menu is wonderful, with selections like Pilsner steamed Prawns, beef or chicken satays, steak and mushroom stew, fabulous salads and sandwiches including English corned beef, juicy warm roast beef or the classic BLT..plus a variety of English pot pies and "bangers" - sausages served with mashed potatoes, onion gravy and vegetables and daily homemade desserts. The Bull & Finch, Mt. Pleasant's only authentic English Pub features 14 British and Irish beers, 11 ten year old single malt scotches and 8 small batch bourbons plus an exotic martini selection that will bring the queen herself to her knees.

APPETIZERS

POTATO CRISPS - housemade potato chips loaded with cheddar, chili, onions, sour cream, diced tomatoes and jalapenos 4.95
SPRING ROLLS - shrimp and vegetables spring rolls with a spicy cucumber sauce 6.95
ALE PRAWNS - grilled ale marinated prawns wrapped with applewood bacon 6.95
BEER BATTERED ONION RINGS - beer battered onions fried to a golden crisp 4.95
BULL CRAB DIP - warm blue crab dip served with toasted baguette points 5.95
PILSNER STEAMED PRAWNS - 1/4 pound chilled beer steamed prawns 6.95
BEEF WELLINGTON TIPS - filet tips and mushroom pate wrapped in puff pastry with onion gravy 6.95
WELSH SEAFOOD CAKE - shrimp, crab and cod seafood cake 6.95
BEEF OR CHICKEN SATAYS - grilled beef skewers with a teriyaki sauce grilled chicken skewers served with a caribbean peanut sauce 4.95

SOUPS AND SALADS

STEAK AND MUSHROOM STEW 2.95
LAGER CHICKEN CHOWDER 2.95
BULL AND FINCH SALAD - fresh greens with beefsteak tomatoes, cucumbers, red onion and mushrooms, cheddar cheese and choice of dressing 6.95
ASIAN CHICKEN SALAD - shredded chicken tossed with cabbage, carrots, onions and sesame noodles in a ginger honey viniagrette 6.50
SPINACH SALAD - fresh spinach with toasted pecans, mushrooms and crumbled bleu cheese in a warm applewood bacon vinaigrette 5.95

SANDWICHES

DEVONSHIRE - warm roast beef with caramelized onion and cheddar cheese on a 9 grain roll 5.95
WIMBLEDON - warm roast beef with sauteed mushrooms and horseradish sauce on a baguette 5.95
GLASGOW - crab salad with swiss cheese and applewood bacon on a toasted english muffin 7.95
CLASSIC CORNED BEEF - warm corn beef with sauerkraut and swiss cheese on grilled rye 5.95
HONG KONG PORK - warm sliced roasted porter hoison pork with sweet/sour cabbage on a baguette 5.95
BANGER SUB - chicken and apple sausage w/ caramelized onions and English mustard 5.95

BULL & FINCH GRILLERS

B & F BURGER - 8 oz. seasoned grilled ground beef on a 9 grain roll with lettuce and tomato $4.95
B & F LAGER CHICKEN - 6 oz. lager marinated grilled boneless chicken breast on a 9 grain roll with lettuce and tomato $4.95

ENTREES

CLASSIC LONDON BROIL - served with vegetable of the day and mashed potatoes $9.95
TRADITIONAL FISH AND CHIPS - fried beer battered cod served with chips and slaw $8.95
NEW WORLD SHRIMP AND CHIPS - golden fried shrimp served with chips and slaw $9.95
BULL AND FINCH COMBINATION - fried cod and shrimp served with chips and slaw $10.95
SCOTLAND YARD - open faced warm roast beef sandwich on double cut cracked wheat bread topped with onion gravy served with colcannon $7.95
CARIBBEAN JERK FISH - grilled fresh fish rubbed with jerk seasonings with a raspberry lambic glaze mkt. price
AMBER ORANGE ROAST CHICKEN - amber ale and orange roasted 1/4 chicken served with mashed potatoes and vegetable of the day $7.95
SCOTTISH BRAISED PORK RIBS - oven braised 1/2 rack of ribs glazed with a sweet bbq sauce with a hint of highland malt scotch served with slaw and chips $9.95
PORTER HOISIN PORK - oven braised pork tenderloin served on a bed of asian slaw $8.95
WELSH SEAFOOD CAKES - shrimp, crab and cod cakes served with a chipolte cream sauce $10.95

BANGERS

TRADITIONAL ENGLISH - made with pork, breading and spices $7.95
HICKORY DUCK AND ORANGE - made with duck, orange and spices $8.95
CHICKEN AND APPLE - made with chicken apple and spices $8.95

PIE AND PASTIES

CUMBERLAND PIE - seasoned ground beef, peas and carrots topped with mashed potatoes and cheddar $5.95
STEAK AND MUSHROOM PIE - steak, mushrooms, tomatoes, herbs and gravy in a pastry shell $5.95
CHICKEN PASTIE - chicken, vegetables and potatoes in a pastry shell $4.95

Café St. Tropez

With it's sophisticated casual atmosphere this quaint little gem is tucked away upstairs overlooking Bohicket Marina on Seabrook Island. Executive Chef Charles Giordano prepares delicious Mediterranean and French Provencal fare with world-class flair. The menu and large variety of seasonal specials are sure to please the most discriminating gourmet.
Great food - great wines - great service, and unparalleled views.

Soups, Salads and Appetizers

Minestrone a la Genovese
cup $4.95 bowl $5.95

Bohicket Crab Soup
cup $4.95 bowl $6.95

Provençal Shrimp Bisque
cup $4.95 bowl $6.95

Lobster Madeira Bisque
cup $6.95 bowl $9.95

Salad of Golden Tomatoes, Seedless Cucumber, Smoked Mozzarella and Grape Tomatoes with Extra-Virgin Olive Oil and Balsamic Vinegar
$9.95

Grilled Shrimp and Feta Cheese Caesar Salad with Garlic Croutons
$9.95

House Smoked Atlantic Salmon with Red Pepper Aiöli, Capers and Mixed Organic Greens
$11.95

Grilled Asian Marinated Beef Tenderloin with Mixed Organic Greens, Grilled Red Onions, Toasted Sesame Soy Vinaigrette and Wasabi Mayonnaise
$11.95

Salad of Mixed Organic Greens and Balsamic Vinaigrette
$5.95

Grilled Portabello Mushroom with Red Onion Reduction Sauce and Shallot Confit
$7.95

Sautéed Escargot in Puffed Pastry with Garlic Herb Cream Sauce and Sautéed Asparagus
$9.95

Entrees

Pepper Crusted Filet of Atlantic Salmon with Moroccan Red Bell Pepper Sauce and Ginger Braised Cabbage
$17.95

Sautéed Loin of Veal with a Wild Mushroom Marsala Sauce and Saffron Whipped Potatoes
$21.95

Grilled 8 Ounce Filet Mignon with Sauce Béarnaise and Saffron Whipped Potatoes
$23.95

Sautéed Breast of and Confit Leg of Duck with Raspberry Port Demi-Glace and Honey Balsamic Lentils
$24.95

Linguini Tossed with a Smoked Salmon Fresh Thyme Cream Sauce
$17.95

Grilled Yellowfin Tuna with Double Roasted Red Peppers and Basil Pesto
$19.95

Grilled Boneless Breast of Chicken and Grilled Eggplant with Tarragon Mayonnaise
$14.95

Fresh Roma and Golden Tomatoes, Sautéed with Garlic, Basil, Extra Virgin Olive Oil and Smoked Mozzarella over Angel Hair Pasta
$14.95

Medallions of Pork Tenderloin Sautéed with a Sundried Tomato Rosemary Sauce
$18.95

Ciopino - Half Maine Lobster, Shrimp, Mussels, Calamari, Diver Scallops and Fresh Fish Sautéed in a Spicy Roma Tomato Fresh Basil Broth
$28.95

Café St. Tropez

SEABROOK ISLAND
1880 Andells Bluff Blvd.
Seabrook Island, SC 29455

PHONE
(843) 768-1500

FAX
(843) 768-1505

HOURS
Daily
5:00 pm-10:00 pm

MEALS SERVED
Dinner

CUISINE
Contemporary
Continental
Mediterranean

DINING INFORMATION
Terrace/Patio Dining
Vegetarian Meals
Seasonal Specials
Extensive Wine Selection

LOUNGE BAR
Daily
5:00 pm-10:00 pm

ADDITIONAL SERVICES
Private Parties

ATTIRE
Casual

RESERVATIONS
Suggested

SMOKING
Bar Only/Terrace

HANDICAP FACILITIES

CREDIT CARDS
American Express
Visa
Master Card
Diners Club

California Dreaming

CHARLESTON
#1 Ashley Pointe Drive
Charleston, SC 29407
PHONE
(843) 766-1644
FAX
(843) 571-2232
WEBSITE
www.californiadreamings.com
HOURS
Sunday-Thursday
11:00 am-10:00 pm
Friday & Saturday
11:00 am-11:00 pm
MEALS SERVED
Lunch
Dinner
CUISINE
American
DINING INFORMATION
Take Out Meals
Childrens Menu
LOUNGE BAR
Restaurant Hours
ATTIRE
Casual
RESERVATIONS
Not Required
SMOKING
Smoking Section
CREDIT CARDS
American Express
Visa
Master Card
Discover Card
CHECKS
Not Accepted

Sit beside the Ashley River and enjoy an unmatched view of the Charleston Harbor in the only Restaurant in Charleston where every table has an excellent waterfront view!

• APPETIZERS •

Onion Ring Loaf 4.50
Peel and Eat Shrimp 7 shrimp 4.95 / 11 shrimp 7.95
Tijuana Chicken Wings 4.95
Chicken Strips 5.50
Bowl of Chili 3.95
Baked Potato Soup 3.25
Basket of Croissants 3.50
Traditional Nacho 5.95
Fresh Salmon Nacho 7.95
BBQ Chicken Nacho 7.50
Creamed Spinach Nacho 6.95

• ENTREE SALADS •

California Dreaming Salad 6.95
Ice cold mixed greens topped with chopped eggs, cured ham, turkey, Cheddar and Monterey Jack cheeses, toasted almonds, tomatoes and finished off with fresh cooked Hormel® bacon and ham.

Broiled Breast of Chicken Salad 6.95
Our chicken is marinated 48 hours, broiled to order and served hot over mixed greens, hearts of palm, fresh mushrooms, scallions and chopped tomatoes.

Caesar Salad *w/Broiled Marinated Chicken Breast* 7.50 / *w/ Freshly Battered Fried Shrimp* 8.95
Classic Caesar dressing topped with fresh, imported Romano cheese and homemade fresh croutons, instead of croissant.

Our Special House Salad 4.95
Mixed greens, chopped eggs, almonds, tomatoes, Hormel® ham and real bacon.

Soup and Special House Salad 6.95

Broiled Salmon Salad 8.95
Mixed greens, hearts of palm, fresh mushrooms, scallions, and chopped tomatoes.

• SANDWICHES •

Broiled Marinated Chicken 6.95
New Orleans Shrimp "Po Boy" 7.95
Club Sandwich 6.95
Sliced Prime Rib Sandwich 8.50
Broiled Salmon Sandwich 8.75

• BURGERS •

American Burger 5.95
Barbecue Bacon Cheeseburger 6.95
Chili Burger 6.95

• STEAKS •

New York Strip 15.95
Filet Mignon *9oz. Barrel Cut* 19.95
Marinated Sirloin *11 oz.* 12.75

• OUR FAMOUS BABY BACK RIBS •

We use only the shorter Danish full flavored ribs and grill them with the classic charred exterior. Topped with our honey tinted barbecue sauce. Our ribs are so "Fall-off-the-bone" tender they can be eaten with a fork.

One Rack 11.50 **Two Racks 15.95**

• HOUSE SPECIAL PRIME RIB •

California Dreaming's #1 beef item is slow cooked in Alto Shaam™ ovens. To insure top quality, we only serve prime rib at dinner.

11 oz. Cut 13.95
16 oz. "Proprietor's Cut" 16.95

• CHICKEN & SEAFOOD •

Marinated Chicken 9.50
Giant 12 oz. double breast of chicken marinated 48 hours in fruit juices, fresh garlic, soy sauce and spices.

Chicken Quesadilla 8.95
Spiced chicken blended with mixed cheeses, scallions, jalapenos and sautéed in a flour tortilla. Sour cream, green onions, and tomatoes on the side.

Chicken Parmesan 10.95
Fresh 8 oz. skinless breast of chicken is dipped in batter, Italian bread crumbs and Romano cheese and topped with marinara sauce and mozzarella cheese. Served with fettuccine marinara unless other side item requested.

Chicken Marinara 9.95
Broiled chicken in homemade classic tomato sauce over angel hair instead of a side item. Topped with fresh chopped scallions.

Chicken Strips Platter 9.75
Large order of batter-fried strips of fresh marinated chicken tenderloins.

Barbecue Chicken 9.50
Giant 12 oz. fresh double breast of chicken marinated in fruit juices and covered with our honey tinted barbecue sauce.

Fried Shrimp Platter 13.95
Large shrimp battered to order. Served with french fried potatoes and your choice of cocktail or tartar sauce.

Broiled Salmon A.Q.
Broiled 10 oz. cut. Served with your choice of steam mixed vegetables or creamed spinach.

Shrimp San Francisco 12.95
Shrimp are sautéed with mushrooms, garlic, white wine, real butter and more garlic. Served over angel hair with Romano cheese.

Fresh Fish of the Day A.Q.
Ask your server for today's variety. Your choice of creamed spinach or steamed mixed vegetables.

Carolina's

Voted "1999's Best Restaurant." For thirteen years, Carolina's Restaurant has charmed patrons with cuisine that fuses Chef Rose Durden's Asian heritage with her love of southern foods. The wine list is extensive and accessible; the decor is stylistically warm and inviting. Let Carolina's Cartering bring their best to your home or favorite place, making your next special occasion an unforgettable event. Visit The Upper Perdita's Room above Carolina's Restaurant to experience an invigorated twist in private group dining.

Appetizers

Spinach Crepe filled with Pork, Shrimp, Wild Mushrooms served with Smoked Onions and Red Pepper Sauce 10.95

Shrimp and Crabmeat Wontons on a Lime Ginger Sauce 7.50

Crowder Pea Cakes with a Cucumber Yogurt Sauce and Avocado Salsa 7.25

Caribbean Shrimp and Scallops with Black Beans and *Carolina Rose Tropical Fruit Chutney*....9.50

Soups and Salads

Grilled Marinated Shrimp and Scallops over Fresh Greens and Citrus-Ginger Vinaigrette 13.75

Grilled Sliced Lamb Tenderloin with Fried Goat Cheese Cake, Balsamic Vinergerette over Fresh Greens, *Carolina Rose Eggplant and Sun-dried Tomato Chutney*™ 16.95

Carolina's Black Bean Soup with Sour Cream and Fresh Salsa 4.50

Pastas

Sauteed Chicken Tenders with Fresh Herbs, Spinach Shiitake Mushrooms and Tomatoes over Penne 10.95

Seasonal Vegetables Sauteed in Extra Virgin Olive Oil and Soy Sauce, Shiitakes, Tomatoes, Fresh Herbs over Asian Angel Hair Pasta 9.95

Entrees

Asian Seafood Pot with Shrimp, Scallops, Grouper and Calamari accompanied with Jasmine Rice 21.95

Sweet Potato Crusted Filet of Flounder with Avocado Salsa, Rice, Vegetables, and Lemon Butter Sauce 19.00

Seared Sesame Crusted Tuna (Cooked Rare) with Asian Stir Fried Vegetables and Wasabi 19.95

Sauteed Local Grouper Encrusted in Almond Black Sesame Seed Topped with Crabmeat, Lemon Butter Sauce, and *Carolina Rose Tropical Fruit Chutney*™ 21.50

Grilled Jerk Chicken Breast, Black Beans and Rice 11.50

Grilled and Smoked Jamaican Jerk Pork Tenderloin with *Carolina Rose Caribbean Pepper Jam*™ and Caribbean Black Beans 17.50

Grilled Boneless Loin of Lamb, Mashed Potatoes, Collard Greens, and *Carolina Rose Eggplant and Sun-Dried Tomato Chutney*™ 18.50

CHARLESTON
10 Exchange Street
Charleston, SC 29401

PHONE
(843) 724-3800

FAX
(843) 722-9493

HOURS
Monday-Thursday
5:30 pm-until
Friday-Sunday
5:00-until

MEALS SERVED
Dinner

CUISINE
Contemporary
Eclectic

DINING INFORMATION
Heart Smart Meals
Vegetarian Meals
Take Out Meals
Childrens Menu
Extensive Wine Menu

ADDITIONAL SERVICES
Full Service Catering
Private Parties

ATTIRE
Resort Casual

RESERVATIONS
Suggested

SMOKING
Smoking Section
No Cigar or Pipe Smoking

HANDICAP FACILITIES

CREDIT CARDS
American Express
Visa
Master Card
Discover Card
Diners Club Card

CHECKS
Not Accepted

Charleston Chops

"Friendly Fine Dining" exemplifies the experience we strive to give all our guests. It is an experience achieved through fabulous food, wonderful wines, exciting entertainment and stellar service. Corporate Chef Jeffery Gibbs and Executive Chef Brian Hallam serve only the best in **Certified Angus Beef™**, *wild game and seafood entrees. We also feature different crème brulees nightly and other treats to enhance your dinner experience. Our culinary creations pair perfectly with over 220 wines from around the world as well as fine cognacs, small batch bourbons, and single malt scotches.*

Our professional pianists will entertain you throughout the evening with your favorite contemporary and classical tunes. We invite you to experience an exquisite evening of "Friendly Fine Dining" at Charleston Chops.

Appetizers

Canadian Mussels Steamed in $10
Saffron and Toasted Coconut Broth

Garlic Rubbed Grilled Portobella with $7
Roasted Red Peppers, Fresh Mozzarella and Blueberry Balsamic Reduction

Lowcountry Crabcake $9
with Spicy Corn Coulis

Black Angus Tartar with Truffle Oil, ... $10
Shaved Parmesan and Traditional Garnish

Lightly Fried Calamari with $8
Baby Mesclun, Banana Peppers and Lemon Asiago Vinaigrette

Ostrich, Wild Mushroom and Pineapple .. $10
Brochette with Port Glaze

Chilled Jumbo Shrimp Cocktail with $10
Horseradish Chili Sauce

Cold Water Lobster Strudel $13
with Roasted Pepper Coulis

Shepherd's Pie of Lamb, Veal, Venison $9
and Beef with Whipped Potatoes, Roasted Corn and Veal Glacé

Soups

Shrimp Chowder $6
Chef's Selection

Charleston Chops

CHARLESTON
188 East Bay Street
Charleston, SC 29401
PHONE
(843) 937-9300
FAX
(843) 937-9308
WEBSITE
www.charlestonchops.com
HOURS
Sunday-Thursday
5:30 pm-10:00 pm
Friday-Saturday
5:30 pm-11:00 pm
Bar Opens Daily at 5:00 pm
MEALS SERVED
Dinner
CUISINE
American
Steak House
Eclectic
DINING INFORMATION
Extensive Wine Menu
LOUNGE BAR
Sunday-Thursday
5:00 pm-11:00 pm
Friday & Saturday
5:00 pm-12:00 pm
LIVE MUSIC
Sunday-Thursday
6:00 pm-10:00 pm
Friday-Saturday
7:00 pm-12:00 pm
ADDITIONAL SERVICES
Private Parties

ATTIRE
Resort Casual
RESERVATIONS
Suggested
SMOKING
Smoking Section
HANDICAP FACILITIES
CREDIT CARDS
American Express
Visa
Master Card
Discover Card
Diners Club Card
CHECKS
Not Accepted

Salads

Caesar Salad $6

Baby Mixed Greens with Seasonal $6
Fruit and a Raspberry, Walnut Vinaigrette

Spinach Salad with Feta and Warm $6
Tomato, Pancetta Vinaigrette

Chilled Iceberg and Hearts of $6
Romaine with Roma Tomatoes and Clemson Bleu Cheese Dressing

Wild Game Specials

Wild Game Meatloaf with Grilled $16
Onions, Blue Cheese over Herb Whipped Potatoes and Roasted Corn

Herb Crusted Wild Salmon $19
Over Mushroom and Tasso Stone Ground Grits with Cranberry Jalapeno Chutney

Grilled Marinated Wild Boar Chops .... Mkt.
with Smoked Gouda Potatoes and Pommeray Mustard Demi Glacé

Charleston Chops' Finest 21 Day Aged *Certified Angus Beef*™

Grilled Filet served 10oz. $24 7oz. $20
with Asparagus, Portobella and Roasted Shallot Whipped Potatoes

Prime Rib served 16oz. $22 12oz. $18
with Baked Potato and Au Jus

Ribeye 15 oz. with Seasonal $21
Vegetables and Marinated Steak Fries

New York Strip 16 oz. served with $25
Sautéed Wild Mushrooms and Tobacco Onions

Porterhouse 28 oz. with .... Market Price
Whipped Potatoes and Tobacco Onions

Chops Bone-In Ribeye 22 oz. ..... Market Price
with Marinated Steak Fries

Also Available

Onion Rings with Bourbon Honey Mustard .. $6

"Oscar Style" Asparagus, ... $6
Crabmeat and Béarnaise

Chops' Specialties

Peanut Crusted Rare Tuna $19
served with Garlic Chili Aioli and Sesame Capallini

Grilled Marinated Veal Chop over $24
Herb Mashed Potatoes with Wild Mushroom and Leek Fricassee

Pistachio Crusted Grouper served with $19
Whipped Sweet Potatoes, Asparagus and Citrus Ginger Beurre Blanc

Grilled Center Cut Bone-In Pork Chops .. $18
with Sweet Potatoes, Sautéed Spinach and Smoked Tomato Bourbon Butter

Jumbo Shrimp and Scallops Sautéed $20
with Sun Dried Tomatoes, Mushrooms and Leeks served over Angel Hair Pasta

Slow Roasted Rack of Lamb $25
with a Rosemary Whole Grain Mustard Crust, Morel Port Glacé and Tomato, Artichoke Hash

Lowcountry Crabcakes $19
with Stone Ground Yellow Grits and Sweet Roasted Corn Coulis

Grilled Chicken Breast Over Whipped $17
Potatoes, Haricotverts and Fresh Roma Tomatoes topped with Tobacco Onions and Thyme Beurre Blanc

Mixed Grill of Jumbo Shrimp, ... $23
Lobster Tail and Seasonal Fish served with Crawfish Risotto, Sautéed Spinach and Tomato Beurre Rouge

Pan Seared Duck Breast $22
and Braised Duck Leg with Whipped Sweet Potatoes, Sesame Wafers and Caramelized Ginger, Duck Glacé

Grilled Marinated Seasonal Vegetables ... $13
with Sweet Basil and Wild Onion Risotto

Veal Osso Bucco Roasted with $23
Caramelized Vegetables and Port Wine over Wild Mushroom Risotto

Steamed 2-3 Pound .... Mkt.
Live Maine Lobster served with Roasted Corn and Asparagus Salad

Charleston Grill

Join us for cocktails, live jazz and wonderful Lowcountry cooking. The extraordinary complexities of Chef Bob Waggoner's cuisine represent an evolution of his travels throughout the culinary world including France's top kitchens and Nashville's five-diamond The Wild Boar.

Now, Bob is receiving national recognition for bringing Charleston the only Mobil Four-Star restaurant in the state of South Carolina for the second consecutive year and a Restaurant Wine and Spirits Chef of the Year award from *Santé Magazine*. Chef Bob is marrying the purest flavors imaginable with some of the most superb presentations in the nation. Our guests are raving! Come indulge while relaxing in our spectacular dining room where candlelight glows throughout and the atmosphere exudes warmth. Larger parties enjoy the intimacy of the Vintner's Room featuring walls of glass-fronted wine cellars showcasing its impressive stock of vintages from around the world.

Plan to dine with us soon to see why the Lowcountry loves Charleston Grill!

APPETIZERS & SOUPS

Coastal Carolina White Shrimp and Lobster Bisque 6.50

Maine Lobster Tempura over Lemon Grits and Fried Mini Green Tomatoes in a Yellow Tomato Tarragon Butter 12.95

Pan Seared Duck Foie Gras with a Hushpuppy Stuffed with Caramelized Figs in a Whipped Pomegranate Cream 14.95

Sautéed Southern Frog Legs on a Mousseline of Roasted Garlic in a Light Chardonnay Parsley Butter 10.50

Oven Roasted Lamb Sweetbreads and Escargot over Truffled Stone Ground Grits in a Light Reduction of Fresh Morels 10.00

Russian Malosal Caviar served with small Buckwheat Blinis
1 ounce Osietr 37.00 1 ounce Beluga 65.00

Charleston Grill

SALADS

Warm Sautéed Rock Shrimp over Micro-sprouts with Charleston Grill Potato Skins in a Lemon-Thyme, Ginger Cream 11.00

Stuffed Parma Prosciutto with Goat Cheese, Roasted Pecans and Sunflower Sprouts in a Sherry Vinegar and Virgin Pecan Oil Vinaigrette 10.00

Baby Lola Rosa Leaves with Clemson Blue Cheese, Marinated Shiitakes and Roasted Hazelnuts in a Sweet Port and Fresh Rosemary Sauce 9.25

Chilled Goat Cheese Mousse with Currant Tomatoes, Opal, Basil and Baguette Chips 8.25

Kennerty Farms Local Young Lettuces in a Balsamic Vinegar and Extra Virgin Olive Oil Sauce 7.25

Aged Swiss Dried Beef Tenderloin with Chilled Chanterelle Mushrooms and Miniature White Asparagus in a Roasted Garlic-Baryuls Vinaigrette 12.00

Southern Fried Chicken Livers over Frisse and Young Mache with Apples, Bacon and Walnuts in an Aged Red Wine Vinaigrette 7.50

ENTREES

Dayboat Fluke Flounder Fillet over a Caramelized Fennel and Vidalia Onion Ragout with Maine Lobster in a Dijon Mustard and Garden Thyme Sauce 25.00

Sautéed Monkfish Loin with Roasted Diver Scallops on a Braised Eggplant Mousseline with Young Asparagus in a Sun Dried Tomato, Green Olive and Sage Butter 24.00

Pan Seared Carolina Golden Trout over Buttered Young Vegetables in a Grapefruit Reduction Scented with Pink Peppercorns 23.00

Local Burlill Duck and Vidalia Hash Pie in a Warm Apple Smoked Bacon and Sherry Pecan Vinaigrette 24.00

Fresh Elk Tenderloin over Caramelized Granny Smiths with Maple-Sweet Potato Mousseline in a Diced Apple and Apricot Glaze 29.00

Grilled Lamb Tenderloin over Lowcountry Succotash Scented with Thyme in a Smoked Heirloom Tomato Coulis and Roasted Garlic Cream 24.00

Roasted Prime Angus Beef Tenderloin Medallions over Opal Basil and Smoked Bacon Whipped Potatoes in a Seared Shallot and Walnut Jus 25.00

Darlington City Poussin Breasts Painted with Tapenade and Skillet Fried Thighs over Southern Fried Green Tomatoes in a Miniature Caper Jus 23.00

Seared Angus Beef Tongue over Heirloom Yellow Tomatoes and Asparagus Tips in a Chardonnay Reduction with Mustard, Capers and Chive Blossoms 23.00

...ON THE SIMPLER SIDE

Vegetarian Tasting Plate with Wild Mushrooms and Local Produce Prepared with our Garden Herbs 17.95

Traditional Fish Soup with Local Shrimp, Scallops, and Mussels 22.00

Simply Grilled Atlantic Salmon with Red, Orange and White Baby Carrots in a Lemon and Fresh Dill Butter 22.00

Slowly Grilled Veal Tenderloin Rolled in Our Garden Herbs over Braised Wild Mushrooms in a Light Summer Truffle Jus 29.00

SIDE DISHES

Wadmalaw Collards Braised in Palmetto Amber with Cabernet Pigs Feet 4.00

Roasted Corn with Smoked Bacon and Caramelized Vidalia Onions 4.00

Smoked Duck Whipped Potatoes with Fresh Chives 4.50

Pencil Asparagus, Roasted Peppers, and Pine Nuts 5.00

Baked Grits with Sundried Tomatoes, Garlic and Fresh Goat Cheese 4.50

CHARLESTON
224 King St.
Charleston, SC 29401

PHONE
(843) 577-4522

FAX
(843) 724-8405

WEBSITE
www.charlestongrill.com

HOURS
Sunday-Thursday
6:00 pm-10:00 pm
Friday & Saturday
6:00 pm-11:00 pm

MEALS SERVED
Dinner

CUISINE
Contemporary Lowcountry

DINING INFORMATION
Vegetarian Meals
Seasonal Menus
Extensive Wine Menu

LOUNGE BAR
Daily
4:00 pm-12:00 am

ENTERTAINMENT
Live Jazz
Weekdays
7:00 pm-11:00 pm
Weekends
8:00 pm-12:00 am

ADDITIONAL SERVICES
Vintner's Room Available for Large Private Parties
Regular Special Events
In-Room Dining Available to Hotel Guests During Regular Dinner Hours

ATTIRE
Casual Elegant

RESERVATIONS
Required

SMOKING
Permitted In Bar/Lounge Only

VALET PARKING

HANDICAP FACILITIES

CREDIT CARDS
American Express
Visa
Master Card
Discover Card
Diners Club Card
Carte Blanche

CHECKS
Not Accepted

Charleston Crab House

JAMES ISLAND •
145 Wappoo Creek Drive
Charleston, SC 29412
PHONE
(843) 795-1963
MT. PLEASANT •
Highway 17
(1 block past
IOP Connector)
1101 Stockade Lane
Mt. Pleasant, SC 29464
PHONE
(843) 884-1617
SUMMERVILLE •
800 North Main Street
Summerville, SC 29483
PHONE
(843) 873-5122
HOURS
Monday-Thursday
11:30 am-10:00 pm
Friday-Saturday
11:30 am-10:30 pm
Sunday
11:30 am-9:30 pm
MEALS SERVED
Lunch
Dinner
CUISINE
Lowcountry
Seafood
Southern
DINING INFORMATION
Terrace/Patio Dining
Heart Smart Meals
Vegetarian Meals
Take Out Meals
Kids Menu
ADDITIONAL SERVICES
Private Parties
Banquet Facilities
Private Rooms
Meeting Facilities
ATTIRE
Casual
RESERVATIONS
Call Ahead Seating
SMOKING
Smoking Section
HANDICAP FACILITIES
CREDIT CARDS
American Express
Visa
Master Card
Discover Card
CHECKS
Not Accepted

Proud to be locally owned and operated since 1991, The Charleston Crab House features fresh "Southern Seafood." Enjoy our famous She Crab Soup, Lowcountry crab cakes, steamed blue crabs, seafood platters, pastas and much more. The Charleston location is Charleston's only restaurant on the Intracoastal Waterway with dockside dining. Come visit Charleston Crab House where it's Southern Seafood, Sensible Prices, and a Darn Good Time!

Crab-a-tizers

Crab Dip & Crackers 4.95
Fresh crabmeat mixed with mayonnaise & Lowcountry spices. An "Old Charleston Recipe"

"Buffalo Style" Fried Oysters 5.95
Select oysters deep fried and served with hot sauce, bleu cheese dressing & celery

Fried Calamari 5.95
Crispy fried calamari served with marinara sauce

Crab Stuffed Mushroom Caps 6.95
Fresh mushroom caps with crabmeat stuffing baked with melted cheeses

Barbeque Shrimp & Grits 6.95
Sautéed popcorn shrimp and barbeque sauce served over creamy grits and topped with melted cheddar cheese

Charleston She Crab
"A Charleston Tradition" Cream base soup with blue crabmeat & a dash of sherry 3.95

Single Select Oysters
1/2 Dozen raw 4.95
Dozen raw or steamed 8.95

Crab House Steamers

Alaskan Snow Crab Legs
Alaskan snow crab legs steamed hot, served with melted butter 16.95

Steamed Charleston Blue Crabs
1/2 dozen Split and cleaned local Blue Crabs covered with Old Bay seasoning & steamed hot 17.95

Steaks & Chicken

Prime Rib
13 oz. 14.95

Grilled Chicken Breast
Grilled chicken breast marinated in our special ginger teriyaki, fruit juice sauce 8.95

Broiled Seafood Platter

Altantic Flounder 13.95

Fresh Shrimp 14.95

Large Sea Scallops 14.95

Seafood Platter 15.95
Shrimp, flounder and sea scallops

Southern Fried Seafood Platters

Clam Strips 12.95
Lightly breaded and fried

Select Oysters 13.95
Select oysters, lightly breaded and fried

Atlantic Flounder 13.95
Atlantic flounder lightly breaded and fried

Fresh Shrimp 14.95
Large shrimp, lightly breaded and fried

Large Sea Scallops 14.95
Large sea scallops lightly fried

"The Fried Seafood Platter" 15.95
Your choice of any 3 of the above

Jumbo Seafood Platter 19.95
Oysters, shrimp, flounder, deviled crab & sea scallops

Seafood Specialties

Grilled Atlantic Salmon
10 oz. cut of fresh Atlantic salmon, grilled and topped with oriental honey glaze 12.95

Crispy Fried Whole Flounder
16 oz. whole local flounder, scored and deep fried 13.95

Charleston Grouper
Fresh filet of local grouper, lightly breaded, and sautéed and baked to golden brown 14.95

Lowcountry Crab Cakes
Two pan sautéed Lowcountry style crab cakes served over a creamy shrimp sauce 14.95

"Billy's" Big Crab & Shrimp Feast
A cluster of steamed Alaskan snow crab legs, pan sautéed Lowcountry crab cakes, and lightly fried fresh large shrimp 17.95

Shrimp & Scallop Pasta 12.95
Sautéed shrimp and sea scallops in white wine, olive oil, garlic, feta cheese, tomatoes and black olives over fresh linguini

---

This is just a small sample of the fine cuisine available at Charleston Crab House.

Easterby's

STEAKS • SEAFOOD
BARBECUE • CATERING

A Lowcountry favorite! Casual atmosphere, the service is true southern hospitality and priced to give you your money's worth! Their lightly battered fried shrimp and oysters are the talk of the town along with their mouth watering baby back ribs.

APPETIZERS

Bohicket Crab Dip	3.95
Buffalo Wings	4.95
Shrimp or Oysters (12)	5.95
Grilled, Fried or Broiled (24)	8.95
Bacon Stuffed Shrimp	5.75
Cheese Sticks	4.95
Barbecued Shrimp and Grits	6.25
Sauteed or Fried Mushrooms	6.25
Crab Legs (2 Clusters)	Market Price
Fried Onion Loaf	3.50
Potato Skins	4.75
Nacho Platter	5.95
Crab Cakes	5.75
Chicken Fingers	5.50
Mugga Oysters	6.25
Steak Cut Fries	1.30

SOUP OF THE DAY/SALADS

Cup	2.95
Bowl	3.50
Chicken, Shrimp, Scallops, Steak, or Mahi	5.50
Aunt Patsy Special - combination	5.95
Cold Plate - chicken or tuna	5.75
Chef Salad	5.75

SANDWICHES

	Sand	Pork
Barbecued Pork	3.25	4.70
Homemade Burger		
8 oz.	4.75	6.20
5 oz.	2.25	3.70
Hot Ham	3.75	5.20
Turkey 'n Cheese	3.75	5.20
Chicken, Tuna, or Shrimp	3.25	4.70
Turkey or Ham Club	4.85	6.30
Bacon, Lettuce, Tomato	2.25	3.70
Grilled Cheese	1.95	3.40
Grilled Marinated Chicken	3.65	5.10
Fried Oyster, Scallop or Shrimp	3.75	5.20
Fried Chicken Breast	3.65	5.10
Corn Dog	1.75	3.20
Fried or Grilled Flounder	3.75	5.20

SEAFOOD - Grilled, Fried or Broiled

Shrimp or Oyster Platter	
Twelve	7.95
Twenty-Four	11.95
Thirty-Six	15.95
Bacon Wrapped Stuffed Shrimp (8)	9.75
Scallop Platter (10-12)	11.95
Flounder or Mahi Platter (8 oz)	9.75
Make Your Own Platter	
Choice of Two	10.95
Choice of Three	13.95
Choice of Four	16.95
Crab Legs 1 lb	Market Price
Crab Cake Platter	8.50

STEAK, CHICKEN AND PORK SPECIALITIES

10 oz Ribeye	9.50
10 oz Grilled Prime Rib	9.75
14 oz New York Strip	12.95
8 oz Filet Mignon	15.95
Smoked Sausage 'n Shrimp	8.95
Beef or Chicken Tips	7.50
Hamburger Steak	7.25
Grilled Marinated Chicken Breast	
one	7.25
two	8.25
three	9.95
Surf 'n Turf	15.50
Barbecued Pork Platter	5.95
1/2 Chicken Platter	5.95
St. Louis Style Ribs	
Order	8.25
Double Order	13.25

PASTA

Shrimp or Scallops over Linguine with an Alfredo Sauce 8.95

Combination add 1.00

CHILDREN'S MENU

Shrimp, Flounder, Chicken Fingers, Corn Dogs, Hamburger or Cheeseburger
3.50

•WEST ASHLEY
2388 Ashley River Road
West Ashley, SC

PHONE
(843) 556-5707

•JAMES ISLAND
1977 Maybank
James Island, SC

PHONE
(843) 762-4890

HOURS
Monday-Saturday
11:00 am-10:00 pm

MEALS SERVED
Lunch
Dinner

CUISINE
American
Barbeque
Seafood/Steak House

LOUNGE BAR

DANCING
New Years Eve
and Private Parties

ADDITIONAL SERVICES
Full Service Catering
Private Parties
Private Rooms
Meeting Facilities

ATTIRE
Casual

RESERVATIONS
Not Required

SMOKING
Smoking Section

HANDICAP FACILITIES

CREDIT CARDS
American Express
Visa
Master Card
Discover Card
Diners Club Card

CHECKS
Accepted

Elliott's on the Square

CHARLESTON
The Westin Francis Marion
387 King Street
Charleston, SC 29403
PHONE
(843) 724-8888
FAX
(843) 724-8880
HOURS
Breakfast
6:30 am-10:30 am
Lunch
11:30 pm-2:30 pm
Dinner
5:30 pm
MEALS SERVED
Breakfast
Lunch
Dinner
CUISINE
American
Contemporary
DINING INFORMATION
Seasonal Menus
ADDITIONAL SERVICES
Full Service Catering
Private Parties

ATTIRE
Casual
RESERVATIONS
Not Required
Suggested
SMOKING
Smoking Section
VALET PARKING
HANDICAP FACILITIES
CREDIT CARDS
American Express
Visa
Master Card
Discover Card
Diners Club Card
CHECKS
Not Accepted

ON THE SQUARE

Post & Courier restaurant critic Peter Herman recently raved about dinner at Elliott's on the Square. Herman praises Elliott's as "a superb place to frequent." His comments have added to the buzz around town about Elliott's as one of the best places to eat. The contemporary American cuisine earns his praise as being "creative, beautifully plated and served by attentive staff in a comfortable setting." Dessert lovers can top off their meal with desserts like the ginger creme brulee or bananas foster bread pudding. It's easy to understand why Herman exclaims, "Choices, choices, choices!" Breakfast, Lunch and Dinner every day.

Soups, Salads & Appetizers

Seafood Chowder
sausage, corn, potatoes & tarragon
cup $3.95 bowl $5.25

Chef's Daily Soup
cup $3.50 bowl $4.95

Classic Caesar Salad
with Parmesan curls, anchovies
& foccacia croutons $6.95

Hearts of Romaine Salad
with crumbled gorgonzola and herb vinaigrette $6.50

Mixed Green Salad
mixed greens with house vinaigrette $4.95
with creamy blue cheese and croutons $5.95

Citrus Salad
citrus segments & mixed greens over bibb lettuce with almonds $5.95

Seared Tuna Wonton
with Asian slaw, seared rare tuna & wasabi drizzle $8.50

Lowcountry Fried Oysters
smoky tomato remoulade and jicama salad $7.95

Maverick Mussels
served sizzling hot at your table - shallots, white wine,
garlic & butter $7.95

Tuscan Shrimp
shrimp, gorgonzola sauce, tomatoes, capers & crostini $8.50

Small Plates

Lumpmeat Crabcake
with Cajun succotash & smoky remoulade $10.50

Pork Tenderloin
wrapped in smoked bacon with Jack Daniel's B.B.Q. sauce,
seasonal greens & crispy onions $8.25

Hoisin B.B.Q. Duck
sesame green beans, shiitake mushrooms & shallots $8.50

Grilled Portobello Mushroom
over fresh ratatouille & finished
with a balsamic vinegar reduction $8.50

Shrimp & Grits
with smoky lobster sauce, andouille sausage,
peppers & tomatoes $8.95

Hanger Steak au Poivre
with crispy shoe string sweet potoato fries $12.50

Mustard Chicken
served with a warm Creole slaw
& stone-ground mustard aioli $6.95

Main Courses

Pan Seared Salmon
over sweet potato hash with creole butter $16.95

Roasted Grouper
over Vidalia onion potato cake topped
with yellow tomato vinaigrette $18.95

Sicilian Roasted Chicken
with polenta "fries," green beans & roasted garlic sauce $15.95

Honey Chipotle Glazed Pork Chop
house mashers, wilted spinach, fried onions $16.95

Tuna Sake
seared tuna with sake-braised shiitake mushrooms & house mashers
smaller $13.25 main $18.95

Blackened Filet of Beef
smoked onion jus, yellowstone grits, braised greens garnished
with fried oyters 6 oz. $16.95 8 oz. $19.95

N.Y. Strip
with house mashers, gorgonzola butter & balsamic grilled onions
$21.95

Sides

House Mashers
$2.75

Spinach
$3.50

Green Beans
$2.95

Polenta Fries
$3.95

Desserts

Sorbet
Chef's selection offered daily $5.00

Ginger Crème Brulee
with candied ginger $5.00

Chocolate Hazelnut Mascarpone Cheescake
nut crust & fresh berry coulis $6.00

Flourless Chocolate Cake
served with a citrus granita $6.00

Bananas Foster Bread Pudding
topped with vanilla bean ice cream $6.00

Lemon Cake
chantilly cream & warm berry compote $6.00

Ellis Creek Bistro

Ellis Creek Bistro embodies a refined balance which emerges from collaboration. Peter Stone and Alan Balch have produced an unexpected and affordable dining experience while maintaining a casual atmosphere. The Bistro is ideally located near downtown Charleston yet removed from its traffic. Chef Peter Stone brings his years of experience in Atlanta restaurants together with his success at Magnolia's to yield a creative cuisine matched only by the Bistros diverse list of wines. The menu is able to impress any palate and includes several vegetarian selections. All Breads and Desserts are Produced In-House.

Ellis Creek
BISTRO

CHARLESTON
807 Folly Road
Charleston, SC 29412
PHONE
(843) 795-3838
FAX
(208) 246-3877
HOURS
Monday-Saturday
5:30 pm-10:00 pm
MEALS SERVED
Dinner
CUISINE
American
Contemporary
DINING INFORMATION
Vegetarian Meals
Take Out Meals
Seasonal Menus
Extensive Wine Menu
LOUNGE BAR
ADDITIONAL SERVICES
Private Parties

ATTIRE
Casual
RESERVATIONS
Not Required
Suggested
SMOKING
Smoking Not Permitted
HANDICAP ACCESSIBLE
CREDIT CARDS
American Express
Visa
Master Card
CHECKS
Accepted
(Local checks)

Appetizers and Small Plates

Sweet Potato and Crab Soup — ***$3.50***

Tossed Greens — ***$3.50***
With Spiced Pecans. Crumbled Blue Cheese and Lemon Thyme Vinaigrette

Romaine Lettuce — ***$4.00***
With Buttermilk Caesar Dressing and Sourdough Croutons

Crab and Zucchini Pancakes — ***$8.00***
With Sweet Pinot Noir Glaze and Chive Cream

Goat Cheese Raviolis — ***$7.50***
With Sautéed Fennel, Cracked Black Pepper and Orange Zest

Pan Roasted Mussels — ***$8.00***
With Andouille Sausage, Yellow Peppers, Red Onions, Thyme and White Wine

Portabella Mushroom Rockefeller — ***$6.50***
With Spinach Herbed Cream Cheese and a Balsamic Glaze

Smoked Salmon Quesadilla — ***$7.50***
With Aged Wine Cheddar, Tomato Relish, and Cilantro Sour Cream

Pan Seared Jumbo Scallops — ***$9.00***
With a Fricassee of New Potatoes, Buttery Leeks, Bacon, and a Roast Tomato Vinaigrette

Entrees

Pan Roasted Grouper — ***$18.00***
With Sautéed Leeks, Saffron Israeli Cous Cous, and a Pinot Noir Sauce

Crispy Catfish — ***$14.00***
With a Soy-Ginger Glaze, Grilled Shiitake Mushrooms, Sautéed Spinach, and a Sesame Rice Cake

Cracker Crumb Salmon — ***$15.00***
With a Fricassee of Spicy Black Beans, Sweet Corn, and Leeks, Scallion Mashed Potatoes, and a Chipotle Pepper BBQ Sauce

Pan Seared Cajun BBQ Jumbo Scallops — ***$17.50***
With White Cheddar Grit Cakes and Sautéed Zucchini Noodles

Pan Roasted Chilean Sea Bass — ***$18.50***
With Sautéed Asparagus, Scallion Mashed Potatoes & a Curry Lemongrass Broth

Parmesan Crusted Pork Chop — ***$16.00***
With Braised Wadmalaw Greens, Caramelized Shallot Mashed Potatoes & a Whole Grain Mustard Sauce

Char Grilled Tenderloin or Beef — ***$18.50***
With Roasted Garlic-Blue Cheese Crust, Bacon-Scallion Mashed Potatoes, Grilled Asparagus, and Ellis Creek Worcestershire Sauce

Pan Roasted Maple Leaf Duck Breast — ***$17.00***
With a Warm Grilled Mushroom Salad, Crispy Potato Cake, and a Citrus-Ginger Sauce

Tri-Colored Orzo Pasta — ***$11.50***
With Organic Sweet Peas, Wild Mushrooms, Red Onions, and Parmesan Cheese

Vegetable Napolean — ***$11.00***
Of Braised Tofu, Winter Squash, Cornbread Dressing, a Sesame Rice Cake, Sautéed Red Cabbage, and a Soy Ginger Glaze

Garibaldi Cafe

CHARLESTON
49 S. Market Street
Charleston, SC 29401
PHONE
(843) 723-7153
FAX
(843) 720-1951
HOURS
Open Every Night
@ 5:30 pm
MEALS SERVED
Dinner
CUISINE
Italian
Seafood
DINING INFORMATION
Terrace/Patio Dining
Vegetarian Meals
Take Out Meals
Seasonal Menus
Childrens Menu
Extensive Wine Menu
ADDITIONAL SERVICES
Private Parties

ATTIRE
Casual
SMOKING
Smoking Section
CREDIT CARDS
American Express
Visa
Master Card
CHECKS
Not Accepted

Since 1978 Garibaldi Cafe has been a local favorite for fresh local seafood and comforting Italian fare. Garibaldi has three distinct settings, each one lively and romantic, replete with Charleston charm and sparkling with candlelight. A cozy cafe adjoins an inviting outdoor courtyard overlooking the historic city market and an upstairs dining room has the proportions and trappings of an elegant downtown home. The focus is on local daily caught seafood such as snapper au poivre and the famous crispy flounder. Crispy flounder is scored to the bone and the crispy outside keeps the tender meat moist and is glazed with an apricot shallot sauce. Attempt by others to duplicate it have enhanced its legendary status.

The Menu

Appetizers

Shrimp Savannah	6.50
Deep Fried Artichoke Hearts	4.95
Deep Fried Zucchini	3.95
Stuffed Mushrooms	4.95
Mushrooms stuffed with Escargot	6.25
Smoked Salmon	6.95

Salads

Pimento and Anchovy	4.95
Garden Salad	3.95
Tomato and Mushroom	3.95
Hearts of Palm	4.95

Soups

Gazpacho	4.25
French Onion	4.25

Entrees

Veal Murat	15.25
Veal Marsala	14.95
Veal Franchese	14.95
Veal Piccata	14.95
Veal Parmigiana	14.95
Shrimp Marinara	14.95
Coquilles St. Jacques	14.95
Scampi	14.95
Chicken Parmigiana	12.75
Chicken Rabini	12.95

Pasta

Fettuccine Alfredo	8.95
Fettuccine Carbonara	9.25
Fettuccine Chicken and Peas	10.50
Fettuccine Fresh Seafood	14.95
Spaghetti Tomato Sauce	8.25
Spaghetti Meat Sauce	8.25
Spaghetti Italian Sausage	9.50
Lasagne	11.95

Famous Nightly Specials

Caesar Salad

Baby Greens with Gorgonzola, Pine Nuts and Raspberry Vinaigrette

Crab Bisque

Crispy Flounder with Apricot Shallot Sauce

Stuffed Grouper with Blue Crab and Ricotta Cheese

Red Snapper Au Poivre

Linguine with Lobster, Shrimp, Mussels and Shiitakes in a Lobster Butter

NY Strip with Shiitakes and Gorgonzola Cream Sauce

Mussels Provençal

Soft Shell Crabs in a Caper & Onion Beurre Blanc

Pan Seared Trout with Corn Crab Fritters and Spicy Cucumber Salad

Penne with Rock Shrimp and Sausage and a Sweet Pepper Cream Sauce

Tuna with Spinach and Tomato Balsamic Vinaigrette

Almond Salmon with Amaretto Hollandaise

Rigatoni with Chicken, Caramelized Onions, Shiitake and Marsala Cream

Steak Diane

Linguine with Shrimp, Artichoke, Tomato and Goat Cheese, White Wine Butter Sauce

Seared Salmon with Cucumber Salad over Risotto

Almond Tilapia with Jumbo Shrimp and Herb Butter

Osso Buco with Creamy Rissoto, Caramelized Carrots and Green Beans

Tiramisu

RISTORANTE

FINE ITALIAN CUISINE

Gennaro's has been serving Fine Italian Cuisine in the Charleston area for 16 years. In a warm cozy atmosphere, Chefs Michael and Robert Gennaro and Hostess Linda Gennaro work diligently at providing a wonderful dining experience. From Veal to grilled Seafood or a wonderful Black Angus Steak, you will certainly appreciate the quality at Gennaro's and the perceived value. See why Charlestonians always come back to Gennaro's.
Thursday night enjoy Live Big Band Jazz.

Hot Appetizers

ZUPPA DE CLAMS 6.95
Clams Steamed in a Hot and Spicy Tomato and Red Wine Sauce

MUSSELS IN WHITE WINE SAUCE 7.95
Mussels Steamed in Butter Garlic and White Wine When Available

FRIED CALAMARI 6.50
Strips of Squid fried in a light breading "You Will Love It"

MINI CALZONE 5.95
Small Meatball, Sausage, Ricotta and Mozzarella Filled Pizza Dough Fried and Served with Tomato Sauce

SPINACH & ARTICHOKE DIP W/ GARLIC TOAST 5.50

MINESTRONE SOUP CUP 1.50 BOWL 2.75

CAESAR SALAD 3.50

Veal Specialties Ala Gennaro

VEAL PICCATA 16.95
Breaded Thinly Sliced Fresh Veal Sauteed in Olive Oil, Garlic Butter and White Wine, Squeezed Lemon Juice and Garnished with Parsley and Lemon Slices

VEAL MARSALA 16.95
Thinly sliced Fresh Veal Rolled with Ham, Ricotta, Mozzarella and Seasoning, Breaded, Fried and Topped with Alfredo Sauce

VEAL DIANE 17.95
Fresh Veal Cutlet (Veal Parmigiana) Served Over Eggplant Ala Michael

Steaks

CHARBROILED RIBEYE 14-16 OZ CUT 16.95
Served with Side of Spaghetti or Steak Fries

STEAK PIZZIOLA 16.95
Ribeye Steak sauteed in Mushrooms, Red Wine and Tomato Sauce and Served with Side of Spaghetti

N.Y. STRIP 16.95
13-15 oz. Angus Strip Served with Mixed Vegetables, Pasta or Steak Fries

SURF & TURF 18.95
Filet Mignon and Fried Shrimp with Mixed Vegetables

From The Sea

	1/2 ORDER	DINNER
SHRIMP ALA MARINARA	8.95	14.95

Sauteed Shrimp, Fresh Fettuccine Noodles, Fresh Heavy Cream and Imported Romano Cheese

	1/2 ORDER	DINNER
SHRIMP SCAMPI, LINGUINE	8.95	14.95

Succulent Shrimp Sauteed in Garlic Butter and White Wine with Linguine Pasta

LINGUINE WITH RED CLAM SAUCE 13.95

MUSSELS MARINARA 13.95
Mussels Steamed in our Marinara Sauce Over a Bed of Linguine

SEAFOOD SCAMPI 17.95
Shrimp, Scallops, Mussels and Clams in Butter, Garlic and White Wine Over Linguine

Chicken Specialties Ala Gennaro

CHICKEN PARMIGIANA 13.95
Breast of Chicken Breaded, Fried and Topped with Mozzarella Cheese and Our Special Tomato Sauce

CHICKEN WITH ROASTED PEPPERS OVER LINGUINE 15.95
Sauteed Breast of Chicken with Onions and Roasted Peppers, Tossed in Olive Oil in a Light Crushed Tomato Sauce - Spicy

CHICKEN BOLOGNESE 15.95
Boneless Chicken Breast rolled with Ham, Ricotta, Mozzarella & Seasoning - Breaded, Fried and Topped with Alfredo Sauce

Italian Specialties

BAKED MANICOTTA 10.50
Pasta Crepe Filled with Ricotta Cheese, Seasonings and Topped with Tomato Sauce and Mozzarella Cheese

FETTUCCINE ALFREDO 12.95
Fresh Heavy Cream and Imported Romano Cheese

EGGPLANT ALA MICHAEL 12.95
Layers of Fried Eggplant, Ricotta Cheese, Sliced Meatballs and Sausage Topped with Tomato Sauce and Mozzarella Served with Side of Spaghetti

Gennaro's Italian Ristorante

NORTH CHARLESTON
8500 Dorchestor Rd.
North Charleston, SC 29418
PHONE
(843) 760-9875
HOURS
Tuesday-Thursday
4:30 pm-10:30 pm
Friday
4:30 pm-11:00 pm
Saturday
3:30 pm-11:00 pm
Seasonal Lunch Hours
Tuesday, Wednesday & Thursday
11:30 pm-2:30 pm
MEALS SERVED
Dinner
CUISINE
Continental, Italian
DINING INFORMATION
Childrens Menu
Extensive Wine Menu
LOUNGE BAR
Daily
4:00 pm-11:00 pm
LIVE MUSIC
Thursday
Swing, Jazz Band
ADDITIONAL SERVICES
Banquet Facilities

ATTIRE
Casual
RESERVATIONS
Suggested
SMOKING
Section Available
HANDICAP FACILITIES
CREDIT CARDS
American Express
Visa
Master Card
Diners Club Card
CHECKS
Accepted

This is just a small sample of the fine cuisine at Gennaro's Italian Ristorante.

Geralyn's

MOUNT PLEASANT
202 Coleman Blvd.
Mount Pleasant, SC 29464
PHONE
(843) 881-8981
FAX
(843) 881-8982
HOURS
Lunch
Monday-Saturday
11:30 am-3:00 pm
Dinner
Monday-Saturday
5:30 pm-until
MEALS SERVED
Lunch
Dinner
Late Night Dining
CUISINE
American
Lowcountry
Southern
DINING INFORMATION
Terrace/Patio Dining
Take Out Meals
Seasonal Menus
Childrens Menu
ENTERTAINMENT
Friday-Saturday
Nights on Deck
(Weather Permitting)
ADDITIONAL SERVICES
Private Parties

ATTIRE
Casual
RESERVATIONS
Not Required
SMOKING
Smoking Section
No Cigar or Pipe Smoking
HANDICAP FACILITIES
CREDIT CARDS
American Express
Visa
Master Card
CHECKS
Accepted
(Local)

Located in Mt. Pleasant's famous Shem Creek Village, just minutes away from Historic Charleston, Isle of Palms, and Sullivan's Island. Geralyn's offers Lowcountry and traditional southern cuisine with a contemporary flair. Proprietors Geralyn Weis and Chefs/Proprietors Jassen and Chad Campbell infuse ingredients indigenous to the lowcountry region of South Carolina. Geralyn's offers inside or outside casual upscale dining. Whether a night out with friends or a romantic dinner for two, look no further than Geralyn's, located in the heart of Mt. Pleasant.

STARTERS

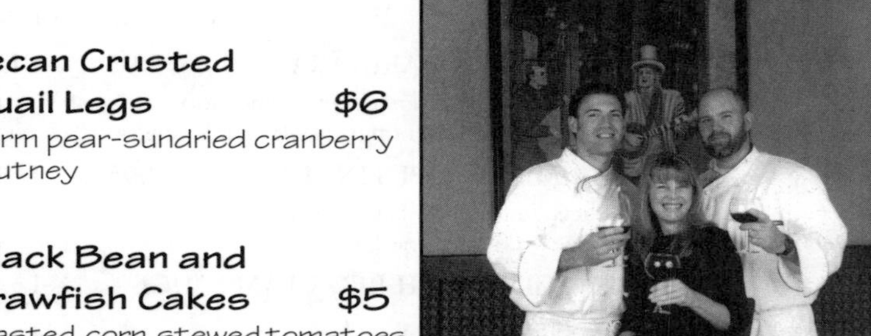

Pecan Crusted Quail Legs **$6**
warm pear-sundried cranberry chutney

Black Bean and Crawfish Cakes **$5**
roasted corn, stewed tomatoes, and tasso ham

Four Cheese, Crab, Spinach Dip **$6**
with confetti chips

Southern Fried Green Tomatoes **$5**
white cheddar grits, caramelized onions and fire roasted peppers

SOUP AND SALADS

Charleston She Crab Soup **$3**
laced with sherry whipped cream

Chef's Soup of the Day **$4**

Bleu Cheese Oyster Stew **$5**
garnished with applewood smoked bacon in a warm bouli

Spinach & Grilled Shiitake Mushroom Salad **$6**
shaved red onions, avocados, clemson blue cheese & dried berry vinaigrette

SANDWICHES

Fried Green Tomato and Applewood Smoked Bacon **$6**
white cheddar, roasted red pepper remoulade on grilled foccia

Grilled Marinated Chicken **$7**
fresh sprouts, avocado-tomato salsa on a toasted kaiser roll

Oyster Po Boy **$8**
cajun fried oysters, asiago cheese, toasted hogie roll with clemson bleu cheese dressing

Grilled Portabello Mushroom **$7**
with goat cheese, sprouts, and tomatoes on grilled foccia

Parmesan Dusted Flounder **$7**
with cilantro-garlic mayonnaise, fresh sprouts and gold tomatoes on a kaiser roll

ENTREES

Pan Fried Carolina Crabcakes **$16**
sweet red pepper remoulade, cilantro oil and hoppin' john

Charleston Spiced Shrimp and Scallops **$16**
warm black bean-roasted corn relish and fried smoked mozzarella raviolis

Parmesan Dusted Flounder **$15**
sauteed crab and rock shrimp brown butter sauce with hoppin john

Opal Basil-Garlic Marinated Ribeye **$17**
bbq steak butter, shaved fried onions and parmesan-chive smashed potatoes

Trio of Duck **$19**
grilled breast, foie gras, roasted leg with accompanying sauces, parmesan-chive smashed potatoes

Lowcountry Shrimp and White Cheddar Grits **$17**
stewed tomatoes, applewood smoked bacon, crispy leeks

Charleston Fishwater **$17**
fresh catch, rock shrimp, scallops, crawfish, oysters in a spicy tomato broth with honey-charleston pepper cornbread

Palmetto Beer Battered Shrimp **$16**
cajun spiced aioli and sweet potato fries

GIBSON CAFE

Gibson Cafe Restaurant is a small charming cafe located in the heart of Sullivan's Island. Joe and Gay Slough opened the cafe five years ago as a gourmet shop that quickly expanded into a full service restaurant and bar. With a warm and friendly atmosphere, this spot has become a favorite of locals and tourists alike. Serving only the freshest of ingredients and creative cooking, the staff is proud to accommodate your needs. Come experience "Gourmet the Island Way."

APPETIZERS

TOMATO BASIL SOUP ... 1.50/3.00
HOUSE SALAD WITH TOMATO BASIL VINAIGRETTE ... 2.50
DATES STUFFED WITH CHORIZO SAUSAGE AND WRAPPED IN BACON ... 4.75
SPINACH SALAD WITH SMOKEY CAESAR DRESSING & BACON POLENTA CROUTONS ... 4.95
ARTICHOKE SALAD WITH GOAT CHEESE DRESSING ... 4.95

HOUSE SPECIALITIES

GROUPER MARTINIQUE ... 17.00
with grilled bananas, tomatoes and hollandaise with potatoes
SHRIMP AND GRITS ... 15.00
with tasso ham gravy
CRAB CAKES ... 17.00
with tomato basil tartar sauce with whipped butternut squash
BEEF TENDERLOIN ... 17.50
stuffed with brie, toppped with mushroom demi glace with potatoes
CRAB CRUSTED SCALLOPS ... 17.00
with mushroom ravioli in sundried tomato sauce
PARMESAN CRUSTED TUNA ... 17.00
cooked medium rare, with a sundried tomato sauce

PASTAS

SHRIMP AND SCALLOPS ... 15.00
with a pesto sauce
VEGETABLES ... 13.00
tossed with a tarragon-sundried tomato sauce
CHICKEN & TASSO HAM ... 13.50
with a creamy shiitake/pepper/artichoke sauce
PASTA WITH ALFREDO SAUCE ... 9.00

FISH AND SHELLFISH

PARMESAN CRUSTED SCALLOPS ... 17.00
over greens with a lemon vinaigrette dressing
SALMON FILET ... 16.00
topped with shrimp and scallops piccata sauce over grits
SCALLOPS ... 16.00
sautéed with a mango/orange sauce with nuts over greens

BEEF PORK AND CHICKEN

CHICKEN ... 13.50
stuffed with herbed goat cheese, breaded, served with dill cream sauce
RIBEYE 14 OZ. ... 17.50
served with roasted peppers and mushrooms
BURGER 8 OZ ... 6.95
with your choice of cheese

OTHER SELECTIONS

GROUPER SANDWICH ... 7.25
with tomato basil tartar sauce
GRILLED CHEESE ... 4.50
with chips

Gibson Cafe Restaurant

SULLIVAN'S ISLAND
2213 Middle Street
Sullivan's Island, SC 29482
PHONE
(843) 883-3536
FAX
(843) 883-3790
E-MAIL
gibsoncafe@aol.com
HOURS
Lunch
Monday-Saturday
11:00 am-3:00 pm
Dinner
Tuesday-Saturday
5:30 pm-Until
MEALS SERVED
Lunch
Dinner
CUISINE
American
French
Seafood
DINING INFORMATION
Terrace/Patio Dining
Vegetarian Meals
Take Out Meals
Seasonal Menus
LOUNGE BAR
ADDITIONAL SERVICES
Full Service Catering
Private Parties

ATTIRE
Casual
RESERVATIONS
Suggested
SMOKING
Smoking Section
No Cigar or Pipe Smoking
HANDICAP FACILITIES
CREDIT CARDS
Visa
Master Card
Discover Card
CHECKS
Accepted

Gilligan's Steamer & Raw Bar

It's our privilege to serve you! We've worked hard to build our reputation as a fine family restaurant by serving the best food available in a friendly casual atmosphere. From our fresh local seafood to special children's meals and a warm, welcoming staff, our goal is to provide you with an unforgettable dining experience.

APPETIZERS

Oysters

Steamed tray (Seasonal)	8.95
Dozen on 1/2 shell	6.95
One-half dozen	4.95

Oysters Gilligan
Oysters on the 1/2 shell, baked with bacon, onions, mushrooms and cheddar

One dozen	8.95
One-half dozen	5.95

Clams
Steamed in a garlic butter

One dozen	8.95
One-half dozen	4.95

Chicken Fingers
Fried strips of chicken breast with honey mustard. **4.95**

Fried Grouper Fingers
Our succulent grouper fried to perfection **5.95**

Steamed Shrimp "Hot or Cold"

1/2 lb.	7.95
1/4 lb.	4.95

Crab Legs **6.95**
One cluster of legs

Mussels–Steamed
One dozen in garlic butter sauce **4.95**

Shrimp Dip
Chopped shrimp with shredded cheese, celery, green onion and secret spices. **4.95**

Buffalo Wings
Wings served with Bleu Cheese and celery. Hot or mild. **4.95**

Fried Calamari
Tossed in a pepperoncini and red onion vinaigrette. **5.95**

SOUPS & SALADS

Soup of the Day
Ask your server

Cup	2.95
Bowl	3.95

House Salad **2.95**
Crisp greens topped with fresh produce, cheese, and croutons.

Gilligan's Deluxe Salad **8.95**
Our signature salad. Crisp greens topped with shrimp, fresh produce, cheese, sliced egg and croutons.

Grilled Chicken Salad **7.95**
Strips of grilled chicken on a bed of lettuce mixed with fresh produce, cheese, sliced egg and coutons.

Shrimp Salad **8.95**
Creamy shrimp salad topped with cheese, fresh produce and sliced egg all on a bed of lettuce.

Gilligan's also offers a full lunch and children's menu.

Gilligan's Steamer & Raw Bar

ENTREES

All entrees served with cole slaw, corn on the cob, green beans and your choice of red rice, baked potato or french fries. No substitutions, please, but if you must, "add a dollar so our chef won't hollar" (including house salad for cole slaw).

From the Steamer

Gilligan's Stew 8.95
A lowcountry tradition. Shrimp, sausage, potatoes and onions all steamed with lowcountry seasonings. No broth.

Steamed Shrimp & Vegetables 9.95
A healthy combination of shrimp and assorted vegetables steamed with bay spices.

Steamed Shrimp Dinner
We cath 'em you peel 'em! 1/2 lb. 9.95
Steamed with bay spices. 1 lb. 14.95

Steamed Seafood Platter 13.95
A large cluster of crab legs, steamed oysters and steamed shrimp.

Crab Legs Market Price
Three clusters of Crab legs steamed and served with warm butter.

Shellfish Pot 16.95
Oysters, shrimp, crab legs, clams and mussels. All steamed together and served in a cast iron pot.

From the Grill

Catch of the Day Priced Daily
We serve what the locals caught. Blackened add a dollar.

Gilligan's Burger 7.25

Marinated Chicken Breasts 8.95
Two boneless chicken breasts marinated in Gilligan's sauce and then grilled to perfection.

Grilled or Fried Sea Scallops 13.95
A hearty portion of juicy sea scallops cooked to perfection.

Ribeye 12.95
A 12-14 oz. ribeye steak grilled to your liking.

Steak And Shrimp 15.95
A Gilligan's Ribeye served with 1/4 lb. of steamed, fried or grilled shrimp.

Steak And Crab Legs 15.95
A Gilligan's Ribeye served with a cluster of crab legs.

Grilled Trio Priced Daily
Our fresh fish of the day, shrimp & scallops grilled to perfection. *Blackened add $1.00*

From the Fryer

Fried Shrimp
Lightly battered & fried 1/2 lb. 9.95
1 lb. 13.95

Fried Flounder 10.95
An 8 oz. portion lightly battered and fried.

Fried Catfish 11.95
A hearty portion of Southern Fried white, flaky farm-raised catfish.

Fried Seafood Combo 11.95
Combination of any two: shrimp, flounder, oysters or scallops.

Fried Seafood Platter 14.95
Combination of shrimp, flounder, oysters & scallops.

Fried Oysters 9.95

Fried Grouper Fingers 13.95
A generous portion of succulent fried grouper

OUR SEASONAL FAVORITES

Fish in a Bag 13.95
A must at Gilligan's. An 8 oz. filet of Grouper and assorted vegetables uniquely baked and served in a brown paper bag.

Pasta–bilities Priced Daily
Ask your server. Served with slaw.

Shrimp & Beef Stir–Fry 11.95
Fresh shrimp and steak stir fried with oriental style vegetables, served over a bed of rice.

Lowcountry Stir–Fry 11.95
Grilled shrimp, sausage and shredded cabbage seasoned with Cajun spices, served over red rice.

- **JOHNS ISLAND**
160 Main Rd.
Johns Island, SC 29455
PHONE
(843) 766-2244
- **LADSON**
3852 Ladson Rd.
Ladson, SC 29456
PHONE
(843) 821-2244
- **MT PLEASANT**
1475 Long Grove Dr.
Mt Pleasant, SC 29464
PHONE
(843) 849-2244

WEBSITE
www.gilligans.net

HOURS
Monday-Saturday
11:30 am-10:00 pm
Sunday
11:30 am-9:00 pm
Ladson Location
Sunday-Thursday
11:30 am-9:00 pm
Friday & Saturday
11:30 am-10:00 pm

MEALS SERVED
Lunch
Dinner

CUISINE
Seafood
American

DINING INFORMATION
Terrace/Patio Dining
(Mt. Pleasant only)
Heart Smart Meals
Take Out Meals
Childrens Menu

LOUNGE BAR

ENTERTAINMENT
Mt. Pleasant Location

ADDITIONAL SERVICES
Full Service Catering
Private Parties
Private Rooms

ATTIRE
Casual

RESERVATIONS
Not Required

SMOKING
Smoking Section

HANDICAP FACILITIES

CREDIT CARDS
American Express
Visa
Master Card
Discover Card

CHECKS
Not Accepted

High Cotton

Our High Cotton, like the time-honored phrase, is first class, high spirited, livin' large. It's an unabashedly masculine and American Saloon. Mahogany woodwork, thick old brick walls, ancient heart pine floors and high ceilings evoke feelings of warmth and well-being. The food, prepared by Chef Jason Scholz, is straightforward, virile and robust. Red meat. Game. Fresh fish. No confetti on the plates or in the descriptions. Familiar, irresistible desserts. This is the top of the food chain in quality and preparation. The wine list is equally compelling. Come back often to High Cotton. Enough times so we know your name, your table, your drink. It may be a new joint, but its soul is as old as a Lowcountry oak.

STARTERS

LOWCOUNTRY CLAM CHOWDER 7

LOBSTER BISQUE 8
blue crab dumpling

CHILLED POTATO LEEK SOUP 4/6

FRIED ABBEY EGG SALAD 7
curly endive with warm bacon dressing

BEEF CARPACCIO 8
Harry's Bar classic

TERRINE OF FOIE GRAS 16
tiny green beans and toast points

HOUSEMADE SAUSAGE AND GRITS 7

HIGH COTTON SHRIMP COCKTAIL 9
with tomato sorbet

COLD SMOKED SALMON 8

BROILED CRAB-STUFFED SHRIMP 9
bacon wrapped, finished with BBQ sauce

BUTTERMILK FRIED OYSTERS 7
watercress and green goddess dressing

SALADS

HIGH COTTON CAESAR 7
sourdough croutons, Parmesan, traditional dressing

KITCHEN SINK SALAD 6
green goddess, French, chunky blue cheese, oil and vinegar

BIBB LETTUCE AND WATERCRESS SALAD 6
walnut oil, apples, aged goat cheese, pickled beets

ON THE SIDE

Beer Battered Onion Rings 3
Stone Ground Grits 2
Tiny Green Beans 3
Sauteed Spinach 3
Lyonnaise Potatoes 2
Sauteed Mushrooms 3

High Cotton

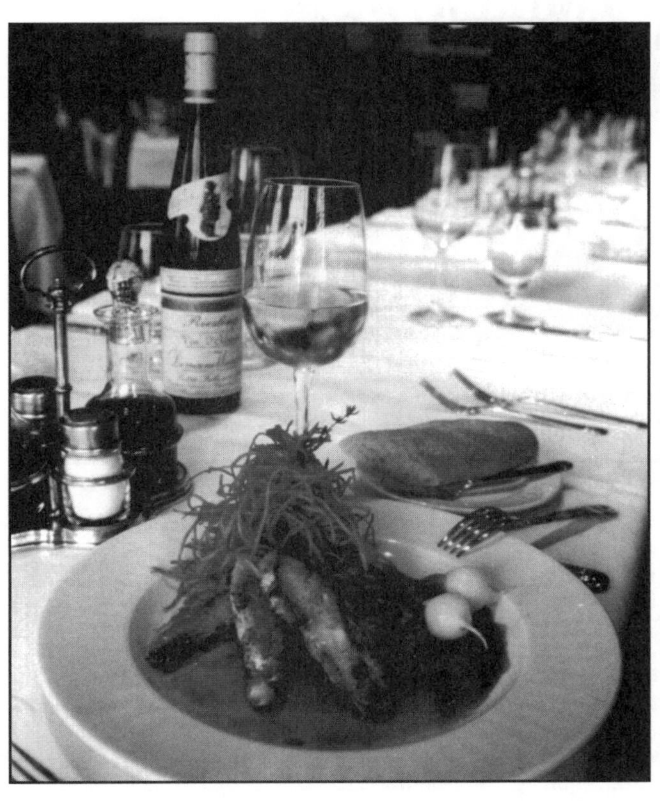

SEAFOOD

ROASTED GROUPER
melted leeks, orange tarragon butter, tiny green beans
21

GRILLED SALMON
grits, wild clams, chive scented broth, shoestring potatoes
18

SEARED TUNA
lentils, shrimp, asparagus and garlicky basil butter
19

GRILLED DOLPHIN
roasted fingerling potatoes, white wine herbs and butter
17

LIVE MAINE LOBSTER

broiled or steamed lemon and drawn butter
[market price]

NIGHTLY SUPPERS

SUNDAY - Spit-roasted Leg of Lamb, risotto, grilled vegetables, Dijon jus 16

MONDAY - Grilled Hanger Steak, skillet fries, sauteed spinach, Henry Bain 15

TUESDAY - Broiled Stuffed Flounder, deviled crab, sweet basil butter 20

WEDNESDAY - Batter-fried Fan-Tail Shrimp, angel hair slaw, green beans, Charleston tartar sauce 19

THURSDAY - Roasted Prime Rib, twice-baked potato, squash casserole, pan drippings, horseradish cream 20

SOMETHING WILD

LOCAL RABBIT LOIN
pan-fried with black-eyed peas, crispy sweet potatoes, Marsala sauce
23

SOUTH CAROLINA SQUAB
poached cabbage and natural jus
22

VENISON MEDALLIONS
root vegetables and juniper reduction
24

FROM THE SPIT

PALMETTO POUSSIN 14
five fresh herbs, garlic and lemon

1/2 ROASTED DUCK 16
Lowcountry spice rub with duck gravy

MEAT

Your choice of maitre d' butter, or sauces including: bearnaise, mushroom, cabernet or Henry Bain.

BEEF

CENTER CUT FILET MIGNON
10 oz. Cut 27 7 oz. Cut 20

DRY AGED 12 OZ. NY STRIP
26

22 OZ. TRUE PORTERHOUSE
34

14 OZ. RIBEYE
20

VEAL

THICK CUT VEAL CHOP
27

LAMB

RIB CHOPS
27

PEPPER-SEARED LOIN
24

PORK

TWO CENTER CUT CHOPS
18

SOUFFLES

Crown your evening with the dessert of kings - a souffle made to your order. Our specality takes time, so choose one of our daily flavors.

CHARLESTON
199 E. Bay Street
Charleston, SC 29401

PHONE
(843) 724-3815

FAX
(843) 724-3816

WEBSITE
www.high-cotton.net

HOURS
Dinner Nightly
from 5:30 pm
7 nights a week

MEALS SERVED
Dinner

CUISINE
American

DINING INFORMATION
Extensive Wine Menu

LOUNGE/BAR
4:00 pm-1:00 am

ADDITIONAL SERVICES
Full Service Catering
Private Parties
Banquet Facilities

ATTIRE
Casual

RESERVATIONS
Suggested

SMOKING
Smoking Section

VALET PARKING

HANDICAP FACILITIES

CREDIT CARDS
American Express
Visa
Master Card
Discover Card
Diners Club Card

CHECKS
Not Accepted

Hyman's Seafood Co.

Voted The Best Seafood Restaurant in S.C..

by *Southern Living Magazine* Survey 3 years in a row!

Mention Charleston Cuisine
& recieve a free appetizer Offer expires 12/31/2000

APPETIZERS

Fried Shrimp, Scallops or Oysters	4.50
Combo of all 3 above	11.95
Fried Green Tomatoes	3.50
Crab & Shrimp Dip	4.25
★ Sauteed Cajun Shrimp	4.95
Fried Calamari	3.95
Stuffed Mushrooms Wrapped in Bacon	5.50
Smoked Salmon, Nova, Lox with Lemon Wedge	4.95
Pickled Herring	3.95
♥ Shrimp Cocktail	3.95
Scallop Scampi	4.95
Shrimp Scampi	4.50
♥ Shrimp Creole	5.95
Fried Soft Shell Crab	Mkt
Single Deviled Crab	3.95
Shrimp or Salmon and Grits	4.95
Oysters - 1/2 dozen on the half shell	4.35
Oysters - 1 dozen on the half shell	7.95
Sauteed Mussels (seasonal)	4.50
Basket of Hushpuppies	1.95

A LA CARTE ITEMS

CRUSTACEANS

Fresh Steamed Shrimp

Regular (7oz)	6.95
Large (14 oz)	10.95
Jumbo (21 oz)	14.95

HOMEMADE BUFFALO WINGS

Half dozen	4.25
1 dozen	7.25
3 dozen	20.25

FOR THE FISHERMAN

Preparation Options

Fried, Broiled, Cajun, Lightly Cajun, Scampi, Sauteed, Caribbean Jerk, Dry Broiled or Steamed

CHOOSE ONE:

Baked Potato, French Fries, Red Rice or Grits.
All seafood meals include Cole Slaw & Hush Puppies
A Salad can be substituted for $1.95

	Regular	Large
♥ Fish #1	6.95	10.95
♥ Fish #2	8.95	12.95
♥ Fish #3	10.95	14.95
Devil Crab Dinner	2/10.50	4/15.95
Shrimp	11.95	15.95
Sea Scallops	11.95	15.95
Calamari (fried only)	9.95	13.95
Oysters (fried only)	11.95	15.95
Sauteed Mussels	10.95	13.95
★ Shrimp & Grits or Salmon & Grits		10.95
Snow Crab Legs		Mkt. Price
Soft Shell Crab		Mkt. Price
★ Crispy Flounder (#1 Best Seller)		14.95

(15-25 different fish to choose from daily.)

★ Large Combo Platter (all cooked one way you choose)

3 above	14.95
5 above	21.95
7 above (for two)	28.95
Seafood Fettuccine Alfredo	13.95
Seafood Fettuccine Marinara	13.95

(Mix & Match Fish and/or Shellfish from above)

with scallops, shrimp and 2 fish. Served w/garlic bread and coleslaw. (Seafood Fettuccine Alfredo)

FOR THE FARM BUOYS

Chicken Fettuccine Alfredo	11.95
♥ Chicken Fettuccine Marinara	11.95
Mrs. Barbara's Meatloaf	8.95
Fried Chicken Breast	7.95
Fettuccine Alfredo	9.95

Comments From The Critics:

Southern Living Magazine...Readers poll survey out of 18 states Hyman's is No.1 in S.C. and No.2 out of all the southeast. 1994 Life Magazine...Full page pictorial Jan. '94. Travel & Liesure..."throughout our tour of the southeast, Hyman's Seafood was one of the most interesting restaurants we've encountered." Chicago Sun Times..."There are a lot of good restaurants in Charleston but, there is a good reason why there is always a line outside." Travel Magazine..."Some of the best She-Crab Soup we've tried anywhere." Atlanta Journal..."Definitely tops in town. No fancy sauces of the likes, just great food at even better prices." Charlotte Observer..."When in Charleston, you've missed out if you don't find the opportunity to try Hyman's Seafood and Aaron's Deli." Raleigh News Observer..."Hyman's is the exception to the rule that seafood must be spicy to be good...Excellent food in a casual atmosphere." 1990 News & Courier...***1/2 Food, **** Value. "When a good seafood dinner is in order, there's no doubt Hyman's Seafood is the place." AAA , Mobile Guide, Frommers and Conde Nast Approved. Any many, many more.

Hyman's Seafood Co.

CHARLESTON
213-217 Meeting St.
Charleston, SC 29401

PHONE
(843) 723-6000

FAX
(843) 958-1533

WEBSITE
www.hymansseafood.com

HOURS
7 Days a Week
11:00 am-11:00 pm
Closed Jewish Holidays
Thanksgiving and Christmas

MEALS SERVED
Lunch
Dinner
Twilight Dinners

CUISINE
Cajun
Deli
Seafood

DINING INFORMATION
Heart Smart Meals
Take Out Meals
Seasonal Menus
Childrens Menu
Extensive Wine Menu

LOUNGE BAR
Oyster Bar

ADDITIONAL SERVICES
Banquet Facilities

ATTIRE
Casual

RESERVATIONS
Not Taken

SMOKING
Smoking Section

HANDICAP FACILITIES

CREDIT CARDS
American Express
Visa
Master Card
Discover Card

CHECKS
Not Accepted

Voted The Best Seafood Restaurant in S.C..

by *Southern Living Magazine* Survey 3 years in a row!

PO-BOY SANDWICHES

- Oysters 7.50
- Calamari 6.50
- Deviled Crab 7.50
- Scallops 7.50
- Fish 5.50
- Shrimp 7.50
- Soft Shell Crab .... Mkt.

All sandwiches served with lettuce and tomato on a French roll with hush puppies.

FISH 'N' CHIPS 6.95

DIETER'S DELIGHT

Large Tossed Salad and Caesar Salads

- Chef Salad 7.50
- Caesar Salad 5.95
- • Add Chicken or Fish 1 & 2 .... 7.95
- • Add Shrimp, Scallops or Fish 3 ...... 10.95

SPECIAL DESSERTS EVERYDAY!

FULL BAR

HOMEMADE SOUPS

• Award Winning Charleston "She" Crab Soup

Charleston 13 Bean Soup

Sarah's Okra Gumbo

3.25/cup 4.50/bowl

FULL CHILDREN'S MENU AVAILABLE

As a participant in the Heart Choice Dining Program, we feature menu items which are consistent with the MUSC Heart Center and The American Heart Association dietary guidelines. To meet these guidelines, when you order your dinner please specify heartchoice and either cook it steamed or dry broiled.

Visit Aaron's Deli

7:00 am–11:00 pm.

BEER, WINE & LIQUOR

Too Many to list.
Please see our table tents.
Our wine prices are comparable to supermarket prices.

Hyman's Half Shell & Raw Bar
Full Bar Open Sunday

All of the brass plaques on the tables are real concerning famous celebrities who have dined with us in the past. They usually stay at the Charleston Place Hotel and enter through our back doors while they are in town filming different movies. To name a few:

Strom Thurmond, Nikhail Barishnikov, Anthony Hopkins, New York Knicks, Martin Sheen, Erma Bombeck, Metallica, Neil Diamond, Oprah Winfrey, Danny Glover, Tanya Tucker, Sinbad, Patti LaBelle, Joe Riley, Steve Gutenburg, Barbara Streisand, Patrick Ewing, Clevone Little, Dan Jansen, Blind Melon, Alan Dershowitz, Colonel Oliver North, David Lee Roth, Billy Joel, Timothy Dalton, Lindsay Wagner, Samuel Jackson, Sam Lender, Jimmy Buffet, Steel Pulse, Pat Conroy, Bob Villa, Hulk Hogan, Kevin Costner, A.C.D.C. (The Band), Tom Berenger, Martha Stewart, Izhak Pearlman, Beach Boys, Neil Young, Sara Jessica Parker, George Seifert, Mathew Broderick

"The only thing we guarantee is our commitment to <u>YOUR</u> satisfaction."

• Due to market price fluctuations beyond our control, we reserve the right to change prices. We apologize. Thank you for your understanding •

Please come early or late to avoid the wait.

OPEN 11:00 am–11:00 pm • 7 days a week
215 Meeting Street • 723–6000
www.hymansseafood.com

Hank's Seafood

CHARLESTON
10 Hayne Street
Charleston, SC 29401
PHONE
(843) 723-FISH/3474
FAX
(843) 723-0613
HOURS
Sunday-Thursday
5:00 pm-10:30 pm
Friday & Saturday
5:00 pm-11:30 pm
MEALS SERVED
Dinner
CUISINE
American Seafood
DINING INFORMATION
Seasonal Menus
Childrens Menu
Extensive Wine Menu

ATTIRE
Resort Casual
RESERVATIONS
Required
SMOKING
Smoking Section
No Cigar or Pipe Smoking
HANDICAP FACILITIES
CREDIT CARDS
American Express
Visa
Master Card
Discover Card
Diners Club Card

Located in a turn of the century warehouse overlooking the Historic Market, Hank's has been renovated to an ambiance that reflects Charleston's seaside history and family roots. Named to Esquire's "1999 Best New Restaurants," this sister restaurant of the renowned Peninsula Grill, recreates a classic Charleston fish house with an old fashioned saloon-style bar, hollywood booths and an exhibition raw bar. Friendly service and a unique wine list earn this new restaurant a top vote-getter by locals and visitors alike.

"Hank's succeeds on every count but takes the food about three higher..."
Esquire Magazine December 1999

COLD APPETIZERS

SMOKED TROUT DIP w/Celery and Carrots .. $5.25
SEARED RARE TUNA with Sweet n Sour Onions and Tomato Vinaigrette $6.95
SOUTHERN SHRIMP SALAD with Benne Crackers $7.95
SALMON TARTARE with Horseradish Cream and Crispy Crackers $7.95
TUNA CARPACCIO with Arugula and Red Onions $7.95
SMOKED SALMON PLATE with Traditional Garnishes $9.95

HOT APPETIZERS

CHARLESTON OYSTER STEW $5.95
BOWL O' MUSSELS with White Wine, Garlic and Parsley $6.95
BAKED OYSTERS with Horseradish, Leek and Black Pepper Butter $7.95
CRISPY ROCK SHRIMP and Calamari with Spicy Tomato Remoulade $8.95
BBQ SEAFOOD BROCHETTE with Bacon and Creole Mustard Sauce $7.95
PAN FRIED CAROLINA CRABCAKES w/Creamy Mushrooms, Leeks and Bacon ... $9.95

THE RAW BAR

GULF OYSTERS (1/2 doz.) $5.95
GULF OYSTERS (doz.) $9.95
OYSTER SAMPLER (1/2 doz) $8.95
OYSTER SAMPLER (doz.) $13.50
CRAB FINGERS $7.95
LOBSTER CLAW (1 lb.) $9.95
LUMP CRAB COCKTAIL $11.50
JUMBO SHRIMP COCKTAIL $10.50

SEAFOOD A LA WANDO

A delicious combination of seafoods including crab, shrimp, and scallops expertly blended with Sweet Creamery Butter, Tender Spring Onions, and Sliced Button Mushrooms, seasoned to perfection with Fine Sherry. Served in a Piping-Hot Casserole with Fried Grits. $15.95

LOW COUNTRY BOUILLABAISSE

Superior Selection of Fresh Fish, Clams, Mussels, Shrimp and Scallops allowed to simmer in a light tomato, leek and garlic broth. Accompanied by toasted garlic croutons. $19.95

Chef's Specialties

ROAST GROUPER
Wild mushroom medley & parsley-sage broth ... $19.95
RARE SEARED TUNA
Mustard greens, fried green tomatoes and black olive vinaigrette $19.95
SEARED SEA SCALLOPS
Basil Mashed Potatoes and Piquante Tomato Sauce $18.95
CRISP COD FISH
Scallion mashed potatoes and rosemary vinaigrette $17.95
SHELLFISH TRIO LINGUINI
Shrimp, mussels, clams and herbed tomato garlic butter with linguini $16.95
STEAK FRITES
NY Strip steak with shoestring fries $17.95
ROAST CHICKEN
Juicy roasted 1/2 chicken with creamy mashed potatoes $12.95

Fish

LOCAL GROUPER $16.95
YELLOWFIN TUNA $16.95
MAHI MAHI $14.95
ATLANTIC SALMON $13.95
SHAD ROE (in season) .... market price

Shrimp or Crab

JUMBO SHRIMP, grilled $15.50
SHRIMP AND CRAB FINGERS scampi style $15.95
BLUE CRAB FINGERS sauteed with garlic butter $14.95
DEVILED CRAB, Geechee style $16.95
CRAB IMPERIAL $18.95

Seafood Platters

Broiled or Fried (Choice of Four)
Served w/red rice or sweet potato fries & Southern coleslaw
$19.95
select oysters, lump crabcake, grouper filet, local flounder fresh shrimp, sea scallops

Idlewild

With the freshest local ingredients, talented Chef David Porter along with owner Andrew Cook design Idlewild's constantly changing menu along with providing all of the favorites you have grown to love. Sit at the bar for great conversation and to enjoy a meal with a wide variety of fine wines and cocktails. Idlewild Restaurant has a cheerful atmosphere at lunch or a cozy atmosphere for dinner. Come see for your self why we were given a ★★★★ star rating by the Post & Courier's restaurant critic. Located on the corner of Coleman Blvd. and Houston Northcutt.

For Starters

Fried Green Tomatoes over Idlewild blue cheese coleslaw served with tomato concasse 5.95

Artichoke Bottoms filled with spinach and goat cheese served atop roasted tomatoes, onions and garlic 6.95

Hot Smoked Seafood Dip with garlic cheese toast 5.95

Soup of the Day cup 3.25 bowl 3.75

Coastal Carolina Gumbo cup 3.25 bowl 3.75 add red rice .75

Salads and Sandwiches

Steak Sandwich marinated flank steak thinly sliced, sauteed mushrooms, caramelized red onions and bell peppers served in a baguette with melted swiss, white cheddar, and sauce merlot 8.25

Crab Cake Sandwich served on a toasted bun w/lettuce, tomato and a key lime tartar sauce 8.95

Stono Tomato Salad with blue cheese served over mixed greens and vegetables with balsamic vinaigrette. small 3.75 large 7.25

Fried Parmesan Crusted Oysters served over fresh spinach with bacon, caramelized onion, mushrooms and an herbed vinaigrette small 6.95 large 9.95

Large or Small House Salad mixed greens with carrots, red onions, tomatoes, mushrooms, cucumbers, and your choice of freshly prepared dressings small 2.75 large 4.95

Today's Catch your choice of grilled, blackened or sauteed, served in a baguette with lettuce, tomato and tartar sauce 8.50

Pastas Etc.

Pasta Roma bowties tossed with roasted garlic, tomatoes, artichoke hearts, feta and parmesa cheeses small 8.95 large 10.95

Baked Cheese Grits with Shrimp and Andouille Sausage served with a tomato basil cream small 9.95 large 13.95

Pasta Palermo angel hair pasta tossed with sausage, peppers, onions, tomatoes, basil, and parmesan cheese small 8.75 large 10.25

Entrees

Fresh Fish selected from local waters - It arrives twice daily to ensure absolute freshness 16.95

Pan Fried Herb Crusted Flounder with browned lemon caper butter small 10.95 large 16.25

Crab and Scallop Cake with herbed hollandaise small 10.95 large 16.50

The Wando a single crab and scallop cake with a small portion of today's catch anyway you like it, served with any two of our sauces 16.95

Sauteed Gingered Sea Scallops served atop stir fried vegetables and angel hair pasta with toasted sesame seeds 16.95

Grilled Medallions of Tenderloin served atop roasted leek and garlic mashed potatoes topped with sauteed mushroom, caramelized onions and sauce merlot 18.50

Ribeye grilled or blackened served atop grilled blue cheese polenta with sauce merlot and choron 18.50

Chicken Porter double breast filled with spinach, goat cheese, Virginia ham, caramelized onions and mushrooms served on lowcountry wild rice and finished with a wild mushroom veloute 13.75

Domestic Lamb served with roasted leek and garlic mashed potatoes, sauce merlot and seasonal vegetables 17.95

Desserts

Hazelnut Brulee 3.95

White Chocolate Bread Pudding with caramel rum sauce 3.95

Today's Individual "Fresh" Fruit Cobbler with a scoop of vanilla bean ice cream 3.95

Chocolate and Then Some More Chocolate flourless chocolate cake served with a chocolate Bailey's mousse and raspberry anglaise 3.95

MOUNT PLEASANT
976 Houston Northcutt Blvd.
Mt. Pleasant, SC 29464

PHONE
(843) 881-4511

FAX
(843) 881-4799

HOURS
Lunch
Monday-Saturday
11:30 am-3:00 pm
Dinner
Monday-Thursday
5:30 pm-10:00 pm
Friday & Saturday
5:30 pm-11:00 pm

MEALS SERVED
Lunch
Dinner

CUISINE
Southern
New American

DINING INFORMATION
Vegetarian Meals
Take Out Meals
Seasonal Menus
Childrens Menu
Extensive Wine Menu

ATTIRE
Casual

RESERVATIONS
Not Required

SMOKING
Smoking Section

HANDICAP FACILITIES

CREDIT CARDS
American Express
Visa
Master Card
Discover Card

CHECKS
Accepted
(Local Only)

Il Cortile del Re

CHARLESTON
193-A King Street
Charleston, SC 29401

PHONE
(843) 853-1888

HOURS
Tuesday-Saturday
6:00 pm-10:00 pm

MEALS SERVED
Dinner

CUISINE
Italian

DINING INFORMATION
Terrace/Patio Dining
Vegetarian Meals
Seasonal Menus
Extensive Wine Menu

ADDITIONAL SERVICES
Private Parties
Private Rooms

ATTIRE
Casual

RESERVATIONS
Suggested

SMOKING
Smoking Section

CREDIT CARDS
Visa
Master Card

CHECKS
Accepted

Food & Ambiance
by Peter Herman
Post & Courier

IL CORTILE DEL RE
ENOTECA
193-A KING STREET
CHARLESTON, SOUTH CAROLINA
843-853-1888

This family owned and operated Trattoria is tucked away on Historic King Street in the Antique District of Charleston. The restaurant offers intimate indoor dining, as well as outdoors in the romantic courtyard. We feature authentic Roman and Tuscan specialties, hard to find Italian cheeses and an exclusive Italian wine list. Charleston's Post & Courier sums it up best: "Authentic Italian in a romantic setting...Il Cortile del Re is the place to experience the pleasures of Italy while in Charleston."

ANTIPASTI

APPETIZERS

CROSTINI MISTI:
small slices of toasted bread with four different toppings $4.75

COZZE AL VINO BIANCO:
mussels sautéed in olive oil and white wine $8.00

CARPACCIO DI BRESAOLA:
thinly sliced Northern Italian naturally cured beef topped with arugula, parmigiano and a mix of olive oil and lemon $9.50

VOL-AU-VENT GRANCHIO:
two puff pastry shells stuffed with sautéed crabmeat and served with mixed greens and tomatoes $6.50

ANTIPASTO ALL'ITALIANA:
for 2 persons: large plate of select cold meats, marinated artichoke hearts, roasted peppers, cherry mozzarella, black olives and tuna with white beans and onion $12.50

INSALATE

SALADS

CAPRESE:
sliced fresh mozzarella topped with tomatoes, basil and olive oil $6.75 with bufala $7.75

MEDITERRANEA:
mixed garden greens with Kalamata olive, fresh mozzarella, tomatoes and olive oil $6.50

ITALIANA:
mixed garden greens with shredded carrots, tomatoes in an olive oil and vinegar dressing $4.75

PASTA

PRIMI PIATTI

SPAGHETTI ALLA PUTTANESCA:
spaghetti with a sauce of capers, anchovies, black olives and tomato $12.50

PENNE ALLA CERTOSINA:
penne pasta tossed with black olive puree, fresh goat cheese and fresh basil...don't top with other cheese...just enjoy the flavor $12.50

RIGATONI ALL'AMATRICIANA:
tomato based sauce with sautéed onions and pancetta...ask for spicy $12.50

RAVIOLI AI FUNGHI PORCINI:
ravioli pasta stuffed and topped with wild mushrooms in cream sauce $14.50

PENNE AL SALMONE:
a cream based sauce with Scottish smoked salmon and onions sautéed with Brandy $13.50

SECONDI PIATTI

CINGHIALE CON FAGIOLI E POLENTA:
wild boar and cannellini beans stew with polenta in tomato sauce $17.50

LUGANICA E FAGIOLI:
Italian pork sausage with rosemary and garlic sautéed beans $7.50

SOGLIOLA ALLA MUGNAIA:
fresh local flounder, pan seared with butter, garlic and olive oil served with spinach sautéed in olive oil and red pepper $15.50

POLLO AL BALSAMICO E MIELE:
chicken tenderloin strips sautéed with rosemary, Balsamic vinegar and honey $15.50

ARROSTO AL CHIANTI:
slowly roasted beef sliced and topped with a Chianti wine sauce $16.50

Il Pescatore

Italia Ristorante

Il Pescatore (the Fisherman) is located one block East of Mt. Pleasant's scenic Shem Creek. A casual fine dining restaurant that includes a varied menu with a classic Italian focus. Customers recognize the warmth of a neighborhood Italian restaurant while being served generous size helpings of Chef Craig Elwood's nightly specials. Homemade desserts are also featured on the menu. The superb Italian wine list adds to each selection. For those who prefer dining at home, the owners offer a "take out" menu. Catering is also available for small and large parties.

Salads & Appetizers

Mixed Baby Greens with Basil & Roma Tomatoes In a Red Wine Vinaigrette 3.75

Traditional Caesar Salad with Herbed Croutons & Shaved Parmesan 4.75

Fresh Mozzarella, Roma Tomatoes & Basil with Olive Oil & Balsamic Vinegar 4.95
Add Salami & Capicola 6.95

Lightly Dusted & Fried Calamari with Red Pepper Relish 4.95

Steamed Little Neck Clams Marinara 7.75

Homemade Potato Chips with Warm Gorgonzola Sauce 4.95

Grilled Asparagus with Shaved Parmesan & Diced Roma Tomatoes 5.95

Pastas, Etc...

Gnocchi with Meat (Includes Meatball and Sausage) 10.95

Gnocchi Marinara 8.95

Gnocchi Alfredo with Wild Mushrooms 9.95

Classic Four Cheese Lasagna 10.95

Penne with Bacon and Spicy Tomato Vodka Sauce 10.95

Italian Sausages Sweet Peppers & Onions over Spaghettini Marinara 10.95

Linguini Primavera with Artichoke Hearts and Fresh Vegetables 9.95

Penne Il Forno Baked with Mozzarella & Parmesan Topped with Marinara 9.95

Risotto

Wild Mushroom Risotto 9.95
Add Sausage 11.95

Salmon Risotto with Sautéed Spinach and Tomatoes 12.95

Risotto Pescatore with Squid, Shrimp, Clams and topped with Crab Meat 13.95

Meats & Poultry

Pan Seared Veal Chop with a Mustard Port Demi served with Parmesan Potatoes & Roasted Rosemary Eggplant 18.95

Pan Seared 12 oz. N.Y. Strip Pizzaiola served over Linguini 15.95

Chicken Franchese served with Sautéed Spinach and Parmesan Mashed Potatoes 10.95

Chicken Cacciatore served over Spaghettini 11.95

Chicken or Veal Marsala served over Spaghettini 11.95/13.95

Seafood

Golden Salmon with Raisins 12.95

Linguini with Little Neck Clams in a White or Red Sauce 12.95

Shrimp Scampi over Linguini 13.95

Spicy Pescatore Fra Diavolo over Spaghettini 15.95

Grilled Yellow Fin Tuna Pesto Rubbed served over Basil Pesto Risotto 15.95

Seafood Florentina - Shrimp & Yellow Fin Tuna Sautéed in a Light Alfredo Cream Sauce with Fresh Spinach and Diced Tomatoes over Fettucini 14.95

Il Pescatore

MT. PLEASANT
201 Coleman Blvd.
Mt. Pleasant, SC 29464

PHONE
(843) 971-3931

HOURS
5:30 pm-Until
Closed Tuesdays

MEALS SERVED
Dinner

CUISINE
Southern Italian
Northern Italian

DINING INFORMATION
Heart Smart Meals
Vegetarian Meals
Childrens Menu
Extensive Wine Menu

LOUNGE BAR
5:00 pm-Until

ADDITIONAL SERVICES
Full Service Catering
Private Parties

ATTIRE
Resort Casual

RESERVATIONS
Suggested

SMOKING
Smoking Not Permitted

CREDIT CARDS
American Express
Visa
Master Card
Discover Card

CHECKS
Accepted
(Local Checks)

J. Bistro

MT. PLEASANT
819 Colemans Blvd.
Mt. Pleasant, SC 29464
PHONE
(843) 971-7778
FAX
(843) 971-0938
HOURS
Tuesday-Thursday
5:00 pm-10:00 pm
Friday-Saturday
5:00 pm-11:00 pm
Sunday
10:30 am-2:30 pm
5:00 pm-10:00 pm
MEALS SERVED
Dinner
Sunday Brunch
CUISINE
New American
DINING INFORMATION
Vegetarian Meals
Take Out Meals
Seasonal Menus
Childrens Menu
Extensive Wine Menu
ADDITIONAL SERVICES
Full Service Catering

ATTIRE
Resort Casual
RESERVATIONS
Not Required
SMOKING
Smoking Section
VALET PARKING
CREDIT CARDS
American Express
Visa
Master Card
CHECKS
Accepted
(Local only)

J. Bistro

Nestled in the heart of Mt. Pleasant, exists one of Charleston's true culinary treasures, J. Bistro. It was founded about 5 years ago by Chef/Owner, James Burns and has long since been noted for its excellent food, friendly service and prices you just won't find downtown. Some of the favorites at J. Bistro include the Sautéed Grouper with Whipped Potatoes; the Sesame Seared Tuna and Roasted Double Cut Pork Chop.

PART I

Prince Edward Island Mussels with Fennel & Roasted Red Pepper Butter .... $6.
Pan–Fried Green Tomatoes with a Warm Crab & Artichoke Ragout .... $7.
Grilled Portobello Mushroom atop a Roasted Garlic Potato Stem with Balsamic Glaze .... $6.
Eggplant, Tomato, and Goat Cheese "Blintzes" over Caramelized Onions .... $5.
"Kushi–Katsu" Bamboo Skewered and Flash Seared, served with a Trio of Sauces .... $6.
Lobster Won Tons in a Bamboo Steamer with Spinach, Leeks, and Carrots .... $8.
Classic French Onion Soup .... $4.
Freshest Mess of Field Greens with Herbs & Vegetables tossed in Mustard Vinaigrette .... $3.
topped with Crumbled Bleu or Goat Cheese .... $4.
Traditional Caesar Salad with Country Sourdough Croutons .... $4.
Crispy Duck Confit with Granny Smith Apple & Pistachio Marmalade .... $7.

PART II

Sesame Seared Tuna with Greens, Pickled Ginger, and Soy Dipping Sauce .... $14.
Sautéed Grouper on Whipped Potatoes with a Crabmeat & Champagne Cream Sauce .... $14.
Pecan Crusted Catfish Filets over Creamy Grits, finished with a Spicy Hollandaise .... $10.
Pan Fried Flounder "Noisettes" finished with Lemon/Caper Meuniere .... $16.
Salt and Garlic Crusted Salmon with Grilled Fennel & Rock Shrimp Salsa
over Carolina Plantation Rice .... $14.
Prosciutto Wrapped N.E. Cod over Lobster, Bacon, and Chive Potatoes .... $15.

PART III

J. Burger with Grilled Onion, Sautéed Mushrooms, and Home–Made Chips .... $7.
Pan Roasted, Double Cut Pork Chop with Roasted Shallots & Bourbon Glaze .... $14.
Southern Fried Breast of Chicken with Chow Chow and Garlic Whipped Potatoes .... $9.
Sautéed Veal Medallions Stacked atop Whipped Potatoes with Wilted Spinach
finished with a Shiitake Mushroom, Prosciutto, and Basil Jus .... $15.
Pan-Roastd N.Y. Strip Steak over a Medley of Wild Mushrooms
topped with a Truffled Chantrelle Butter .... $19.
Grilled Pork Tenderloin
with Fingerling Potato, Andouille Sausage, and Bell Pepper Hash .... $15.
Pistachio Crusted Duck Breast on Lyonnaise Potatoes
finished with a Black Currant-Cassis Glaze .... $18.

Jasmine

Jasmine restaurant

A new flower is blooming in Charleston! Experience traditional Charleston hospitality in an elegant atmosphere. Jasmine is centrally located at the end of the historic open–air Market and adjacent to the Customs House. Enjoy Chef John Hewson's unique blend of creative, progressive fare based on the classic style such as Seared Scallops with Lobster Mashed Potatoes, Grilled Ribeye with Cheddar and Bacon Potato Gratin, and Lobster Tempura. The Post and Courier and City Paper of Charleston quote: "A Special Night" and "Extremely delicious"

APPETIZERS

Soup of the Day 4.50

Lobster Tempura, Grilled Asparagus and Ginger Wasabi Buerre Blanc 8.95

Lime & Coriander House Cured Salmon on Gold Potato Cakes w/Sour Cream Vinaigrette & Chives 7.25

Pepper and Mustard Seed Crusted Beef Carpaccio w/Dijon Vinaigrette & Green Olive Tapanade 7.50

Barbecued Pork Springrolls with Spicy Cucumber Salad 8.50

Thai Curried Mussels Steamed with Kaffir Lime Leaves, Cilantro and Coconut Milk 7.50

Basil and Ricotta Ravioli with Fresh Vine Tomato Ragout and Shaved Parmesan 7.00

Grilled Chili Spiced Shrimp with Coconut Rice and a Sweet and Sour Eggplant Sauce 8.25

SALADS

Salad of Baby Lettuces w/Vine Ripened Tomatoes, Glazed Pecans, Applewood Smoked Bacon with a Buttermilk Herb Vinaigrette 5.50

Crisp Tossed Salad, Chinois Style with Orange Shrimp 7.95

Salad of Arugula, Orange, Shaved Fennel and Bermuda Onion with a Maytag Blue Cheese 5.95

Warm Goat Cheese Salad of Grilled Eggplant and Tomatoes with a Tomato Basil Vinaigrette 7.50

Grilled Lobster Salad of Baby Greens, Fire Roasted Chili and Corn Tamales with Queso Fresco, Avocado and Lime Vinaigrette and Salsa Verde 16.00

ENTREES

Maple Glazed Duck Breast, Sweet Potato and Duck Confit Gallettes and Sautéed Chard 17.95

Beef Short Ribs Braised in Red Wine with Porcini Potato Puree and Glazed Carrots 17.25

Roasted Chilean Seabass with Ginger Jus and Grilled Jasmine Rice Cakes 18.95

Grilled Cider Cured Pork Tenderloin, Potato Pancake, Sweet Onion Relish & Whole Grain Mustard Sauce 16.25

Grilled 12 oz. Ribeye, Vermont Cheddar and Bacon Potatoes Gratin with Garlic Sauteed Escarole 19.95

Seared Scallops, Lobster Mashed Potatoes and Creole Buerre Blanc 18.95

Grilled Miso Rubbed Tuna, Shiitake Stir Fry and Steamed Jasmine Rice 18.95

Rosemary Scented Grilled Chicken with Creamy Polenta and Sautéed Greens 15.95

Wild Mushroom Meatloaf, Buttermilk Chive Mashed Potatoes, Greens and Gravy 15.95

Citrus Glazed Salmon with Wasabi Mashed Potatoes, Tempura Vegetables and a Chinese Black Bean Sauce 18.95

Prosciutto Wrapped Roasted Halibut Filet with Pearl Cous Cous and Lobster "Risotto" with Garlic Spinach 17.95

Fresh Fettucine with Smoke Roasted Salmon and Asparagus in a Garlic and Lemon Thyme Cream Sauce 14.95

Fresh Angel Hair Tossed with Garlic Shrimp, Vine Ripened Tomato Sauce, Prosciutto, and Italian Parsley 15.95

Linguine Tossed with Roma Tomatoes, Arugula, Radicchio, Roasted Garlic and Balsamic Vinegar 13.95

Roasted Squab with Fresh Ricotta Gnocchi, Wild Mushrooms, Honey Roasted Shallots, Grilled Asparagus and a Pinot Noir Reduction Sauce 19.95

CHARLESTON
16 North Market Street
Charleston, SC 29401
PHONE
(843) 853-0006
FAX
(843) 853-4450
HOURS
Lunch
Monday-Friday
11:30 am-2:00 pm
Dinner
Monday-Saturday
5:30 pm-10:00 pm
Sunday closed
MEALS SERVED
Lunch
Dinner
CUISINE
Progressive American
Seafood
DINING INFORMATION
Extensive Wine Menu

ATTIRE
Elegant Casual
RESERVATIONS
Suggested
SMOKING
Smoking Section
No Cigar or Pipe Smoking
HANDICAP FACILITIES
CREDIT CARDS
American Express
Visa
Master Card
CHECKS
Not Accepted

John's at the Market

CHARLESTON
85 Market Street
Charleston, SC 29401
PHONE
(843) 534-1234
FAX
(843) 534-0000
HOURS
11:00 am-11:00 pm
MEALS SERVED
Breakfast
Lunch
Dinner
Sunday Brunch
Late Night Dining
CUISINE
Lowcountry
Seafood
Steak House
DINING INFORMATION
Terrace/Patio Dining
Heart Smart Meals
Vegetarian Meals
Take Out Meals
Seasonal Menus
Childrens Menu
Extensive Wine Menu
LOUNGE BAR
ENTERTAINMENT
Charleston's Finest Live Jazz
5:00 pm-11:00 pm
DANCING
ADDITIONAL SERVICES
Full Service Catering
Private Parties
Banquet Facilities
Private Rooms

ATTIRE
Resort Casual
RESERVATIONS
Not Required
(Except for Private Parties)
SMOKING
Smoking Section
CREDIT CARDS
American Express
Visa
Master Card
Discover Card
Diners Club Card

Located in historic downtown Charleston at 85 South Market Street, John's at the Market is an excellent steak and seafood restaurant with an upstairs live Jazz Entertainment Room. Our Mission is simple, to provide high-quality food in a convenient and comfortable atmosphere with a responsive staff at a price that's reasonable. To experience the Lowcountry at its best you must experience Johns at the Market.

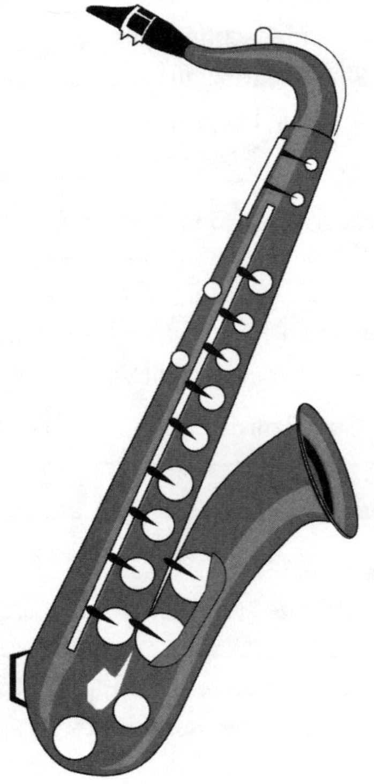

The menu for John's at the Market was not available at publication time. The Restaurant is due to open in March 2000.

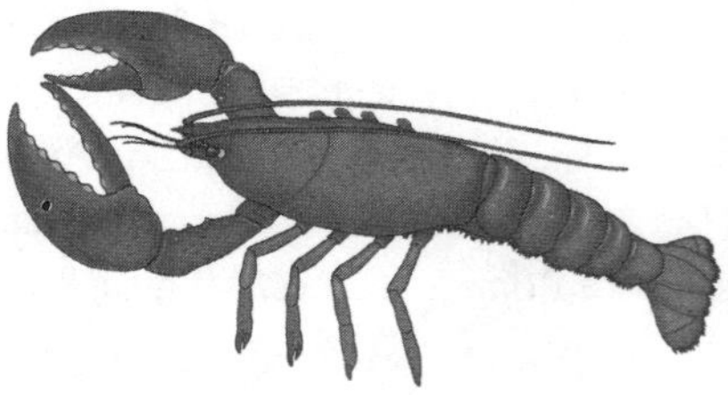

Kaminsky's is a Charleston late-night institution. Featuring a full-service bar that proudly offers a vast selection of wines by the glass, cocktails, specialty coffees including hand crafted cappuccino, espresso, and latte, and award-winning desserts made by our own pastry chefs. Join your friends for coffee, dessert, or a cocktail in this sophisticated bistro atmosphere. The Lowcountry's premier choice for an after-dinner outing.

Desserts

Mountain of Chocolate — $4.50
3 layer chocolate cake with chocolate buttercream icing.

Bourbon Pecan Pie — $3.95
Our version of this southern favorite. Try it warmed with ice cream!

Tollhouse Cookie Pie — $3.75
Watch out chocoholics— this one'll hook ya!!!

Coconut Cream Pie — $3.75
Homemade custard with coconut in a flaky pie crust, topped with whipped cream & toasted coconut

Carrot Cake — $4.95
3 layer spiced carrot cake with raisins, pecans & cream cheese icing.

Fruited Buttercream Cake — $3.95
Layered white cake with buttercream icing & fresh glazed fruit.

Double Chocolate Dare — $3.95
A flourless chocolate torte, drizzled with white chocolate. Go on, we dare you!!!

Hummingbird Spice Cake — $3.95
3 layers of pineapple, apple and banana spice cake, topped with cream cheese icing & crushed pecans

Low Fat Cheesecake — $3.95
Honestly it's only 4 grams of fat per slice!!!

Caramel Chocolate Chip Walnut Pound Cake — $3.95
Homemade traditional sour cream pound cake with the above ingredients. Served warm.

Milkshakes

Kaminsky's Famous Milkshake —$3.95

Voted by the Charleston Post and Courier "Best Milkshake" in Charleston.

Three scoops of Greenwood vanilla bean or coffee ice cream, milk and your choice of flavor(s): chocolate, mocha, vanilla, banana, strawberry, raspberry, almond, hazelnut, caramel, Irish cream, cherry, mint or malt.

Our Most Excellent Specialty Shakes —$6.75
Add Bailey's, Kahlua, Malibu Rum, or your choice of liqueur to any of the above flavors

Brandy Alexander — $6.50
Our own version made with brandy, dark crème de cocoa and three scoops of Greenwood vanilla bean ice cream.

Sundaes

Kaminsky's Most Excellent Brownie —$1.75
A delicious amaretto, fudge, espresso concoction—you'll love it! Served warm with fudge sauce and whipped cream.

Our famous Brownie Sundae — $3.75
Kaminsky's brownie served warm with fudge sauce then a scoop of vanilla bean ice cream and whipped cream. Top with walnuts at no charge if you like.

Ice Cream Sundae — $3.25
Three generous scoops of Greenwood vanilla bean ice cream, with fudge, caramel, raspberry or strawberry sauce, topped with fresh whipped cream and a cookie (and walnuts upon request)

This is Just a small sample of the wonderful desserts that Kaminsky's has to offer.

Kaminsky's also has a wide variety of specialty coffees and liqueurs.

Kaminsky's
Most Excellent Cafe

CHARLESTON
78 N. Market Street
Charleston, SC 29401
PHONE
(843) 853-8270
FAX
(843) 720-7842
MT. PLEASANT
1028 Johnnie Dodds Blvd.
Mt. Pleasant, SC 29464
PHONE
(843) 971-7437
FAX
(843) 856-2444
HOURS
12 Noon-Late
DESSERT SERVED
Lunch
Dinner
Twilight Dinners
Late Night Dining
CUISINE
Dessert & Coffee
DINING INFORMATION
Terrace/Patio Dining
(Mt. Pleasant Location Only)
Take Out Meals
Childrens Menu
Extensive Wine Menu
LOUNGE BAR
ENTERTAINMENT
Cool Jazz
Thursdays Mt. Pleasant
8:00 pm-11:00 pm
ADDITIONAL SERVICES
Private Parties
Wedding and Special
Occasion Cakes

ATTIRE
Casual
RESERVATIONS
Not Required
SMOKING
Smoking Section
Cigar & Pipe Friendly
(Mt. Pleasant Only)
HANDICAP FACILITIES
CREDIT CARDS
American Express
Visa
Master Card
CHECKS
Accepted
(Local Only)

Latasha's Taste of New Orleans

CHARLESTON
43 Cannon Street
Charleston, SC 29403
PHONE
(843) 723-3222
FAX
(843) 723-6006
HOURS
Lunch
Tuesday-Friday
11:00 am-3:00 pm
Dinner
Tuesday-Saturday
6:00 pm-10:00 pm
MEALS SERVED
Lunch
Dinner
CUISINE
Cajun/Creole
Seafood
DINING INFORMATION
Vegetarian Meals
Childrens Menu
ADDITIONAL SERVICES
Full Service Catering

ATTIRE
Casual
CREDIT CARDS
Visa
Master Card
Discover Card
Diners Club Card
Carte Blanche
CHECKS
Accepted

LATASHA'S

A TASTE OF NEW ORLEANS

"Our menu combines the oldest traditional foods of New Orleans, Louisiana, with our newest creations to give our patrons the finest foods, utilizing the very best herbs and seafoods found in our area. We sincerely hope that you enjoy what we think is the best of a New Orleans tradition."

Only Authentic Cajun Restaurant in South Carolina.

APPETIZERS

CREOLE EGG ROLLS
$4.95
DEEP FRIED CRAB FINGERS
$5.95
JALAPENO STUFFED WITH CRAB MEAT
$5.95
FRIED CRAWFISH TAILS
$5.95
DEEP FRIED MUSHROOMS
$4.95
MARINATED CRAB FINGERS
$6.95

DINNER SALADS

C-FOOD SALAD
$6.95
SHRIMP SALAD
$5.95
CHICKEN SALAD
$4.95
GREEN SALAD
$3.95

FROM THE FRYER

JR'S SPECIAL
GOLDEN FRIED PORK CHOPS
WITH CREOLE RICE AND CORN
$7.95
FRIED SHRIMP
$9.95
FRIED SCALLOP
$9.95
FRIED CATFISH
$9.95
FRIED OYSTERS
$10.95
C-FOOD COMBO
COMBINATION OF ANY TWO SEAFOOD ENTREES
$11.95
C-FOOD PLATTER
SHRIMP, SCALLOP, FISH, OYSTER
$13.95

CHEF ROBERT SIGNATURE DISHES

C-FOOD ALA TASHA
SERVED WITH YELLOW RICE AND ONE VEGETABLE,
SHRIMP, SCALLOP AND CRABMEAT IN CASSEROLE
WITH TWO CHEESES AND BREADCRUMBS
$13.95

SHRIMP AND SCALLOP MONICA
SHRIMP AND SCALLOP IN LOBSTER SAUCE
WITH YELLOW RICE AND ONE VEGETABLE
$12.95

C-FOOD CATHERINE
SHRIMP, CRAWFISH AND CRABMEAT
OVER LINGUINE IN A LITE CREAM SAUCE
$13.95

DINNER ENTREES

SHRIMP CREOLE
$10.95
SHRIMP AND CRABMEAT ETOUFEE
$10.95
CRAWFISH ETOUFEE
$10.95
JAMBALAYA
$10.95
GRILLED OR BLACKENED FISH
(OF THE DAY)
$10.95
STUFFED FISH WITH SHRIMP OR CRABMEAT
$13.95
GRILLED OR BLACKENED STEAK
(RIBEYE)
$11.95
GRILLED OR BLACKENED STEAK AND SHRIMP
$13.95
GRILLED OR BLACKENED STEAK AND SCALLOP
$14.95
CREOLE PASTA
CRAWFISH AND SHRIMP IN CREOLE SAUCE OVER
LINGUINE WITH SALAD OR ONE VEGETABLE
$12.95

Library Restaurant

CHARLESTON
23 Vendue Range
Charleston, SC 29401

PHONE
(843) 577-7970

FAX
(843) 577-7346

HOURS
Lunch
7 Days a Week
11:30 am-2:30 pm
Dinner
Monday-Saturday
5:30 pm-10:00 pm
Sunday
5:30 pm-9:00 pm

MEALS SERVED
Lunch
Dinner

CUISINE
Eclectic
Lowcountry

DINING INFORMATION
Terrace/Patio Dining
Heart Smart Meals
Vegetarian Meals
Take Out Meals
Seasonal Menus
Extensive Wine Menu

LOUNGE BAR

ENTERTAINMENT
Seasonal

ADDITIONAL SERVICES
Full Service Catering
Private Parties
Banquet Facilities
Lodging
Private Rooms
Meeting Facilities

ATTIRE
Resort Casual
Semi-Formal

RESERVATIONS
Suggested

SMOKING
Smoking Not Permitted

VALET PARKING

HANDICAP FACILITIES

CREDIT CARDS
American Express
Visa
Master Card
Discover Card
Diners Club Card

CHECKS
Not Accepted

Imaginative American Cuisine with a Southern Flair

"...The Library is a Culinary Bestseller"
-Post & Courier

"...The Library at Vendue satisfies the hunger of imagination"
-Charleston Magazine

- 3 Distinctive Cozy & Unique Dining Rooms
- Available for Group Parties & Corporate Dinners
- Roof Top Bar Overlooking Charleston Harbor

APPETIZERS

Pan-Seared Lump-Crab Medallions
with White Cheddar Cheese and Sweet Pimento with Fresh Corn Relish - 8.00

Pan-Seared Frog Legs
Cayenne Dusted and served with Sweet Onion and Garlic Compote - 9.00

Carpaccio of Yellowfin Tuna
with Fried Artichoke Chips and Wasabi Muse - 7.00

Marinated Asparagus Spears with Portobello Mushrooms
Shaved Parmesan and Crème Fraiche - 6.00

Baked Cheese Tart
of Soft Ripened Blue Cheese, Basil and Sundried Tomatoes with Sliced Chargrilled Pear - 7.00

SOUPS

Charles Towne Original Recipe She-Crab
with Sherry Lace cup $3.75 bowl $4.50

Harvest Sweet Corn Chowder
cup $3.75 bowl $4.50

Low Country Seafood Gumbo
cup $3.75 bowl $4.50

SALADS

Library House Salad
Romaine and Radicchio Lettuces, Almonds, Plum Tomatoes, Portobello Mushroom Slice and Parmesan Cheese - $4.75

Chevre Spinach Salad
with Roasted Peppers, Caramelized Walnuts, Peppered Goat Cheese and Cranberry Cider Vinaigrette - $5.25

VEGETARIAN FRIENDLY ENTREES

Vegetarian Feast
of Grilled Portobello Mushroom and Asparagus with Gorgonzola Cheese, Rosemary Mashed Potatoes and Sautéed Spinach with Herbed Cream - 16.00

Sautéed Mushrooms and Sundried Tomatoes
over Penne Pasta with Toasted Pignolias - 15.00

ENTREES

Vendue Strip Loin of Beef
with Gorgonzola Butter and Portobello Mushroom Ragout - 20.00

Grilled Maple Leaf Breast of Duck
with Sesame Tangerine Honey Glaze - 19.00

Grilled Chicken Havana
with Caramelized Plantains, Garnished with Fresh Mango - 19.00

Crown of New Zealand Lamb
Seasoned with Fresh Rosemary and Rubbed with Fresh Garlic - 22.00

Library Webster-Cut Pork Chop
with Fresh Grated Ginger and Balsamic Vinegar Reduction - 18.00

Peppered Beef Tenderloin
with Vanilla Veal Glace - 22.00

SEAFOOD

Black Grouper
crusted in Blue Crab with Citrus Ginger Mustard - 24.00

Ahi Tuna
grilled with Plum Tomato and Cilantro Relish, garnished with Lime Crème Fraiche - 22.00

Poached Salmon
with Saffron Boursin Cream - 19.00

Seafood Linguini of Scallops, Shrimp, Mussels and Salmon
with Lemon Basil Cream Sauce - 17.00

DESSERTS

Imported Sweet Cheese Plate
with Blackberry Compote and Fruit - 7.00

Rum Roasted Banana Soufflé
with Vanilla Bean Ice Cream and Warm Caramel - 5.00

Pina Coloda Cheese Cake
with Fresh Orchid Raspberry Paint - 6.00

Marquise of Dark Chocolate
With truffle fruit relish and fresh mint - 7.00

Locklear's Fine Seafood

MT. PLEASANT
427 Coleman Blvd.
Mt. Pleasant, SC 29464
PHONE
(843) 884-3346
FAX
(843) 884-8832
E-MAIL
askew5159@aol.com
HOURS
Lunch
Monday-Sunday
11:30 am-3:00 pm
Dinner
Monday-Friday
5:00 pm-10:00 pm
Sunday
12:00 pm-9:00 pm
MEALS SERVED
Lunch
Dinner
CUISINE
American
DINING INFORMATION
Heart Smart Meals
Take Out Meals
Children's Menu
ADDITIONAL SERVICES
Full Service Catering
Private Parties

ATTIRE
Casual
RESERVATIONS
Suggested
SMOKING
Section Available
No Cigar or Pipe Smoking
HANDICAP FACILITIES
CREDIT CARDS
American Express
Visa
Master Card
Discover Card

L O C K L E A R ' S

Featuring the finest in Southern Coastal Cuisine, Locklear's is a tried and true local favorite. Enjoy a relaxed and casual atmosphere where value and quality are number one. Locklear's is a participant in M.U.S.C.'s Heart Choice Dining Program and has been satisfying customers for over eighteen years. Experience an evening not soon forgotten.

Winner of the critics choice for the best SHE-CRAB SOUP

"Locklear's a winner"
The Charlotte Observer July 1994.

The Post & Courier March 1994.
"It's a lock: Locklear's has satisfied diners coming back year after year."

Winner of the first Heart Choice cooking competition.

STARTERS

OYSTER CORN FRITTER $6.99
A GRILLED CORN FRITTER TOPPED WITH FRIED OYSTERS AND CAJUN CREAM

CRAB CAKES $6.10
FRESH PICKLED BLUE CRAB, MIXED DICED VEGETABLES AND HERBS, SERVED ON BLACKBEAN SAUCE WITH SALSA AND LEMON CREME FRAICHE

BLACKENED SHRIMP $6.10
BEAUTIFUL WHITE SHRIMP DUSTED WITH OUR OWN BLACKENED SPICE AND GRILLED, SERVED OVER PREMIUM STONE GROUND GRITS AND DRIZZLED WITH ROASTED GARLIC CREAM

COCONUT FRIED SHRIMP $6.10
FRESH SHRIMP MARINATED WITH COCONUT CREAM AND FRIED, SERVED WITH SPICY MARMALADE

LOCKLEAR'S INCREDIBLE FRIED CALAMARI $4.25
LIGHTLY BREADED AND FRIED TO PERFECTION! SERVED WITH BUTTER AND LEMON

MS. KAREN'S CRAB AND SHRIMP DIP $5.10
FRESH CRAB PICKED AND SHRIMP MIXED WITH CHEESE AND SOUR CREAM. SERVED WITH CRACKERS

BRUCHETTA PROVENCAL .... $4.50 WITH SHRIMP $6.99
SOURDOUGH BRUSHED WITH OLIVE OIL AND TOPPED WITH MUSHROOMS, TOMATO, BASIL, BLACK AND GREEN OLIVES, ARTICHOKE HEARTS, MOZZARELLA AND SHREDDED PARMESAN

AWARD WINNING SHE CRAB SOUP .... PRICED DAILY

SALADS

HOUSE SALAD $3.00
MIXED GREENS TOPPED WITH AN ASSORTMENT OF GARDEN VEGETABLES AND CHOICE OF DRESSING

SPINACH SALAD $3.99
SPINACH WITH BACON, GREEN ONION, ROMA TOMATOES, MUSHROOMS AND BOILED EGG

CHICKEN CASHEW SALAD $6.25
MIXED GREENS WITH A GRILLED CHICKEN BREAST JULIENNE, MUSHROOMS, GREEN ONIONS, CASHEWS, TOMATO AND BOILED EGG

FRIED OYSTER SALAD $7.50
FRESH OYSTERS LIGHTLY BREADED AND FRIED, SERVED OVER MIXED GREENS WITH GARDEN RELISH AND TOMATO. SERVED WITH HOT BACON DRESSING

FRIED SEAFOOD

FRIED SHRIMP $11.25
FRIED OYSTERS $12.99
FRIED SCALLOPS $12.99
FRIED FLOUNDER $13.99
FRIED PLATTER - SHRIMP, OYSTERS, SCALLOPS $14.99
FRIED FEAST $16.99
SHRIMP, SCALLOPS, OYSTERS, FISH & DEVILED CRAB

ENTREES

CHICKEN ITALIANO $10.99
CHICKEN BREAST LIGHTLY BREADED AND FRIED, TOPPED WITH MARINARA, MUSHROOMS, GREEN AND BLACK OLIVES AND SERVED WITH PASTA ALFREDO

CHICKEN CHARLESTON $13.99
CHICKEN BREAST GRILLED AND TOPPED WITH A CRAB CAKE AND MUSHROOM VELOUTE

CHICKEN AND SHRIMP STEPHANIE $13.99
STRIPS OF EGG COATED CHICKEN SAUTEED IN BUTTER AND GARLIC WITH MUSHROOMS AND SHRIMP, SERVED OVER FRESH SPINACH WITH A SIDE OF PASTA ALFREDO

CHICKEN AND SHRIMP WILLIAM $14.99
SAUTEED STRIPS OF CHICKEN AND SHRIMP IN OLIVE OIL WITH GARLIC, GREEN AND BLACK OLIVES, MUSHROOMS, ARTICHOKE HEARTS, TOMATOES AND FETA CHEESE

CATCH HERB $13.99
FRESH CATCH OF THE DAY TOPPED WITH HERBS AND JULIENNE VEGETABLES AND BAKED WITH WHITE WINE, TOMATOES AND BALSAMIC VINEGAR

STUFFED CATCH $14.99
FRESH CATCH OF THE DAY TOPPED WITH A GRILLED BLUE CRAB CAKE AND LACED WITH MUSHROOM VELOUTE ....

GROUPER LOCKLEAR .... PRICED
FRESH LOCAL GROUPER DIPPED IN EGG AND SAUTEED WITH BUTTER, GARLIC, MUSHROOMS AND WHITE WINE. SERVED OVER FRESH SPINACH WITH A SIDE OF ALFREDO

CAJUN SHRIMP AND GRITS $12.99
PREMIUM WHITE SHRIMP WITH MUSHROOMS AND GREEN ONIONS IN A CAJUN CREAM SAUCE SERVED OVER GRITS WITH CORN FRITTERS

BLACKENED STEAK AND FRIED SHRIMP $15.25
MEDALLIONS OF BEEF TENDERLOIN DUSTED WITH BLACKENED SPICES AND COOKED TO ORDER, ACCOMPIANIED BY A GENEROUS PORTION OF FRIED SHRIMP

STEAK LOCKLEAR $15.25
TENDERLOIN MEDALLIONS SAUTEED WITH SHRIMP AND MUSHROOMS ON A BED OF FRESH SPINACH

MIXED VEGETABLE MARINARA $7.99
A COMBINATION OF FRESH VEGETABLES SIMMERED IN OUR OWN MARINARA SERVED OVER PASTA

SHRIMP AND SCALLOPS MARINARA $6.99 $13.99
OUR HOUSE MARINARA MADE WITH ROASTED RED BELL PEPPERS AND EGGPLANT

SHRIMP PARMESAN $6.25 $11.99
SHRIMP AND MARINARA OVER FRIED EGGPLANT WITH PARMESAN

This is a sample of the many menu items offered at Locklear's Fine Seafood

Locklear's Lowcountry Grill

At Locklear's we love our Lowcountry community. That's why we set out to serve the best of its local recipes, many dating back more than 200 years. We dedicated ourselves to preserving this impressive culinary heritage, but delivering delicious tradional foods is only part of our goal. We also serve our community as strong supporters of local groups and charities. We feel it's only right to give back to a place that has given us so much, including a marvelous time-honored cuisine.

STARTERS

BULL'S BAY BBQ OYSTERS 1999 FIRST PLACE FINISH ... $7.99
GRILLED CORN FRITTERS TOPPED WITH OYSTERS SAUTEED IN A SOUTHERN STYLE BBQ SAUCE AND LACED WITH CAJUN CREAM.

BRUSCHETTA PROVENCAL ... $4.99
FRESH BAKED SOURDOUGH BRUSHED WITH OLIVE OIL AND TOPPED WITH MUSHROOMS, TOMATO, BASIL, BLACK AND GREEN OLIVES, ARTICHOKE HEARTS, MOZZARELLA AND SHREDDED PARMESAN.
ADD SHRIMP $6.99

CAJUN SHRIMPS ... $6.99
PREMIUM WHITE SHRIMPS SAUTÉED WITH GREEN ONIONS IN A ZESTY SAUCE.

CRAB CAKES ... $6.50
FRESH PICKED BLUE CRABS MIXED WITH VEGETABLES AND HARBS SERVED ON A BLACK-EYED PEA SAUCE, WITH HOMEMADE SALSA AND CRÈME FRAICHE.

FRIED CALAMARI ... $4.99
LIGHTLY BREADED AND FRIED TO PERFECTION, SERVED WITH DRAWN BUTTER AND PARMESAN.

QUESADILLA OF THE DAY ... PRICED DAILY
A FRESH ASSORTMENT OF FILLINGS EVERDAY, SERVED WITH HOMEMADE SALSA AND CRÈME FRAICHE.

SIDES

BASKET OF FRIES ... $1.50

BAKED POTATO (LOADED) ... $3.00

VEGETABLE OF THE DAY ... $2.00

PLANTATION RED RICE ... $1.50

OLD MILL HOMINY GRITS ... $2.00

CORN FRITTERS WITH TOMATO JAM ... $2.00

SALADS

HOMEMADE DRESSING AVAILABLE: MANGO VINAIGRETTE, HOT BACON, BLEU CHEESE, GREEK, RANCH AND HONEY MUSTARD SERVED WITH CRACKERS

CHICKEN CASHEW SALAD ... $6.25
MIXED GREENS WITH A GRILLED CHICKEN BREAST JULIENNE, MUSHROOMS, GREEN ONION, CASHEWS, TOMATO AND BOILED EGG.

FRIED OYSTER SALAD ... $7.50
FRESH OYSTERS LIGHTLY BREADED AND FRIED, SERVED OVER MIXED GREENS WITH GARDEN RELISH AND TOMATO. SERVED WITH HOT BACON DRESSING.

ENTREES

ALL SERVED WITH HOUSE SALAD

CAROLINA PIE ... $12.99
CHICKEN AND SHRIMPS SAUTÉED IN ROASTED GARLIC CREAM WITH MUSHROOMS AND PEPPERS. SERVED WITH CAROLINA SPOONBREAD.

PECAN PILAU WITH DUCK AND SHRIMPS ... $13.99
DUCK AND SHRIMPS COOKED WITH THE HOLY TRINITY OF SOUTHERN COOKING (CELERY, BELL PEPPER AND ONION), RICE AND SPOONBREAD.

GROUPER LOCKLEAR ... PRICED DAILY
FRESH LOCAL GROUPER DIPPED IN EGG AND SAUTÉED WITH BUTTER, GARLIC, MUSHROOMS, LEMON AND WHITE WINE. SERVED OVER FRESH SPINACH WITH A SIDE OF PASTA ALFREDO.

WHISTLE STOP SIRLOIN ... $13.25
A 10 OZ. SIRLOIN STEAK GRILLED TO YOUR SPECIFICATIONS AND SERVED WITH POTATO AND VEGETABLE.

BLACKENED STEAK AND SHRIMPS ... $15.25
MEDALLIONS OF BEEF TENDERLOIN DUSTED WITH BLACKENED SPICES AND COOKED TO ORDER, ACCOMPANIED BY A GENEROUS HELPING OF FRIED SHRIMPS AND SERVED WITH POTATO AND VEGETABLE.

STEAK LOCKLEAR ... $15.25
BEEF TENDERLOIN MEDALLIONS SAUTÉED WITH SHRIMPS AND MUSHROOMS SERVED OVER FRESH SPINACH WITH POTATO.

ROCKVILLE SHRIMPS AND HOMINY ... $13.99
WHITE SHRIMPS SAUTÉED WITH MUSHROOMS AND GREEN ONIONS IN A CAJUN CREAM SAUCE AND SERVED OVER OLD MILL HOMINY GRITS WITH CORN FRITTERS A DOLLOP OF TOMATO JAM AND VEGETABLE OF THE DAY.

FRIED SEAFOOD

ALL SERVED WITH SALAD, VEGETABLE AND RED RICE OR POTATO

FRIED SHRIMPS ... $12.99

FRIED OYSTERS ... $12.99

FRIED SCALLOPS ... $12.99

FRIED FLOUNDER ... $13.99

FRIED PLATTER ... $14.99
SHRIMP, OYSTERS, SCALLOPS

FRIED FEAST ... $16.99
SHRIMP, SCALLOPS, OYSTERS, FLOUNDER & DEVILED CRAB

THIS IS A SMALL SAMPLE OF THE FINE CUISINE AVAILABLE AT LOCKLEAR'S LOWCOUNTRY GRILL.

CHARLESTON
504 Folly Rd.
Charleston, SC 29412

PHONE
(843) 762-2549

FAX
(843) 762-2549

HOURS
Lunch
Monday-Sunday
11:30 am-3:00 pm
Dinner
Sunday-Thursday
5:00 pm-10:00 pm
Friday & Saturday
5:00 pm-11:00 pm

MEALS SERVED
Lunch
Dinner

CUISINE
Lowcountry

DINING INFORMATION
Terrace/Patio Dining
Take Out Meals

LOUNGE BAR
Restaurant Hours

ADDITIONAL SERVICES
Private Parties

ATTIRE
Casual

RESERVATIONS
Suggested

SMOKING
Smoking Section

HANDICAP FACILITIES

CREDIT CARDS
American Express
Visa
Master Card
Discover Card

CHECKS
Accepted

Louis's Restaurant & Bar

CHARLESTON
200 Meeting Street
Charleston, SC 29401
PHONE
(843) 853-2550
FAX
(843) 722-9485
WEBSITE
www.louiss.com
HOURS
Daily
4:00 pm-Midnight
MEALS SERVED
Dinner
Late Night Dining
CUISINE
Southern
DINING INFORMATION
Seasonal Menus
Extensive Wine Menu
ADDITIONAL SERVICES
Private Parties
Private Rooms
Meeting Facilities

ATTIRE
Casual
RESERVATIONS
Suggested
SMOKING
Smoking Section
Cigar & Pipe Friendly
(In the Bar)
VALET PARKING
HANDICAP FACILITIES
CREDIT CARDS
American Express
Visa
Master Card
Discover Card
Diners Club Card

LOUIS'S
Restaurant

Occupying space in one of the few recently built buildings in the city, Louis's shows that the present is as rich and lush as the past. Created by designer du jour Adam Tihany, Louis's design echoes Chef Osteen's style in its subtle use of unusual, natural materials. Known for his "southern food, more sophisticated, than traditional", the *New York Times* credited Chef Louis Osteen as "the spiritual general of the new Charleston chefs". Or, as one reviewer noted: "Louis Osteen is to Charleston cooking what Donald Trump is to Manhattan real estate." Osteen has been twice nominated by The James Beard Foundation as American Express Best Chef: Southeast for a style described by Helen Schwab of the *Charlotte Observer* as "lush by reason of ingredient, not frill." He is a recipient of *Restaurants & Institutions* Ivy Award and *Nation's Restaurant News* Fine Dining Hall of Fame.

FIRST COURSES

Lobster Bisque with a Rice and Lobster Fritter 6.00
Brown Oyster Stew with Benne Seeds 6.00
Mac 'n Cheese with Lobster and Crab Meat 10.00
Veal Sweetbreads, Braised with Country Ham, Vidalia Onions and Madeira 8.50
Fresh Foie Gras with an Argmanac and Prune Sauce 15.00
Atlantic Littleneck Clams with Fresh Linguine 10.00
Mediterranean Mussels Steamed in Belgian Beer with Saffron and Fennel 9.50
Asian Spiced Giant Scallops with Watermelon & Red Onion Salsa 8.50
McClellanville Lump Crabmeat and Lobster Cakes with Grained Mustard Sauce 12.00

SALADS

Grilled Lobster and Spinach Salad with an Orange and Vanilla Dressing 11.50
Tender Baby Lettuces with a Citrus Vinaigrette 5.00
Grilled Shrimp and Marinated Mushrooms over Baby Field Lettuces 8.00
Grilled Scallop and Arugula Salad with Shaved Red Onion, Julienne Tomato and a Sesame —Soy Vinaigrette 10.00

MAIN COURSES

Blue Ridge Rainbow Trout Stuffed w/Lump Crabmeat and Bacon w/Braised Cipolline Onions 19.50
Monkfish with Potato-Bacon Cake and Red Wine Butter 20.00
Grilled Tuna w/a Succotash of Cherry Tomatoes, a Medley of Beans and Peas, & Sweet Corn 21.50
Horseradish Crusted Salmon with Sweet Brown Butter and Scallion Mashed Potatoes 20.50
Roasted Maine Lobster with Baby Bok Choy and Beet Couscous 33.00
A Platter of Grilled Zucchini, Yellow Squash, and Red Peppers, with Sauteed Spinach, Crispy Fried Angel Hair and Wild Mushrooms 16.00
Grilled Free Range Veal Rib Chip with Wild Mushroom Bread Pudding and Herbed Cream 32.00
Argentine Churrasco Steak with Potato-Onion Hash and Chimichurri Sauce 21.00
Lamb Shank Braised in Red Wine, with Wild Mushrooms and Canellini Bean Puree 19.00
Roasted Black Angus Short Ribs with a Root Vegetable Puree 20.00
Louis's Grilled Pork Porterhouse with Mustard Spaetzle and Baked Apples 18.75
Grilled Filet of Tenderloin Beef with a Cabernet-Shallot Sauce, Haricot Vert and a Potato Gratin 26.00
Properly Aged Black Angus Strip w/Clemson Blue Cheese Sauce, Onion Rings, & Braised Spinach 25.00
Roasted All Natural Free Range Chicken Breast with Walnut Maple Glaze and Brussel Sprout - Wild Rice Stir Fry 19.50

Magnolias
Uptown Down South

From its prestigious location in Charleston's historic district to its dynamic Southern cuisine, Magnolias combines old world charm with contemporary excitement. Chefs Donald Barickman and Don Drake are recognized as pioneers in the creative use of the lowcountry's bounty. Magnolias' main dining room features high ceilings, pine floors, wrought-iron accents and stunning paintings by Taos artist, Rod Goebel. *Southern Living Magazine* sums it up best: "Magnolias...the city's most celebrated restaurant."

Uptown/Down South Starters

Skillet Seared Yellow Grits Cake 6.75
with Tasso gravy and yellow corn relish

Lobster, Hominy and Scallion Fritters 7.95
with buttermilk and tarragon dressed lettuces and a sweet pickle remoulade

Blackened Green Tomatoes 6.50
with creamy white grits, white cheddar cheese and country ham

Down South Eggroll 8.25
stuffed with collard greens, chicken and Tasso served with red pepper puree, spicy mustard and a peach chutney

Pan Fried Chicken Livers 7.50
with caramelized onions, country ham and a Madeira sauce

Soups and Salads

Creamy Tomato Bisque ....cup 3.95
with lump crab meat and a chiffonade of fresh basil

Grilled Portobello Mushroom Cap 9.95
layered with fresh tomato, shaved red onion, mashed avocado and Carolina goat cheese served with spicy tomato chutney

Wadmalaw Field Greens 4.25
with lemon lingonberry vinaigrette

Grits, Gumbos and Pastas

Spicy Shrimp and Sausage 9.95
with Tasso gravy over creamy white grits

Fried Chicken Gumbo 12.95
With Carolina Plantation Aromatic Rice, collard greens and a spicy black water gumbo

This is just a small sample of the fine cuisine available at Magnolias Uptown/Down South.

Down South Dinners

"Double Cut" Smoked Pork Chop ... 19.50
served with a herb butter, collard greens, buttermilk mashed potatoes and a mushroom gravy

Shellfish Over Grits 21.95
sautéed shrimp, sea scallops and lobster over creamy white grits, with a lobster butter sauce topped with fried spinach

Coriander Seared Tuna Filet 19.95
over a pan fried potato cake, and sautéed local greens topped with a jalapeno and mango vinaigrette

Sautéed Grouper w/Shrimp Succotash .. 21.95
Served on a stem of buttermilk mashed potatoes with herb butter

Carolina Carpetbagger Filet 21.95
with fried oysters, green beans, Madeira and Bernaise sauces

Grilled Domestic Lamb Chops 24.95
with a spicy tomato chutney, buttermilk mashed potatoes and collard greens

Grilled Dolphin Filet 19.95
with creamed crabmeat, country ham and pearl hominy hash, local greens and a tomato chive hollandaise

Grilled Game Hen 16.95
with a spicy tomato chutney, fresh green beans, buttermilk mashed potatoes and mushroom gravy

Sautéed Crab Cakes 19.95
with black beans, Carolina Plantation Aromatic Rice, herbed summer squash and a tomato chive butter

Southern Sweets

Pastry Chef, John Cornely

Southern Pecan Custard Pie 5.75
with Vanilla Bean Ice Cream and a Bourbon Sauce

Magnolias' Warm Cream Cheese Brownie .. 5.75
with White Chocolate Ice Cream

Uptown Banana Pudding Napoleon .. 5.75
with Crisp Pastry and Fresh Whipped Cream

Magnolias
Uptown Down South

CHARLESTON
185 East Bay St.
Charleston, SC 29401

PHONE
(843) 577-7771

FAX
(843) 722-0035

E-MAIL
info@magnolias-blossom.com

HOURS
Sunday-Wednesday
11:30 am-10:00 pm
Thursday-Saturday
11:30 am-11:00 pm

MEALS SERVED
Lunch
Dinner
Late Night Dining

CUISINE
American, Contemporary
New Southern

DINING INFORMATION
Vegetarian Meals
Extensive Wine Menu

BAR
Daily
11:30 am-11:00 pm

ADDITIONAL SERVICES
Private Parties
Private Rooms

ATTIRE
Resort Casual

RESERVATIONS
Suggested

SMOKING
Section Available
No Cigar or Pipe Smoking

FREE PARKING AVAILABLE

CREDIT CARDS
American Express
Visa
Master Card
Diners Club Card

CHECKS
Accepted

Maybanks

JAMES ISLAND
1978 Maybank Hwy.
James Island, SC 29412
PHONE
(843) 795-2125
FAX
(843) 795-2124
HOURS
Tuesday-Saturday
5:30 pm-10:00 pm
MEALS SERVED
Dinner
CUISINE
American
French
Southern
DINING INFORMATION
Vegetarian Meals
Extensive Nightly Specials
Extensive Wine Menu
ADDITIONAL SERVICES
Private Parties

ATTIRE
Resort Casual
RESERVATIONS
Suggested
SMOKING
Smoking Section
(Bar only)
HANDICAP ACCESSABLE
CREDIT CARDS
American Express
Visa
Master Card
CHECKS
Accepted
(Local Checks Only)

Featured in April 99
Bon Appetit
Did Honorery
Chaine Dinner

4 Star Review
by Post & Courier

Restaurant

Maybank's restaurant is nestled under live oak trees on Maybank Highway. The interior is cozy with hardwood floors, clean white linens and original artwork painted by local artists. The surroundings are refined but still comfortable and casual.

The owners are Charles P. Youmans, Jr. and Chef Peter Thomason. The Chef has worked at some of Charleston's finest restaurant's such as Restaurant Million, Robert's and The Woodland's. His knowledge of cuisines and local ingredients create dishes that abound with flavor.

Soups

Wild Mushroom soup with fresh chives and truffle oil 4.50
Chilled Gazpacho soup with cilantro, cumin and sour cream 4.50

Salads

Maybank's house salad with Clemson blue cheese dressing, grapes and toasted pecans 5.50
Traditional Caesar salad with hearts of Romaine, roasted garlic crostinies and shaved Parmesan 5.50
Baby spinach salad w/Shiitake mushrooms, grilled purple onion, & a warm bacon & grain mustard vinaigrette 5.95
Hazelnut crusted warm goat cheese salad w/grilled peasant bread and black currant raspberry vinaigrette 7.25
Cold smoked salmon salad with capers, purple onion, fresh dill, cracked pepper and sherry vinaigrette 7.95
Summerfield Farms duck prosciutto w/sweet mango, crunchy pecans & a port wine pistachio vinaigrette 9.95

Appetizers

Seared bronzed Atlantic Salmon on a warm salad of Yukon gold potatoes with fried leeks 6.75
Sautéed black been cake with pulled roasted pork, avocado salsa, fresh cilantro and sour cream 6.95
Sautéed rock shrimp and grits with ripe tomatoes and a sweet corn broth 6.95
James Island Littleneck clams with smoked sausage and sweet corn 7.95
Rosemary grilled portobella and oyster mushrooms with sweet peppers, wilted spinach, roasted garlic, shaved Parmesan and balsamic vinegar 6.95

Pastas

Penne pasta with spit roasted chicken, wild mushrooms and spinach 13.95
Orecchiette pasta with fresh rock shrimp, pancetta, sweet basil and Asiago cheese 14.95
Seafood Alfredo Gratin with Parmesan, tomatoes and tarragon over creamy fettuccine 15.95

Entrees

Grilled marinated vegetable salad with sweet basil, shaved Parmesan, balsamic vinegar and truffle oil 13.95
Pan seared Atlantic Salmon with pancetta, braised leeks, potatoes and a red wine sauce 16.95
Potato crusted lump blue crab cakes w/roasted garlic mashed potatoes, tender baby spinach & a grain mustard sauce 17.95
Sautéed fresh Halibut with a Parmesan and artichoke crust, asparagus with lemon, garlic mashed potatoes and a tomato caper beurre blanc 17.95
Grilled Yellowfin Tuna w/a black bean and avocado salsa, crisp red corn tortillas & a tomato vinaigrette 17.95
Roasted Ashley Farms free range chicken breast with braised cabbage and bacon, garlic mashed potatoes and a sweet sun-dried cherry chutney 14.95
Pan seared Maple Leaf duck breast glazed with wildflower honey, with smokey lentils and a port wine reduction 16.95
Grilled filet of beef with fresh asparagus, portobella mushrooms, new potatoes and a red wine sauce 20.95
Dijon and herb crusted rack of lamb with grilled spring vegetables, red skin potatoes and a lamb jus 22.95

"The Future of American Cuisine"

Locally owned and operated by Herman and Melinda McNeill since 1994, McNeill's: The Restaurant is located in historic downtown Summerville. The quaint 50 seat dining room with it's eclectic and unique furnishings is the perfect place to relax and enjoy your meal. Chef Herman McNeill's distinctive menu features International as well as Lowcountry dishes, prepared traditionally, with new interpretations. Fresh fish is featured in the chef's special, daily creations.

Appetizers and Light Meals

HOUSE SALAD
Mixed Greens, with your choice of our housemade dressings, served on the side....$3.50

SOUP OF THE DAY
$4.00

FRIED FOCACCIA
Strips of our Focaccia Dough, deep fried and served with Marinara and Parmesan Cheese....$5.00

BABY PORTABELLAS
Baby Portabella Mushroom Caps, stuffed with a Feta Cheese, Roasted Red Bell Pepper, and Herb stuffing. Baked in White Wine.....$6.95

SHRIMP AND BACON RAVIOLI
Housemade Ravioli, filled with Shrimp, Bacon, Mozzarella Cheese, and Garlic. Served with an Oregano Cream Sauce.....$7.50

photo by Eleanor Koets

CRAB CAKES PRIMEROSE
Two Crab Cakes, fried to golden brown, served with Granny Smith Apple slices and our Ranch Dressing......$8.50

CHICKEN NINETY NINE
Chicken cutlets and Artichoke Hearts tossed with Pasta, Garlic, Parsley and Cream......$7.95

GRILLED CHICKEN SANDWICH
On Focaccia with Lettuce, Onion, Basil Mayonnaise and Mozzarella, served with fried Potato......$6.95

SEAFOOD RISOTTO
Shrimp, Scallops, and Crab Meat, served in imported, Arborio Rice, with fresh Vegetables, Shrimp Broth, and Basil......$8.25

BOBA FETTUCCINE
Shrimp and Italian Sausage, sautéed with Bell Peppers, Portabella Mushrooms, and Garlic. Tossed with Fettuccine in a Sauce of Madeira Wine, Tomato, and Chicken Broth......$8.25

SHRIMP & GRITS
Shrimp, Peppers, Onions, Stewed Tomatoes and Herbs served in Creamy Grits......$8.25

Entrees

All entrees are served with a House Salad and two Side Dishes

PAN ROASTED CHICKEN
A boneless Breast of Chicken, pan-roasted with an Orange scented Barbecue Sauce and Bacon....$12.95

SHRIMP SCAMPI
One dozen sautéed Shrimp, in a Garlic, White Wine and Butter Sauce....$13.95

FRIED PORK CHOP
Boneless Pork Chop, hand breaded and deep fried. Served with a Honey and Balsamic Glaze....$13.95

CURRIED SCALLOPS
Scallops, pan seared and served in a Sauce of Curry, Parmesan, and Cream....$14.95

VEAL GEOFFREY
Veal Cutlets, dusted in Flour, sautéed with Garlic, Bacon, and Portabella Mushrooms, deglazed with Brandy and Chicken Broth....$15.95

VEAL McNEILL
Veal Cutlets, dusted in Flour, sautéed with Roasted Garlic. Served in a Sauce of Honey, Parsley and Cream....$15.95

VEAL AND SAUSAGE MADEIRA
Veal Cutlets, dusted in Flour, sautéed with Italian Sausage and Basil, deglazed with Madeira Wine.....$16.25

GRILLED RIBEYE
USDA Choice, charcoal grilled. Topped with Shrimp Scampi: add $1.00....$16.95

PRIME RIB
Choice Prime Rib, grilled to your taste, topped with horseradish Sauce.....$17.95

McNeill's

SUMMERVILLE
105 South Cedar St.
Summerville, SC 29483

PHONE
(843) 832-0912

FAX
(843) 821-5180

HOURS
Lunch
Tuesday-Friday
11:00 am-2:30 pm
Dinner
Tuesday-Saturday
5:30 pm-9:00 pm
Closed Sunday & Monday

MEALS SERVED
Lunch
Dinner

CUISINE
American
International
Italian

DINING INFORMATION
Heart Smart Meals
Vegetarian Meals
Take Out Meals
Seasonal Menus
Childrens Menu
Extensive Wine Menu

LOUNGE BAR

ADDITIONAL SERVICES
Full Service Catering
Private Parties

ATTIRE
Casual

RESERVATIONS
Suggested

SMOKING
Smoking Section
No Cigar or Pipe Smoking

HANDICAP FACILITIES

CREDIT CARDS
American Express
Visa
Master Card

CHECKS
Accepted

Meritäge

CHARLESTON
235 E. Bay St.
Charleston, SC 29401
PHONE
(843) 723-8181
FAX
(843) 723-8138
E-MAIL
meritage2@aol.com
HOURS
Full menu
5:00 pm-1:00 am
MEALS SERVED
Dinner
CUISINE
International Tapas
DINING INFORMATION
Terrace/Patio Dining
Heart Smart Meals
Vegetarian Meals
Take Out Meals
Seasonal Menus
Extensive Wine Menu
LOUNGE BAR
5:00 pm-2:00 am
Tuesday-Sunday
ENTERTAINMENT
10:00 pm-2:00 am
Tuesday-Sunday
ADDITIONAL SERVICES
Private Parties
Private Rooms
Outdoor Patio

ATTIRE
Casual
RESERVATIONS
Not Taken
SMOKING
Smoking Section
HANDICAP FACILITIES
CREDIT CARDS
American Express
Visa
Master Card
Diners Club Card
CHECKS
Not Accepted

Meritäge

Meritäge is an Americanized tapas restaurant. The concept that has been popular in Spain for centuries, namely "Tapas" or small plates. Other countries have had similar concepts for instance in the East it is Dim Sum. Our Americanized version has already been readily accepted and is growing by leaps and bounds. Chef John Olsson creates our selections from only the freshest, and highest quality products available, so we have the ability to change and play with the menu frequently. The food is designed for you to experience cuisine from around the world and right here in the Lowcountry. Our menu selections are created to be shared and sampled by groups and intimate diners alike. Above all else Meritäge is a place to relax, enjoy great food and great wine with great company! Please enjoy your Meritäge experience!

Table Dips and Starters

Served for Two or Four

Tzatziki Studded with Coriander Seared Tuna $3.99/$7.99

Brie with Bacon and Peppered Apples $3.50/$6.25

Chilled Selection

Shaved Fennel Salad with Fresh Orange and Basil $2.99

Lobster Salad with Ginger and Wasabi Spiked Rice Noodles $7.99

Smoked Salmon Crepe Folded with Caviar and Chive Creme Fraiche $7.99

Vietnamese Grilled Beef Salad $5.50

New England Lobster Roll 8.99

Classic Shrimp Cocktail 7.99

Tuna Tartare with Herb Salad 7.99

Herb and Spring Greens Salad with Lemon Dressing, Olive Tapanade, and Goat Cheese Toast Points $4.50

Special Offerings

Crab, Gorgonzola and Roasted Corn Dip Baked in Rosemary and Roasted Garlic Tuscan Bread $8.50

Duck Spring Rolls Served with a Chili Orange Sauce $5.95

Sea Scallops Baked with Goat Cheese and Roasted Peppers; Folded in Exotic Mushroom Crepes $7.25

Grilled Jerk Pork Tenderloin Stacked with Grilled Sweet Potatoes and Rum Spiked Demi Glace $6.95

Hot Selection

Pan Seared Crab Cake with Sauteed Spinach, Crispy Onions and Pepper Jam $7.99

Fried Walnut Crusted Goat Cheese with Rosemary Infused Tomato Coulis and Green Tomato Marmalade $5.99

Shrimp and Grits; Bacon and Cheese Grit Cake and Tasso Sauce $7.99

Grilled Vegetable Lasagna $5.50

New Zealand Lamb Shank Braised in a Tomato, White Wine and Roasted Garlic Broth $8.25

Grilled Satays; Served with Sticky Rice and Thai Peanut Sauce
- Chicken $1.25
- Beef $1.50
- Portabello $1.00

Crispy Cornmeal and Ancho Chili Fried Calamari Served with Saffron Aoli $6.50

Crispy Cornmeal Fried Oysters with Green Tomato Marmalade $5.50

Roasted Garlic Bulb with Grilled Tuscan Bread $2.99

Prince Edward Island Mussels Steamed with Garlic, Saffron Spiked Fennel and White Wine $6.99

Crispy Beef Wontons Served with a Chili Orange Sauce $5.50

Fire Roasted Peppers Topped with Garlic Oil and Shaved Regiano Parmigiano $5.99

Seared Filet Mignon Topped with Crabmeat, Gorgonzola Cheese and leeks $9.50

Garlic and Red Wine Roasted Rack of Lamb with a Rosemary Accented Demi Glace $8.99

This is a sample of the 50+ menu items available at Meritäge.

Peninsula Grill

LOCATED IN THE HEART AND SOUL OF DOWNTOWN CHARLESTON IN THE HISTORIC PLANTERS INN, PENINSULA GRILL'S 100 SEAT RESTAURANT AND CHAMPAGNE BAR HAS RECEIVED UNPRECEDENTED NATIONAL ACCLAIM. PENINSULA GRILL, WITH ITS EVOCATIVE LOWCOUNTRY DINING ROOM, VELVET WALLS, AND SEAGRASS CARPET, IS THE PERFECT SETTING FOR CHEF ROBERT CARTER'S REFINED AMERICAN STYLE. WALK DOWN THE GAS-LIT ALLEY, THROUGH THE LUSH COURTYARD, INTO A REFINED SUPPER CLUB ATMOSPHERE REMINISCENT OF THE 1930'S AND 40'S. SUCCULENT LOBSTER, BRILLIANTLY PREPARED OYSTERS OR ANGUS BEEF FILET (WITH A CHOICE OF DELECTABLE SAUCES SUCH AS FOIE GRAS TRUFFLE BUTTER OR RED PEPPER BEARNAISE), AWAIT YOU IN THIS "BEST NEW RESTAURANTS OF 1997" AWARD WINNER FROM ESQUIRE MAGAZINE, WHERE JOHN MARIANI SAYS IT BEST, "THIS IS DEFINITELY WHAT I LIKE ABOUT THE SOUTH."

Starters

WILD MUSHROOM GRITS
with Lowcountry Oyster Stew $7.50

RABBIT LOIN WRAPPED IN VEAL BACON
with Tapenade Linguine and Mustard Vinaigrette $11.00

SEARED CARPACCIO OF LAMB
with Roasted Beet & Goat Cheese Tart, Truffle-Sherry Vinaigrette $11.50

CRISPY VEAL SWEETBREADS
with Roast Garlic-Green Bean Salad, Black Pepper-Cheese Grits and Natural Jus $13.00

LIGHT PORTOBELLO MUSHROOM SOUP
with Smithfield Ham Flan and Fresh Rosemary $5.50

LOBSTER & CORN CHOWDER
with Basil Butter $5.50

SAMPLING TRIO OF TODAY'S SOUPS
$6.50

ROMAINE & RADICCHIO SALAD
with Lemon-Thyme Caesar Dressing $5.50

SUPER CHILLED WEDGE OF ICEBERG
with Smoked Bacon Jerky & Buttermilk Dressing
$5.00

Prime Seafood

LIVE MAINE LOBSTER $$MARKET$$

ATLANTIC SALMON $17.50

BLACK GROUPER $19.50

YELLOWFIN TUNA $18.50

Sauces

ginger-lime butter • toasted pecan-rosemary butter
tomato vinaigrette • horseradish cream sauce
• tapenade

Chef's Suggestions

MARINATED DOUBLE CUT PORK CHOP
with Mac & Cheese Noodle Cake, Peppered Collard Greens and BBQ Jus $22.00

NY STRIP 'AU POIVRE'
with Brandy Pan Sauce, Crispy Potato Cake and Teene Weene Benne Beans $26.50

BOURBON GRILLED JUMBO SHRIMP
with Low Country Hoppin John, Creamed Corn and Lobster-Basil Hushpuppies $23.00

SLICED MEDALLIONS OF MUSCOVY DUCK BREAST
with House Smoked Duck and Potato Strudel, Balsamic Glazed Savoy Cabbage and Natural Jus $24.00

PAN ROASTED YOUNG CHICKEN
with Vidalia Onion-Potato Napolean, Garlic Green Beans and Roast Garlic-Chicken Jus $17.50

SAUTEED CAROLINA MOUNTAIN TROUT
with Creole Crawfish Bread Pudding, Baby Spinach and Tomato-Creole Mustard Sauce $17.50

SAUTEED AMERICAN RED SNAPPER
with Creamer Potatoes, Autumn Vegetable Ragout and Lobster-Crab Butter $26.00

BENNE SEED CRUSTED RACK OF NEW ZEALAND LAMB
with Wild Mushroom Potatoes & Coconut Mint Pesto $28.00

Steaks & Chops

ANGUS BEEF FILET (8 OZ) $24.50

ANGUS NY STRIP (12 OZ) $24.00

USDA 'PRIME' RIBEYE (16 OZ) $27.00

NATURAL VEAL CHOP $24.00

Sauces

blue cheese-balsamic glaze • foie gras-truffle butter
red pepper bearnaise • shiitake mushroom sauce
• zinfandel-peppercorn jus

CHARLESTON
112 N. Market Street
Charleston, SC 29401

PHONE
(843) 723-0700

HOURS
Sunday-Thursday
5:30 pm-10:00 pm
Friday & Saturday
5:30 pm-11:00 pm

MEALS SERVED
Dinner

CUISINE
American
Southern Regional

DINING INFORMATION
Terrace/Patio Dining
Extensive Wine Menu

LOUNGE BAR
4:00 pm-midnight

ADDITIONAL SERVICES
Private Parties
Banquet Facilities
Lodging
Private Rooms
Meeting Facilities
Courtyard Dining

ATTIRE
Semi Formal

RESERVATIONS
Suggested

SMOKING
Smoking Section in Bar Area
No Cigar or Pipe Smoking

HANDICAP FACILITIES

CREDIT CARDS
American Express
Visa
Master Card
Discover Card
Diners Club Card

CHECKS
Accepted

North Towne
Grill & Seafood

NORTH CHARLESTON
2093 Eagle Landing Blvd.
North Charleston, SC
29418
PHONE
(843) 863-1001
FAX
(843) 863-1002
HOURS
Sunday-Thursday
11:00 am-10:00 pm
Friday-Saturday
11:30 am-11:00 pm
MEALS SERVED
Lunch
Dinner
CUISINE
American, Greek
Seafood
DINING INFORMATION
Heart Smart Meals
Vegetarian Meals
Take Out Meals
Seasonal Menus
Childrens Menu
Extensive Wine Menu
LOUNGE BAR
ADDITIONAL SERVICES
Full Service Catering
Private Parties
Banquet Facilities
Private Rooms
Meeting Facilities

ATTIRE
Casual
RESERVATIONS
Not Required
SMOKING
Section Available
CREDIT CARDS
American Express
Visa
Master Card
Discover Card
Diners Club Card
CHECKS
Accepted

Grill and Seafood

OLD TOWNE
Downtown Charleston
(Next to Sak's Fifth Avenue)

NORTH TOWNE
North Charleston
(Across from Northwoods Mall)

Old Towne is the oldest family-owned restaurant in Charleston. The owner-Steve, a fisherman and Spiro, a butcher-are from the island Kefalonia, Greece. Together they bring the best grill and seafood to Charleston. We insist on only the freshest foods in all our entrees. Old Towne specializes in grilled, broiled, steamed, or fried seafood, flame-grilled steaks and shish kabobs, slow-roasted chicken, salads, and the best Greek dishes you've ever tasted.

Plus, we feature over ten delicious desserts, cappuccino, and a full bar.
Old Towne has great prices and a wonderful atmosphere.
Private party rooms are available.

STARTERS

Gyros Appetizer 3.95
Slices of gyro meat topped with chopped vegetables and tzatziki sauce.

Shrimp Cocktail 5.75
Grilled Greek style shrimp served with lemon and cocktail sauce.

Chicken Fingers 5.50
Tender all-breast chicken served with honey mustard.

Feta Appetizer 4.25
Layers of feta cheese served with kalamata olives and pepperocini.

Buffalo Wings 4.95
Spicy wings with celery sticks & bleu cheese dressing.

Cheese Sticks 4.95
Deep fried Kasserri cheese served with our homemade tomato sauce.

Calamari 4.95
Fried baby squid served with lemon and cocktail sauce.

Saganaki 4.95
Sharp Kasserri Cheese baked in a lemon butter sauce flamed to perfection.

Dolmadaki 3.25
Grape leaves stuffed with rice and seasoned with herbs and spices.

Spanakopita 3.25
Fine layers of fillo baked with spinach and feta cheese.

House Sampler 6.75
(For 2 or more)
A rich combination of gyro, feta, spanakopita, and dolmadaki appetizers.

One Menu Availlable At Both Restaurants.
Menu subject to change.

SALADS

Greek Salad 4.95
Lettuce, tomatoes, olives, onions, cucumbers, peppers, and feta cheese with our Greek dressing.

Chicken Salad 6.50
Our garden salad topped with Greek chicken and Tzatziki sauce.

North Towne's Chefs Salad..... 6.25
Gyro meat, boiled eggs, lettuce, tomatoes, olives, peppers, and onions topped with American cheese and your choice of dressing.

Village Salad 6.95
Our Greek Village Salad topped with Kalamata olives, peppers, anchovies, feta cheese, with our Greek dressing.

Soup & Salad 4.25
A bowl of our famous homemade soup and house salad with choice of dressing.

PASTA

Spaghetti Meat Sauce 7.95
Spaghetti noodles topped with our special meat sauce and parmesan cheese.

Spaghetti Meat Balls 7.95
Topped with our homemade meat balls, marinara sauce and parmesan cheese.

Lasagna 8.95
Lasagna noodles layered with a rich combination of three cheeses and our homemade seasoned ground beef sauce.

Manicotti 7.95
Pasta tubes stuffed with creamy cheese and topped with marinara and melted mozzarella. A vegetarian favorite.

Chicken Marinara 8.50
Tender chicken breast strips with marinara and parmesan cheese.

Old Towne
Grill & Seafood

CHARLESTON
229 King Street
Charleston, SC 29401
PHONE
(843) 723-8170
FAX
(843) 577-2078
HOURS
Sunday-Thursday
11:00 am-10:00 pm
Friday-Saturday
11:30 am-11:00 pm
MEALS SERVED
Lunch
Dinner
CUISINE
American, Greek
Seafood
DINING INFORMATION
Heart Smart Meals
Vegetarian Meals
Take Out Meals
Seasonal Menus
Childrens Menu
Extensive Wine Menu
LOUNGE BAR
ADDITIONAL SERVICES
Full Service Catering
Private Parties
Banquet Facilities
Private Rooms
Meeting Facilities

ATTIRE
Casual
RESERVATIONS
Not Required
SMOKING
Section Available
CREDIT CARDS
American Express
Visa
Master Card
Discover Card
Diners Club Card
CHECKS
Accepted

GRILL

Pork Kabob 10.50

Chicken Kabob 10.25

Beef Kabob 11.25

Lamb Kabob 11.25

Combo Kabob 12.25
Beef, shrimp and Greek chicken.

North Towne Kabob 12.25
Lamb kabob with fresh vegetables.

Hamburger Steak 10.75

North Towne's Hamburger Steak 10.95
Hamburger steak mixed with vegetables seasoned with Greek spices and lemon sauce.

NY Steak ... 10 oz. 10.95...14 oz. 12.95

Ribeye ..... 10 oz. 10.95...14 oz. 12.95

CHEF'S CORNER

Chicken Livers 8.95
Grilled with Greek spices and lemon sauce.

Steak and Shrimp 13.95
A 10 oz. New York Strip and our Greek style shrimp.

Mousaka 9.95
Baked layers of eggplant and seasoned ground beef topped with our creamy cheese sauce.

Souvlaki Plate 9.50
Tender chunks of our pork-kabob on pita bread with chopped vegetables and tzatziki sauce.

Roast Leg of Lamb 11.25
Oven baked leg of lamb seasoned with a delicate blend of our spices.

Pizza 8.25
Our delicious homemade pizza with cheeses, tomatoes, pepperoni, and gyro.

Vegetable Lasagne 8.95
A vegetarian favorite.

Spanakopita Plate 7.50
Fine layers of fillo baked with spinach and feta cheese. A vegetarian favorite.

Vegetarian Platter 6.95
Grilled vegetables on pita bread with feta and tzatziki sauce.

All above entrees served with Greek potatoes, rice or fries.

SEAFOOD

Shrimp 12.75
Lightly sauteed in butter, Greek spices and lemon sauce.

Scallops 11.25
Broiled with our Greek spices and lemon sauce.

Calamari 9.95
Fried baby squid served with lemon and cocktail sauce.

Whole Flounder 11.95
Whole fresh flounder broiled with our spices and lemon sauce.

Alaskan Crab Legs .... Market Price
Three clusters of Alaskan crab legs with drawn butter, choice of starch and all the complimentary items.

Shrimp Kabob 12.75

Fried Shrimp 12.75
Lightly breaded shrimp served with lemon and cocktail sauce.

Fried Seafood Platter 12.25
Our fried platter filled with shrimp, scallops, calamari, and fish fillet.

Broiled Seafood Platter 11.95
Our combination of shrimp, scallops and fresh flounder fillet broiled to perfection.

Catch of the Day ...... Market Price
Our fresh catch broiled in olive oil, Greek spices and lemon sauce.

Super Special 12.95
Our most popular item. A platter filled with Greek chicken, pork-kabob, gyros, roast leg of lamb, Greek style shrimp, Greek potatoes, pita bread, soup and Greek salad. It is 12.95 per person and starts from a Super Spiro for one and goes up to any infinite number.

House Special 13.95
A cross section of a few specialties: pasticio, mousaka, dolmadaki, feta cheese, olives, and peppers.

Greek Chicken 9.50
North Towne's famous chicken slowly roasted over our grill from three to four hours.

Gyro Plate 8.95
Our delicious Gyro meat on pita bread topped with chopped vegetables and tzatziki sauce.

Ask to speak to a manager about reserving private parties
Ask your server about our daily specials

OLD TOWNE
Downtown Charleston
(Next to Sak's Fifth Avenue)

NORTH TOWNE
North Charleston
(Across from Northwoods Mall)

Grill and Seafood

Palmetto Café

THE PALMETTO CAFE

Located in the elegant lobby of the Charleston Place Hotel, the Palmetto Cafe specializes in Contemporary American fare. Executive Chef Bill Brodsky blends old world cuisine with the freshest ingredients from South Carolina's "Lowcountry." The dining room's atmosphere is sophisticated yet comfortable. The entire dining room overlooks a lush courtyard complete with circular bronze fountain and impeccably kept gardens. There are additional twenty tables set amongst the foliage where guests can enjoy breakfast, lunch and dinner.

APPETIZERS

Carolina Crab Cakes — 11 -
Trio of Sauces

Ahi Tuna Tartare Napoleon — 11 -
Wasabi Aioli, Sweet Ginger Soy Reduction, Wonton Crisps, Sturgeon Caviar

Raw Oyster Sampler — 15 -
Vermouth Cocktail Sauce, Cranberry, Mignonette

Potato Crusted Diver Scallops with Peekytoe Crab Salad — 13 -
Grilled Mushroom-Tomato Duxelles, Chilled Lemon-Tarragon Emulsion

SOUPS

Traditional Lowcountry She Crab Scented with Sherry — 7 -

Soup of the Day — 7 -

John's Island Heirloom Tomato Gazpacho — 7 -

Palmetto Café

SALADS

Caesar — 15 -
Choice of Two: Grilled Shrimp, Fried Edisto Island Oysters, Grilled Chicken, Duck Confit or Seared Scallops

Duck Confit Cobb — 15 -
Avocado Brie, Micro Sprouts, Pear-Blue Cheese Dressing, Duck Fries

Seasonal Exotic Fruit Sampler — 14 -
Honey-Mint Mascarpone Cheese Canndi

Grilled Lobster and Mango — 18 -
Honey-Lime Vinaigrette, Mizuna

Warm Smoked Salmon — 16 -
Roesti Potato, Pea Tendrils, Caviar Crème Fraiche

ENTREES

Crabmeat Stuffed Salmon Fillet — 18 -
Seared Grit Cakes, Asparagus, Plum Butter, Sweet Soy

Gorgonzola and Herb Encrusted Center Cut Veal Chop — 23 -
Roasted Ginger-Peach Chutney, Baby Vegetables

Sea Bass Tempura with Lobster and Shrimp Stuffing — 20 -
Black Bean and Summer Corn Tamale, Avocado Sauce, Salsa Fresca

Skillet Seared Herb Roasted Lamb Loin — 22 -
Duck Confit-Tri-Potato Hash, Shiitake Sweet Onion Reduction, Steamed Haricot Vert

Pinot Noir Braised Osso Bucco with Crisp Fried Sweetbreads — 25 -
Truffled Goat Cheese Grits, Haricot Vert

Grilled Prime Angus Beef Tenderloin — 25 -
Foie Gras Hollandaise, Roasted Garlic-Thyme Dauphinoise Potato

Exotic Mushrooms En Phyllo — 17 -
Vidalia Onion, Port Wine Reduction Sauce, Summer Squash

Truffled Wild Scottish Pheasant — 28 -
Butternut Squash Mousse, Baby Vegetables

SIDES
(Available with Entrees)

Chilled Asparagus with Balsamic Syrup — 2 -

Smoked Leek Whipped Potatoes — 2 -

Fried Portabella Mushrooms — 4 -

Creamy Tarragon- Porcini Mushroom Scented Grits — 2 -

Fresh Grilled Sweet Corn — 2 -

Chef Bill Brodsky Uses the Finest Local Ingredients the Lowcountry Has to Offer Along With Herbs Grown On Property to Create His Innovative Contemporary American Cuisine

CHARLESTON
130 Market Street
Charleston, SC 29402

PHONE
(843) 722-4900 ext. 7951

HOURS
Breakfast
6:30 am-11:00 am
Lunch
11:30 am-3:00 pm
Dinner
5:00 pm-11:00 pm

MEALS SERVED
Breakfast
Lunch
Dinner
Sunday Brunch

CUISINE
Contemporary American

DINING INFORMATION
Terrace/Patio Dining
Vegetarian Meals
Take Out Meals
Seasonal Menus
Childrens Menu
Extensive Wine Menu

LOUNGE BAR
Sunday-Thursday
1:00 pm-10:00 pm
Friday & Saturday
1:00 pm-11:00 pm

ENTERTAINMENT
Piano
6:00 pm-close

ADDITIONAL SERVICES
Private Parties

ATTIRE
Casual

RESERVATIONS
Suggested

SMOKING
Smoking Section
No Cigar or Pipe Smoking

VALET PARKING

HANDICAP FACILITIES

CREDIT CARDS
American Express
Visa
Master Card
Discover Card

CHECKS
Not Accepted

Privateer Seafood Restaurant

SEAFOOD & STEAK HOUSE

Savor our sunset and pamper your palate with The Privateer's world-famous gourmet Lowcountry cuisine. Vacationers return every year to enjoy our fabulous seafood, friendly service and sunsets more spectacular than Key West. The Privateer overlooks a deep water harbor at Bohicket Marina, just minutes from the gates of Kiawah and Seabrook.

The Sunset Lounge, the island's favorite "watering hole," is above The Privateer Restaurant. Enjoy sporting events on our big-screen TV, great music and a friendly game of darts. Our well-stocked bar offers 13 kinds of domestic beers, 7 imports, premium and bar-brand liquors, a sizable wine selection and good-natured bartenders who specialize in frozen tropical drinks.

Appetizers

Jumbo Shrimp Cocktail...7.99
Court Bouillon Simmered and Served with Our House Cocktail Sauce

Fresh Oysters
On the Half Shell
Half Dozen...5.99...Dozen...10.99

Bahamian Shrimp...6.99
Mildly Spiced and Fried

Crispy Fried Clam Strips...5.99
Served with House Remoulade Sauce

Shrimp and Clam Strips Combination...9.99
Generous Portions; Served with House Firecracker and Remoulade Sauces

Jumbo Chicken Wings...6.99
Served Plain, Mild, or Hot with Celery Sticks and Bleu Cheese Dressing

Crab Dip...5.99
Creamy Cheeses and Rich Lump Crab in a Brandy Enhanced Base Served Warm

Filet Mignon Tips...7.99
Marinated Tips with Wild Mushrooms in a Rich Burgundy Demi-Glace

Oysters Rockefeller...7.99
Fresh Oysters Topped with a Spinach-Bacon Veloute, Bronzed with Hollandaise; Local's Favorite!

Portabello Mushroom Cap...5.99
Whole Cap Grilled, Topped with a Tomato-Basil Sauce and Shredded Cheeses

Fresh Steamed Mussels...6.99
With John's Island Tomatoes, Garlic and Fresh Herbs

Fried Green Tomatoes...5.99
Cornmeal Encrusted John's Island Tomatoes with Firecracker Sauce

Privateer Seafood Restaurant

SEABROOK
Bohicket Marina Village
1882 Andell Bluff Blvd.
Seabrook, SC 29455

PHONE
(843) 768-1290

FAX
(843) 768-9567

HOURS
Daily (Seasonal)
5:00 pm-10:00 pm

MEALS SERVED
Dinner
Twilight Dinners

CUISINE
Seafood, Steak, Pasta

DINING INFORMATION
Lite Meals
Vegetarian Meals
Take Out Meals
Seasonal Menus
Childrens Menu
Extensive Wine Menu

LOUNGE BAR
4:30 pm-Until

DANCING
9:00 pm-Until (Seasonal)

ADDITIONAL SERVICES
Full Service Catering
Private Parties
Banquet Facilities
Private Rooms
Meeting Facilities

ATTIRE
Resort Casual

RESERVATIONS
Suggested

SMOKING
Section Available
Cigar & Pipe Friendly

HANDICAP FACILITIES

CREDIT CARDS
American Express
Visa
Master Card
Discover Card
Diners Club Card

Salad & Soups

Superb She Crab Soup
Cup 4.50...Bowl 5.50
Combination of Jumbo Lump Crab Meat, Heavy Cream, Sherry and Mixed Spices; A Lowcountry Speciality

Black Bean Soup
Cup 3.50...Bowl 4.50
Creamy and Distinctive; Served with Sour Cream and Chives

Soup D'Jour
Cup...3.50...Bowl...4.50
Chef's Creation using the Freshest Local Ingredients

Privateer House Salad...4.50
Boston and Romaine Greens with Tomatoes, Cucumbers, and Baby Shrimp

Mesclun Salad of Baby Greens...4.99
Accented with Walnut Oil and Balsamic Vinaigrette

Chilled Salmon Salad...13.99
Served Over Mesclun Greens with an Herb-Dijon Dressing

Classic Caesar Salad
Classic...5.99
With Shrimp or Grilled Chicken...7.99

From The Grill

Tender Filet Mignon...17.99
Hand Trimmed, Nestled in Bacon and CharBroiled to Perfection

Black Angus New York Strip...17.99
Perfectly Marbled and Grilled

Black Angus New York Strip Au Poivre...18.99
Enhanced with a Rich Reduction of Brandy, Shallots, Heavy Cream and Peppercorns

Filet Mignon with Jumbo Shrimp...21.99
CharBroiled to Your Specifications

Surf and Turf...Mkt. Price
Includes a Broiled Cold-Water Lobster Tail and a Tender Filet Mignon

Lowcountry Surf and Turf...24.99
Tender Filet Mignon with our Signature Crabcakes

Whole Pork Tenderloin...17.99
Marinated in Herb and Spices and Roasted to Perfection

Riviera RibEye...18.99
Generous 14 oz; Marinated in Mediterranean Spices and Seared to Capture the Spectacular Flavor

Prices subject to change without notice. Items may be limited by availability.

Pastas

Sauteed Chicken Breast in a Mushroom Cream Sauce...14.99
Served over Linguine

Vegetarian Pasta...12.99
Fresh Steamed Vegetables Served with Basil-Pesto and Linguine

Seafood Pasta with Jumbo Shrimp, Mussels and Fresh Fish Selections...17.99
Served in a Tomato-Basil Sauce; Tossed with Linguine

Pan Seared Jumbo Shrimp...16.99
In a Lobster Cream Sauce over Linguine

Jumbo Shrimp Sauteed in a Tomato-Basil Sauce...16.99
Served with Linguine

Alfredo Carbonara...14.99
Linguine with Bacon and Mushrooms in a Creamy Alfredo Sauce

From The Sea

Shrimp Privateer...15.99
Jumbo Shrimp Sauteed with Garlic, White Wine, Lemon, Butter and Mushrooms; Served with Rice

Dijon-Herb Crusted Salmon...16.99
Generous Filet, Broiled and Served with Buerre Blanc

Butterflied Jumbo Shrimp...15.99
Beer Battered and Breaded in a Tangy Mixture of Mild Spices

Privateer Crabcakes...22.99
The Finest Jumbo Lump Crab and Fresh Spices Blended into Cakes and Sauteed. The House Specialty

Mahi Mahi...16.99
Blackened with Cajun Spices and Served with Linguine and a White Clam Sauce

Honey-Ginger Glazed Jumbo Shrimp...16.99
Roasted and Served with Snowpeas and Rice

Alex Newberg...19.99
Lobster, Jumbo Shrimp and Lump Crab in a Sherry Cream Sauce

Australian Cold Water Lobster Tails...Mkt Price
Twin Broiled and Served with Clarified Butter

Lowcountry Catfish Filets...15.99
Cornmeal Encrusted and Served with Housemade Remoulade

Sauteed Grouper Filet...18.99
Local Favorite; Served with Steamed Snowpeas and Hollandaise

Poogan's Porch

CHARLESTON
72 Queen Street
Charleston, SC 29401
MAILING ADDRESS
P.O. Box 534
Charleston, SC 29402
PHONE
(843) 577-2337
FAX
(843) 577-2493
E-MAIL
BBall29464@aol.com
HOURS
Lunch
7 days
11:30 am-2:30 pm
Dinner
7 days
5:30 pm-10:00 pm
Sunday Brunch
10:30 am-2:30 pm
MEALS SERVED
Lunch
Dinner
Sunday Brunch
CUISINE
Lowcountry
Seafood
Southern
DINING INFORMATION
Terrace/Patio Dining
Vegetarian Meals
Seasonal Menus
Childrens Menu
Extensive Wine Menu
ADDITIONAL SERVICES
Full Service Catering
Private Parties
Banquet Facilities
Private Rooms
ATTIRE
Casual
Resort Casual
RESERVATIONS
Suggested
CREDIT CARDS
American Express
Visa
Master Card
CHECKS
Not Accepted

Nestled in the heart of Old Charleston, and named for the dog who sat on its porch, Poogan's Porch has been a "must eat" establishment since it opened in 1976. We specialize in creole, jambalaya, gumbo, she crab soup, fresh seafood, quail, alligator, peanut butter pie and other very Southern things. Dine indoors or outdoors on our porches and patio. Open daily for lunch and dinner plus Sunday brunch. Don't forget to ask about our ghost!

Appetizers

Issac's Old Fashioned Okra Gumbo $2.50
with smoked sausage and chicken

Lowcountry Mushrooms $5.75
stuffed with crabmeat

Fresh Garden Salad $2.50
served with peach poppy seed dressing

Carolina Alligator $5.95
fried in seasoned buttermilk batter, served with honey-jalapeno dressing

Albertha's She Crab Soup $3.50
topped with dry sherry

BBQ Shrimp & Andouille Sausage $5.95
over cheddar cheese grits

Oyster Queen Street $5.50
lightly battered and baked w/ bacon, green peppers & cheese in a crab sauce

Carolina Crabcake $7.95
sauteed in old Southern tradition, served w/ black bean salsa and honey-jalapeno dressing

Bronzed Carolina Quail $6.95
served w/ country ham, over cheese grits

From the Sea

All entrees served with appropriate sides & homemade buttermilk biscuits (broiled or fried)

Seafood Specials of the Day....... Market Price

Carolina Coastal Shrimp $14.95

Sea Scallops $14.95

Select Bay Oysters $13.95

Seafood Combination Platter $17.95
a bountiful selection of scallops, oysters, shrimp, crabcake & filet of fresh fish

Desserts

Bread Pudding $3.25
with bourbon sauce. An old southern favorite

Praline Cheesecake $3.95

Triple-Layer Chocolate Cake $3.95

Peanut Butter Pie, Kahlua Pecan Pie, Key Lime Pie $3.25

From the Lowcountry

Cajun Shrimp $14.95
Poogan's Best! Sauteed with red peppers, garlic & scallions. Hot & Spicy!

Creole Jambalaya $15.95
Highly seasoned and strongly flavored with shrimp, smoked sausage, oysters & chicken served over rice

Shrimp Creole, an old Southern favorite $13.95

Cajun Duck $13.95
boned breasts of duck marinated in Cajun spices, served over speckled cheese grits

Chicken Charleston $11.95
boneless breast of chicken sauteed in white wine & cream with fresh mushrooms and artichoke served over rice

Southern Fried Catfish (farm-raised) $11.95

Carolina Crab Cakes $16.95
sauteed in old Southern tradition, served with black bean salsa and jalapeno-honey sauce

Heavenly Scallops $15.95
sauteed in a saintly blend of wine, scallions & cheeses

Vegetarian Creole $9.95

Brace of Carolina Quail $14.95
with country ham, cheddar grits, & black bean relish

Apple-Glazed Pork Tenderloin $14.95
center cut pork medallions sauteed with apples & selected spices in a whiskey sauce

Filet Mignon (8 oz. choice cut) $18.95
topped w/ Madeira demi-glaze & sprinkled w/ Clemson blue cheese

Bronzed Shrimp & Scallops $15.95
with roasted red pepper cream sauce, over linguini

Tomato Basil Cream Pasta $9.95
.... with chicken $11.95 with shrimp $14.95

Cajun Surf & Turf $18.95
a taste for every bud...blackened filet mignon with our famous Cajun shrimp!

Red Sky Grill

Located at Seabrook's Village Center, Red Sky Grill features delicious American fare, in a casual setting. Enjoy fresh seafood, pasta and choice steaks prepared by Chef George Odachowski and his talented staff.

Appetizers

Hot Soup du Jour 3.95
House garden salad 4.25
Caesar Salad 4.95
Goat cheese, tomato & olive gratin with grilled bread 6.95
Vietnamese style shrimp & chicken egg rolls with peanut & soy dipping sauces 8.25
Wild Mushrooms in a sherry cream sauce with puff pastry 7.95
Mussels steamed in white wine & cream finished with Gran Marnier fennel butter 7.95
Roquefort & Pear Salad with spiced pecans & a honey lemon vinaigrette 7.95
Deep Fried Oyster salad with Tasso ham & a maple cider vinaigrette 8.95
Risotto of the day .... Market price

Main Courses

Bow Tie Pasta with chicken breast, tomatoes, artichoke hearts, assorted Greek olives, Feta cheese, white wine & garlic 13.95

Linguine with white clam sauce 14.95

Penne Pasta with shrimp, peas, sun dried tomatoes, pesto & Ricotta Salata cheese 14.95

Balsamic Rubbed Chicken Breast with grilled vegetables & a Parmesan Polenta cake .. 15.95

Grilled Black Angus Strip Steak with a Cabernet mushroom sauce & potato gratin 19.50

Braised Center Cut Pork Chop with dried fruits and sage mashed potatoes 16.95

Sauteed Salmon with a mustard horseradish crust, Basmati rice & a cucumber, dill salsa 16.95

Southwestern Seafood & Chicken Stew with shrimp scallops, mussels and fish filet steeped in a rich tomato, pepper & corn broth 16.95

Grilled Rare Tuna atop a scallion potato cake with sauteed spinach & a sauce Pinot Noir heightened with grilled Portobello mushrooms 17.95

Sesame Coated Sea Scallops with a spicy orange sauce & peppered fettucine 17.95

Grilled Hamburger platter served with french fries and cole slaw (add .50 for cheese). 7.50

A children's menu is available for those under 10 years.

SEABROOK ISLAND
1001 Landfall Way
Seabrook Island, SC 29455
PHONE
(843) 768-0183
FAX
(843) 768-0184
HOURS
Lunch
Monday-Friday
11:30 am-2:30 pm
Dinner
Monday-Thursday
5:30 pm-9:00 pm
Friday & Saturday
5:30 pm-10:00 pm
Closed Sundays
MEALS SERVED
Lunch
Dinner
CUISINE
American
Eclectic
DINING INFORMATION
Take Out Meals
Childrens Menu
LOUNGE BAR

ATTIRE
Casual
RESERVATIONS
Suggested
(for parties of
6 or more only)
SMOKING
Smoking Section
at bar only
HANDICAP FACILITIES
CREDIT CARDS
American Express
Visa
Master Card
CHECKS
Not Accepted

Reminisce

SUMMERVILLE
214 North Cedar Street
Summerville, SC 29483
PHONE
(843) 821-4388
FAX
(Call First)
(843) 821-4388
E-MAIL
ronladygin@prodigy.net
HOURS
Lunch
Thursday-Sunday
Dinner
Thursday-Saturday
MEALS SERVED
Lunch
Dinner
Sunday Brunch
CUISINE
Classic
Continental
French
International
Lowcountry
DINING INFORMATION
Terrace/Patio Dining
Heart Smart Meals
Vegetarian Meals
Take Out Meals
Seasonal Menus
Childrens Menu
Extensive Wine Menu
ADDITIONAL SERVICES
Catering
Private Parties
Private Rooms
Meeting Facilities
Weddings & Receptions
(Gazebo Garden area also)

ATTIRE
Casual
RESERVATIONS
Suggested
SMOKING
Smoking Not
Permitted Inside
Smoking Section on Porch
HANDICAP FACILITIES
CREDIT CARDS
American Express
Visa
Master Card
Discover Card
CHECKS
Accepted

Enjoy wonderful Victorian splendor when you walk into the period decorated dining rooms of this 112 year old house. The Ambiance - Beautiful! The diverse menu features lowcountry cuisine with French, Italian, and American influences. Our efficient wait staff will fill your every need, as you enjoy the atmosphere and delicious food and wines. Our garden gazebo offers a setting for romantic weddings and garden parties. There is ample - Free and safe parking.

Appetizers

Shrimp Cocktail $6.95
Lowcountry spicy Shrimp. Served with a special Cocktail sauce and a Lemon wedge.

Spanakopita $4.50
Layers of buttered Filo Pastry, filled with sauteed chopped Spinach, Onions, Spices, Feta Cheese and Old Country, Greek Spices.

Oysters Rockefeller $7.95
Oysters on the Half Shell. Served with a mix of Onions, Spinach, Pernod with selected Sauces and Seasonings. Broiled to perfection.

Mushrooms Stuffed with Crab $6.95
Stuffed with succulent Crabmeat, special Herbs and Monterey Jack Cheese. Then broiled to marry the flavors. Served with Honey Jalapeno sauce.

Escargot Chanbertin $6.95
Succulent Escargot - marinated in Sauvignon Blanc Wine & broiled in seasoned Garlic Butter. Topped with Puffed Pastry Hats.

Charleston She Crab Soup $4.95
This is a Lowcountry favorite. It has Vegetable and Onions Dry Sherry Wine and is complemented with a Heavy Cream Topping.

Dinner Salads

Chicken Teriyaki Salad $9.95
Garden fresh Greens and Tomatoes. Red Kidney Beans & Onions. Montery Jack cheese & Cheddar cheese. Topped with marinated Teriyaki Chicken Breast, Croutons and crowned with our house Teriyaki Sauce.

Greek Isle Salad $10.95
Garden fresh Greens with Tomatoes & Black Olives. Pepperoncini, Red Onions, Feta Cheese and chunks of Chicken Breast and Lowcountry Shrimp. Croutons and Aegean Greek Dressing.

Black Angus Steaks

King Cut Filet Mignon $17.95
10 oz. Steak - Bacon wrapped on request

Prime Rib Steak $16.95
16 very tender oz. Slow cooked for 12 hours to perfection. Available at your choice of cooking temperature.

Queen Cut Filet Mignon $14.95
8 oz. Steak, Bacon wrapped on request

Black Angus Ribeye $17.95
This is real Beef Lovers treat. It is Smothered in sauteed Onions and grilled.

Special Beef Selections

Chateaubriand with a Bourbon Mustard Sauce $21.95
Served with a Salad and Roasted Garlic Potatoes.

Beef Wellington for Two $49.95
A 24 hour advance order is required. Black Angus Beef Tenderloin with a seasoned Pate'. Baked in flaky pastry.

Special Reminisce Entrees

Shrimp Scampi $13.95
Lowcountry Shrimp - Sauteed in butter, garlic and White Wine. Served over Angel Hair Pasta.

Norwegian Baked Salmon $14.95
Seasoned and marinated with Dill Butter and fresh Seasonings. Over Wild Rice.

Paella $13.95
A feast that features saffron rice topped with Shrimp, Chicken, Seafood and Andouille Sausage.

Grilled Tuna Three Ways $13.95
1. Cajun 2. Teriyaki 3. Lemon Garlic Butter. Served over wild rice.

Tipsy Marinated Shrimp $13.95
Lowcountry Shrimp. Marinated in Bourbon Mustard Sauce. Grilled to pink perfection. Served with Creamy Stone Ground, Slow cooked, Southern Grits.

Vegetable Lasagna $10.95
Sauteed Vegetables. Layered between Pasta and Cream Sauce with Mozzarella Cheese. With Salad.

Chicken Reminisce $13.95
Sauteed Ballantine of chicken breast. Topped with Crabmeat, Asparagus Spears & Reminisce's Chef's Bearnaise Sauce.

Chicken Crepes $11.95
Three crepes filled with Breast of Chicken. Sauteed with Onions and Mushrooms. Topped with Chardonnay Herb Sauce & Parmesan Cheese.

Carpetbagger A La Reminisce $19.95
Oysters sauteed in Wine and Butter Sauce and then stuffed between two grilled Filet Mignon & served over a bed of Wild Rice or Roasted Garlic Potatoes. Topped with our own Bearnaise Sauce.

Chicken Scallopini Marsala $12.95
Balentine of Chicken Breast - Sauteed in Marsala Wine with Scallions & Mushrooms. Topped with Fresh Parmesan Cheese over Angel Hair Pasta.

This is a small sample of the wonderful cuisine offered by Reminisce

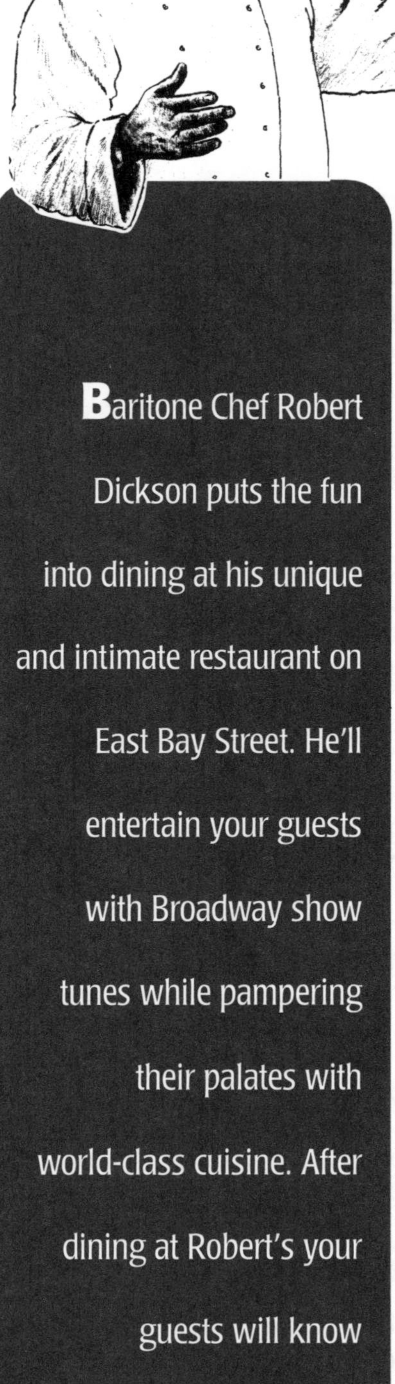

Music Creates Memorable Dining

Robert's Prix Fixe Menu

Dinner Menu and Wine Changes Frequently

- Sea Scallop Mousse, Main Lobster Sauce

  1998 Australian Penfolds Semillion/Chardonnay or Non-Alcoholic California Chardonnay

- Warm Semolina Bread baked in our kitchen
- Roasted Breast of Duckling with Orecchiette Pasta
  Cremini mushrooms, spinach and yellow pepper sauce
- A Salad of Mesclun Greens, Jicama Root and Grape Tomatoes
  Goat's cheese, crustini, virgin olive oil, white balsamic vinegar and sweet basil dressing

  1994 R.H. Philips Cabernet Sauvignon

- Roasted Tenderloin of Beef, Port Wine Sauce
  Haricot verts and wild rice
- Chocolate Paté stuffed Crepe with Apricot & Orange Sauce
  White chocolate cream and almond praline
- Lavazza Italian Coffee or a Selection of Teas

Please call us for your next intimate dinner, private party or gift certificate.

Baritone Chef Robert Dickson puts the fun into dining at his unique and intimate restaurant on East Bay Street. He'll entertain your guests with Broadway show tunes while pampering their palates with world-class cuisine. After dining at Robert's your guests will know why... *Music creates memorable dining.*

Robert's of Charleston

CHARLESTON
182 East Bay Street
Charleston, SC 29401

PHONE
(843) 577-7565

FAX
(843) 723-0530

WEBSITE
www.robertsofcharleston.com

HOURS
7.30 pm-Dinner

MEALS SERVED
Five Course Dinner

CUISINE
Continental

DINING INFORMATION
Gourmet Dining with Entertainment

VOCALIST
Nightly

ADDITIONAL SERVICES
Private Parties

ATTIRE
Casual

RESERVATIONS
Required

CREDIT CARDS
American Express
Visa
Master Card

Rosebank Farms Café

Bohicket Marina Village

Executive Chef John Cuff

Rosebank Farms Cafe, located on the picturesque Bohicket River and just a short drive from historical downtown Charleston, offers the best in local Southern cuisine. Owner Julie Limehouse, native to the Lowcountry, insists on only the freshest; thereby local product. Rosebank's atmosphere is friendly, comfortable and inviting. Come and enjoy the best in Southern cuisine in the Charleston area.

Taking advantage of local specialties, we offer our customers only the freshest and highest quality ingredients. Occasional substitutions may be required due to seasonal availability or market conditions.

STARTERS

Carolina Lump Cake and fried green tomato with cucumber, tomato salsa and creamed corn........................ 9.95

Southern Fried Quail with blackeyed pea chili....................................... 8.50

Sauteed Shrimp and Crawfish in a spicy tasso cream over yellow grits 7.50

Lowcountry Blackeyed Peacakes with sour cream and salsa.................. 7.00

Pan seared, Buttermilk Marinated Chicken Livers with shiitake mushrooms, red eye gravy and yellow grits 7.25

Old Bay Spiced Chilled Shrimp and fried green tomato Napolean with a spicy remoulade sauce 8.25

GARDEN GREENS

House salad of local baby greens with your choice of dressing.............. 4.75

Southern Caeser with tasso ham, pecarino romano cheese and grit croutons 5.00

Baby Spinach Salad with toasted pecans, egg and fresh tomatoes with smoky tomato-bacon vinaigrette...5.75

Rosebank Farms Café

SEABROOK ISLAND
1886 Andell Bluff Blvd.
Seabrook Island, SC 29455
PHONE
(843) 768-1807
FAX
(843) 768-1371
HOURS
Lunch
11:00 pm-2:30 pm
Dinner
5:30 pm-9:30 pm
MEALS SERVED
Lunch
Dinner
CUISINE
Lowcountry
Southern
DINING INFORMATION
Terrace/Patio Dining
Vegetarian Meals
Seasonal Menus
Extensive Wine Menu
LOUNGE BAR

ATTIRE
Resort Casual
RESERVATIONS
Not Taken
SMOKING
Section at Bar
HANDICAP FACILITIES
CREDIT CARDS
American Express
Visa
Master Card
Discover Card
Diners Club Card
CHECKS
Accepted

SOUPS

Local Seafood Chowder with grouper, tuna, dolphin, salmon and blue crab.... .... cup 3.25 bowl 4.25

Wild Mushroom Bisque with frizzled leeks .... cup 3.25 bowl 4.25

GRITS FITS

Carolina Lumpcrab Cakes with cucumber tomato salsa, yellow grits and fried leeks 20.00

Fricassee of Local Shrimp, Scallops and Sausage with apple smoked bacon, tomato, and green onion and yellow grits 18.00

Chili Rubbed Beef Tenderloin Medallions, frizzled leeks, fresh corn and pepper sauce and yellow grits 20.00

Cornmeal Fried Catfish Fillets, creole sauce and yellow grits 20.00

Grilled Double Cut Smoked Pork Loin Chop, green tomato chutney, blackeyed pea salad and yellow grits 19.00

Cajun Spiced Salmon fillet, herb butter and yellow grits 17.00

ENTREES

Marinated and Grilled Pork Tenderloin with garlic yukon mashed potatoes, sweet creamed corn and hard cider apple chutney 18.00

Grilled Local Yellowfin Tuna with drunk butterbeans and rice, black strap molasses BBQ sauce and tobacco fried onions 18.50

Benne Seed and Herb Crusted Local Grouper over hoppin john with seasonal vegetable and tomato-goat cheese fondue 18.50

Seared Rack of Lamb with goat cheese yukon mashed potatoes, sweet creamed corn and fresh rosemary demi-glaze 22.95

Honey Buttermilk Fried Breast of Chicken with garlic yukon mashed potatoes, cole slaw, and peppered gravy 16.00

Grilled Filet of Beef Tenderloin, garlic yukon mashed potatoes and seasonal vegetable .... with corn and pepper sauce 21.00
.... with candied shallot demi glace 21.00
.... with Clemson blue cheese crust 22.00

Saracen

CHARLESTON
141 East Bay Street
Charleston, SC 29401
PHONE
(843) 723-6242
FAX
(843) 723-6244
HOURS
Closed Sunday & Monday
Tuesday-Saturday
6:00 pm-10:00 pm
MEALS SERVED
Dinner
CUISINE
Contemporary
Eclectic
DINING INFORMATION
Seasonal Menus
Extensive Wine Menu
LOUNGE BAR
7 Days a Week
5:00 pm-2:00 am
ADDITIONAL SERVICES
Private Parties
Private Rooms

ATTIRE
Casual
RESERVATIONS
Suggested
SMOKING
Smoking Section
CREDIT CARDS
American Express
Visa
Master Card
Diners Club Card
CHECKS
Not Accepted

S·A·R·A·C·E·N

A culinary jewel located in a National Historic Landmark. Enjoy the most enticing array of appetizers and light meals to exotic culinary creations. The freshest seasonal ingredients and influences from the Lowcountry to the Orient. A Mecca of sensual delights…

◆ APPETIZERS ◆

GRATIN OF OYSTERS WITH CRABMEAT AND CHEDDAR STUFFING 9.95
TWICE BAKED GOATS CHEESE & CARAMEL ONION SOUFFLE WITH PLUM COMPOTE 8.95
BAKED BRIE, CRAB & ARTICHOKE DIP WITH CRISP PITA CHIPS 8.50
VIETNAMESE IMPERIAL ROLLS FILLED WITH PORK, VEGETABLES AND CELLOPHANE NOODLES 6.95
BLUE CHEESE FONDUE TOPPED W/ROASTED SHALLOTS & SERVED WITH TOASTED WALNUT BREAD 8.95
SALMON NAPOLEON SMOKED SALMON LAYERED WITH SALMON MOUSSE WITH DILL OIL 9.95
BUBBLY GARLIC BREAD 4.25
PISTACCHIO CRUSTED JUMBO SHRIMP WITH PINK GRAPEFRUIT AIOLI 8.95
PORTOBELLO, FETA & SPINACH BEGGARS PURSE WITH RED PEPPER COULIS 9.50

◆ SOUP & SALADS ◆

CHARLESTON SHE CRAB BISQUE CUP 4.25 BOWL 5.25
SOUP OF THE DAY CUP 4.25 BOWL 5.25
BUFALA MOZZARELLA & ROASTED RED PEPPER SALAD BASIL OIL & BALSAMIC VINEGAR 9.50
CAESAR SALAD 5.50
WADMALAW ISLAND SALAD WITH HONEY–BLACK PEPPER OR BALSAMIC VINAIGRETTE 4.75
BABY SPINACH W/GOATS CHEESE, CANDIED PECANS, MEDJOOL DATES & MAPLE VINAIGRETTE 8.50

◆ PASTA & GRAINS ◆

SARACEN PASTA OF THE DAY COMPOSED & PRICED DAILY
SHRIMP & GRITS W/TOMATOES, TARRAGON, CREAM, TASSO AND A TOUCH OF SHERRY VINEGAR 17.95
WILD & EXOTIC MUSHROOM RISOTTO WITH MADEIRA GLAZE, PARMESAN & CRISPY LEEKS 16.95

◆ MAIN COURSES ◆

HONEY & SESAME CRUSTED SEA BASS WITH MOROCCAN–SPICED OIL & BEET COUSCOUS 19.95
VEAL SCALLOPINI WITH CARAMELIZED SHALLOTS & MARSALA SAUCE 21.95
GRILLED SALMON WITH ORANGE-BASIL GLAZE 17.95
SAUTEED SEA SCALLOPS WITH ASIAN VINAIGRETTE & WILTED GREENS 21.95
CORIANDER CURED MUSCOVEY DUCK BREAST WITH BOURBON & SWEET POTATO SAUCE 21.95
GRILLED AGED BEEF TENDERLOIN PORTOBELLO FRIES & PORT-CHOCOLATE GLACE 22.95
PORTUGESE PORK TENDERLOIN & CLAMS WITH WHITE WINE, LINQUICA & TOMATOES 19.95
GARLIC-CURED LAMB LOIN GRILLED WITH SUN-DRIED CHERRY & RED WINE SAUCE 20.95
STEAK & FRITES GRILLED ANGUS RIBEYE WITH GARLIC HERB BUTTER & CRISPY FRENCH FRIES 17.95

Seafare
Seafood Buffet & Oyster Bar

NORTH CHARLESTON
6258 Rivers Ave.
North Charleston, SC 29406
PHONE
(843) 566-7840
FAX
(843) 554-1055
HOURS
Oyster Bar
Monday-Thursday
11:00 am-Midnight
Friday & Saturday
11:00 am-2:00 am
Sunday
1:00 pm-Midnight
Restaurant
Monday-Thursday
4:00 pm-9:30 pm
Friday
4:00 pm-10:30 pm
Saturday
3:00 pm-10:30 pm
Sunday
1:00 pm-9:30 pm
MEALS SERVED
Lunch
Dinner
CUISINE
American, Seafood
Lowcountry
DINING INFORMATION
Take Out Meals
Childrens Menu
LOUNGE BAR
ENTERTAINMENT
Live Bands
Wednesday-Saturday
8:00 pm-1:00 am
ADDITIONAL SERVICES
Private Parties

ATTIRE
Casual
RESERVATIONS
Not Required
SMOKING
Smoking Section
No Cigar or Pipe Smoking
HANDICAP FACILITIES
CREDIT CARDS
American Express
Visa
Master Card
Discover Card
Diners Club Card
CHECKS
Accepted

All-U-Can Eat Buffet

Seafare Famous Seafood Buffet has a unique dining room. The decor is a nautical theme with many ships, tackle, brass, pictures and flags. The 70 item seafood buffet is designed to resemble a clipper ship complete with mast and tackle. Our newly completed oyster bar has the same natical decor with a beautiful mahogany bar and cabinets. We also feature live local blues talent Wednesday through Saturday.

ALL-YOU-CARE-TO-EAT SEAFOOD BUFFET
70 Item Seafood Buffet with Crab Legs

Steamed Oysters
Crawfish
Mussels
Clams
Peel & Eat Shrimp
Broiled Salmon
Snapper
Mahi-Mahi
Jumbo Stuffed Shrimp
Crab Imperial
Oysters Rockerfeller
Fresh Roast Beef
Bar-B-Que Ribs
Baked Chicken
Fresh Vegetables Galore

$19.95
Includes:
Outrageous Soup, Salad, Dessert & Fruit Bar

OYSTER BAR MENU

APPETIZERS
CHICKEN WINGS *$3.95*
OYSTERS ON THE HALF SHELL .... *ONE HALF DOZ $3.50* *FULL DOZ $5.95*
OYSTER SHOOTERS *$4.25*
CRAB DIP *$4.25*
PEEL-N-EAT SHRIMP .... *1 LB. $11.95* *1/2 LB $8.50*

SOUPS
CLAM CHOWDER .... *CUP $3.50* *BOWL $4.50*
SHE CRAB SOUP .... *CUP $3.50* *BOWL $4.50*

SALADS
GRILLED CHICKEN SALAD *$7.95*
SHRIMP SALAD *$8.95*

FRIED SEAFOOD
FRIED OYSTERS *$6.95*
FRIED SHRIMP *$8.95*
THE CAPTAIN'S FAVORITE *$12.95*

SANDWICHES
GRILLED CHICKEN *$4.95*
FRIED CHICKEN SANDWICH *$4.75*
HOT HAM AND SWISS *$4.95*
SMOKED TURKEY *$4.95*
HAMBURGER *$5.75*
CHEESEBURGER *$5.95*
BACON CHEESEBURGER *$6.25*
MUSHROOM SWISS BURGER *$6.50*
FRIED OYSTER PO BOY *$5.95*
FRIED SHRIMP PO BOY *$5.95*

SEAFOOD BUCKETS
CAJUN CRAWFISH BUCKET *$10.95*
SHRIMP IN HOT BUTTER *$11.95*
CRAB BUCKET .... *$11.95 BY THE lb.*
BLACK MUSSELS .... *$7.95 BY THE lb.*
STEAMED OYSTERS .... *2 doz. $8.95*

Sermet's Corner

CHARLESTON
276 King Street
Charleston, SC 29401
PHONE
(843) 853-7775
FAX
(843) 853-7770
HOURS
Lunch
Daily
11:00 am-3:00 pm
Dinner
Sunday-Thursday
4:00 pm-10:00 pm
Friday & Saturday
4:00 pm-11:00 pm
Mezzane
Nightly
5:00 pm-2:00 am
MEALS SERVED
Lunch
Dinner
CUISINE
Eclectic
DINING INFORMATION
Vegetarian Meals
Take Out Meals
Childrens Menu
Extensive Wine Menu
ENTERTAINMENT
Live Jazz Upstairs at
Mezzane 5:00 pm-2:00 am

ATTIRE
Casual
RESERVATIONS
Not Required
SMOKING
Smoking Section
(Bar Area Only)
No Cigar or Pipe Smoking
HANDICAP FACILITIES
CREDIT CARDS
American Express
Visa
Master Card
CHECKS
Accepted
(Local)

Sermet's CORNER

When you walk into Sermets, you are immediately surrounded by his paintings on the wall and on your table top. The colorful restaurant design by Sermet offers true Mediterranean Cuisine that has maintained the integrity and spirit of it's peasant roots…fresh, informal and healthy. Try his baked artichoke torta and grilled calamari and you mustn't miss his lavender, honey and black pepper marinated pork tenderloin or the citrus tahini crusted salmon. Sermet's Corner…where art meets the palate.

Mediterranean cuisine at its finest.
Everything made fresh daily from the best ingredients of the season.
Come try some of our favorites.
Appetizers: $4-$9 Entrees: $9-$16

❖ *Lavender scented pork tenderloin*
❖ *Toasted nut encrusted salmon*
❖ *Grilled calamari Appetizer*
❖ *Baked artichoke torta*
❖ *Sautéed shrimp, chicken, and seafood pastas*
❖ *Fresh mixed greens topped with homemade vinaigrettes*

During lunch we also serve a variety of paninis and burgers.
Join us upstairs at the Mezzane for an evening of live jazz.

The Mezzane will be serving a unique selection of tapas and desserts to accompany a wonderful selection of wines and cocktails.
Don't forget to taste:

❖ *Marinated mushrooms*
❖ *Artichoke torta with fresh mozzarella, tomatoes and basil pesto*
❖ *Eggplant campanata*
❖ *Fresh fruit and cheeses*

Creative salads, soups, pastas and entrees are created daily for your enjoyment.
Our versatile menu has something everyone will enjoy.
We are a vegetarian friendly restaurant and also have a children's menu.

Slightly Up The Creek

The Atlanta Journal-Constitution proclaims, Slightly Up The Creek has "a knack for filling warm plates with hard-to-forget eats, remarkable kick-in-the-pants cuisine." Located on a tidal creek at Charleston Harbor, Slightly Up The Creek is the waterfront version of Charleston's Slightly North of Broad. Enjoy innovative regional dishes featuring fresh fish and seafood from the Maverick Southern kitchen of Chef Lee. The outdoor bar, "Without a Paddle" offers frosty cold beverages on summer evenings while enjoying sunset views of the shrimping fleet.

Appetizers and Small Plates

Crab Soup
celery, onions, crab with a touch of cream & sherry — cup $3.95 bowl $4.25

House Salad
mesclun lettuce w/Roma tomatoes, croutons & choice of chunky bleu cheese, balsamic or Asian soy dressing — $3.95

Seared Sea Scallops
apple smoked bacon & tiny green beans tossed with sherry wine vinegar and walnut oil — $7.25

Mussels
poached mussels with white wine, garlic, parsley, tomatoes & a touch of butter — $6.95

Maverick Crab and Artichoke Dip
warm dip with artichoke, crab & crispy tortilla chips — $6.25

Oyster BLT
cornbread layered with pickled okra remoulade, crispy bacon, arugula, piled high with fried oysters and tangy Q sauce — $7.95

Beef Carpaccio
thinly sliced raw beef with horseradish cream, shaved romano, cracked pepper and toast points — $8.25

Main Courses

Crab Stuffed Dolphin
with shiitake mushrooms, tomatoes and basil butter — $16.95

Crispy Whole Fried Flounder
with angel hair slaw and housemade tartar sauce — $16.50

Grilled BBQ Tuna
mustard Q glaze, topped with fried oysters, country ham & green onions — Main $16.95 smaller $13.50

Horseradish Encrusted Salmon
served over creamy leeks — $14.75

Pan Roasted Supreme Cut Chicken Breast
over roasted garlic mashed potatoes with country gravy — $12.95

Grilled Pork Tenderloin
with a tasso cheddar grit cake finished with port wine sauce — $15.75

Maverick Beef Tenderloin
grilled, topped with deviled crab cake & béarnaise, complemented with green peppercorn sauce — Main $18.50 smaller $15.50

Southern Vegetable Plate
a variety of the best local vegetables we can find — $12.50

Side Dishes

Mashed Potato $1.50
Sautéed Spinach $2.95
Seasonal Vegetable $2.25
Stone Ground Grits $1.50

MT. PLEASANT
130 Mill Street
Mt. Pleasant, SC 29464

PHONE
(843) 884-5005

FAX
(843) 856-9828

HOURS
7 nights per week
from 5:30 pm

MEALS SERVED
Dinner

CUISINE
Seafood

DINING INFORMATION
Terrace/Patio Dining
Seasonal Menus

ADDITIONAL SERVICES
Full Service Catering
Private Parties

ATTIRE
Casual

RESERVATIONS
Suggested

SMOKING
Not Permitted

HANDICAP FACILITIES

CREDIT CARDS
American Express
Visa
Master Card
Discover Card
Diners Club Card

CHECKS
Not Accepted

Slightly North of Broad

Charlestonians flock to award-winning Slightly North of Broad for the eclectic atmosphere and Chef Lee's maverick Southern menu. Innovative regional dishes like Maverick Grits and Grilled Barbecue Tuna are menu headliners. Indulge in desserts--Triple Chocolate Cake with Raspberry Sauce and the Key Lime Tart with Pecan Sandy Crust. Fabulous wines by the glass too.

Winner of GQ Magazine's Golden Dish Award for Maverick Grits.

"A happening place where the unexpected is a key element of the setting and menu."
Southern Living.

"Exceptional" *N.Y. Times.*

Soups, Salads & Appetizers

Red Bean Soup
slow cooked with peppers, onions, celery & garlic
with tomato jalapeno salsa & sour cream — Cup: $3.50 Bowl: $4.25

Charleston Okra Soup
cooked to order, with shrimp, oysters, celery, sweet peppers, onions & tomatoes — $6.95

House Salad
fancy mixed greens tossed with a choice of Caesar, ranch, honey mustard,
balsamic vinaigrette or Asian soy dressing — $3.75

Oven Roasted Clams
with smoked sausage, zucchini, bell pepper, country ham & garlic — Large: $12.95 Smaller: $6.50

Mussels
poached mussels with white wine, garlic, parsley & a touch of butter — $7.25

Sautéed Shiitake Mushrooms
filled with foie gras mousse sautéed spinach with port wine reduction sauce — $8.50

Mâverick Paté
accompanied by a salad of tiny green beans, sweet pepper relish,
whole grain mustard & toast points — $6.50

Crostini
grilled sourdough bread, goat cheese, topped with wilted spinach,
marinated tomatoes, red onions, pecorino romano cheese, calamata olives — $6.25

Slightly North of Broad

CHARLESTON
192 E. Bay Street
Charleston, SC 29401
PHONE
(843) 723-3424
FAX
(843) 724-3811
HOURS
Lunch
Monday-Friday
11:30 am-3:00 pm
Dinner
Nightly from 5:30 pm
MEALS SERVED
Lunch
Dinner
CUISINE
Southern
DINING INFORMATION
Seasonal Menus

ATTIRE
Casual
RESERVATIONS
Not taken
except for parties of 6 or 8
SMOKING
Smoking not permitted
HANDICAP FACILITIES
CREDIT CARDS
American Express
Visa
Master Card
Discover Card
Diners Club Card
CHECKS
Not Accepted

Small Plates

Carpaccio of Beef Tenderloin
thinly sliced raw beef, EV olive oil, romano & grilled bread — $7.95

Grilled Marinated Portobello Mushroom
grilled onions & peppers with balsamic & mixed greens — $8.25

Grilled Southern Medley
chicken breast, zucchini, eggplant, tomatoes, goat cheese croutons with pesto, romano & balsamic vinaigrette — $10.50

Maverick Grits
local yellow grits with shrimp, scallops, smoked sausage & country ham — $9.75

Sautéed Squab Salad
with frisée and sherry-walnut oil vinaigrette — $9.95

Pad Thai
classic Thai dish combines shrimp & pork with rice noodles, Thai fish sauce, eggs, mung bean sprouts, green onions & peanuts (vegetarian with Tofu) — $11.25

Sesame Crusted Tuna Medallions
with nori rolls, housemade kim chee, cucumber salad, miso, pickled ginger & wasabi — $9.50

Main Courses

Southern Vegetable Plate
a variety of the best local vegetables we can find — $13.25

Grilled BBQ Tuna
glazed with mustard Q, topped with fried oysters, country ham & green onions — Main: $17.50 Smaller: $14.00

Sautéed Salmon
encrusted with horseradish & breadcrumbs, served over creamy leeks — $15.75

Coastalina Deviled Crab Cakes
on spicy Charleston Creole, sautéed blue crab claw meat seasoned with bell peppers, Tabasco, lemon & mustard — Main: $16.75 Smaller: $9.25

Sautéed Grouper
glazed with whole grain mustard & topped with lemon dill butter — Main: $16.75 Smaller: $13.50

Sautéed Palmetto Squab
over spinach with coriander enhanced natural reduction sauce — $22.00

Lamb Tenderloin
bacon wrapped, over butternut squash puree, red wine reduction sauce — $17.75

Mixed Grill
housemade sausage over cabbage, brace of quail stuffed with mushroom duxelles, apple smoked bacon sauce — $17.25

Grilled Porterhouse Pork Chop
12 oz. glazed with sweet pepper relish, over white bean-tomato-mushroom ragout — $15.75

Maverick Beef Tenderloin
grilled, topped with deviled crab cake, béarnaise, complemented with green peppercorn sauce — Main: $20.00 Smaller: $17.00

Grilled N.Y. Strip
with buttermilk blue cheese & red wine sauce — $17.25

Rack of Veal
pan roasted 12 oz. rack with mashed rutabagas & chive mustard cream — $27.50

Sautéed Duck Breast
with leg confit & natural jus — $15.95

Desserts

Triple Chocolate Cake — $5.00
Sour Cream Apple Pie — $5.00
Key Lime Tart — $4.50
Creme Brulee — $4.50
Ice Cream — $3.25
Sorbets — $3.25
Seasonal Fruits — $3.75

Southend Brewery & Smokehouse

CHARLESTON
161 East Bay St.
Charleston, SC 29401
PHONE
(843) 853-4677
FAX
(843) 853-3516
WEBSITE
www.southendsc.com
HOURS
Lunch
Sunday-Saturday
11:30 am-4:00 pm
Dinner
Sunday-Thursday
5:00 pm-10:00 pm
Friday-Saturday
5:00 pm-11:00 pm
MEALS SERVED
Lunch
Dinner
CUISINE
American
Microbrewery
Seafood
DINING INFORMATION
Take Out Meals
Childrens Menu
LOUNGE BAR
11:30 am-2:00 pm
ADDITIONAL SERVICES
Full Service Catering
Private Parties
Banquet Facilities

ATTIRE
Casual
RESERVATIONS
Not Required
SMOKING
Section Available
Cigar & Pipe Friendly
CREDIT CARDS
American Express
Visa
Master Card
Discover Card
CHECKS
Accepted

Southend Brewery and Smokehouse is rated #1 Microbrewery in the South. We serve regional American Cuisine in a three-story landmark building in Historic Charleston. Enjoy pastas, wood oven pizzas, fresh daily fish and speciality in-house smoked BBQ ribs, chicken and sausage. Visit our third floor Harborview Bar and enjoy a premium cigar and a game of billiards. We offer live entertainment. Plan your party here for 100+ people.

STARTERS

Oriental style shrimpcakes with ginger soy aioli 6.95

Grilled rosemary & garlic portabello mushroom with Charleston grits, grilled roma tomatoes and balsamic vinaigrette 5.95

Firecracker BBQ buffalo wings with ranch dressing and celery sticks 5.95

BBQ Babyback Rib appetizer 6.95

SALADS

Mixed seasonal greens with glazed pecans & asiago cheese 4.95

Oriental smoked chicken salad with Thai vinaigrette 8.95

Blackened salmon on local baby greens with orange sherry vinaigrette, local chevre red onions and seasonal berries 10.95

WOOD OVEN PIZZAS

Applewood-smoked bacon, smoked chicken & mushrooms 9.25

Pepperoni & sausage with mozzarella cheese 8.95

Artichokes, gorgonzola, roasted garlic & rosemary 8.75

Smokehouse pizza with B.B.Q. chicken, red onions & cilantro 8.95

Seasonal grilled vegetables with sundried tomatoes and goat cheese 8.75

** Our pizza dough is made fresh daily with fresh brewed Southend Scarlet ale **

SANDWICHES

Carolina burger with housemade chili & slaw (1/2 lb. Certified Angus beef) 7.95

Grilled blackened chicken with Cajun aioli 7.75

Smoked BBQ pork sandwich with Carolina mustard sauce 7.95

** Most sandwiches are served with french fries.*

WOOD BURNING GRILL

Southwestern pork chops with mashed potatoes, pico de gallo salsa and roasted garlic jus 16.95

Grilled chicken breast with tropical fruit salsa, Santa Fe rice & vegetables 12.95

Grilled Blackened Salmon with pico de gallo salsa, mashed potatoes and vegetables 15.95

Daily fish special .... Priced Daily

Add a dinner mixed green or Caesar salad to any entree for $2.95

SMOKEHOUSE SPECIALS "BREW B QUE"

Ale-steamed sausage with Santa Fe rice, red & black beans, salsa and guacamole 10.95

Sliced BBQ beef brisket with mashed potatoes 13.95

Southend B.B.Q. combo: ribs, chicken & sausage with fries & slaw 18.95

Add a dinner mixed green or Caesar salad to any entree for $2.95

PASTA

Tri-color ricotta cheese ravioli with a pesto cream sauce 10.95

Capellini with grilled chicken, artichokes, garlic, basil & roma tomatoes 12.95

Garlic fettucine with shrimp, sea scallops and roma tomatoes 13.95

HANDCRAFTED BEERS

Carolina Blonde 3.50/pint

Carolina Blonde Light 3.50/pint

Ironman Wheat 3.50/pint

Scarlet Ale 3.50/pint

Bombay Pale Ale 3.50/pint

East Bay Brown 3.50/pint

O'Ryans Stout 3.50/pint

SpiritLine Dinner Cruise

Charleston's premier dining experience aboard the "Spirit of Carolina!" Cruise by Charleston's beautiful and intriguing waterfront as you enjoy an exquisite meal prepared to order onboard. Enjoy live entertainment, dancing, and your favorite beverages on Charleston's largest, most elegant dining yacht. The 3-hour SpiritLine Dinner Cruise departs from Patriots Point. Free parking. Reservations required.

Price includes soup, salad and choice of entrée

Soup

Charleston She-Crab Soup (A local favorite)

Ship's Salad

Baby Spinach Greens with Fresh Mushrooms, Bacon and Blue Cheese. Served with an Herbed Red Wine Vinaigrette.

Entrees

Filet Mignon

A Beautiful Cut of Beef Grilled to perfection Topped with Roasted Pistachio and Sunflower Seed Cabernet Sauce. Served with our Horseradish Smashed Baby Red Potatoes and Fresh Vegetable Medley.

Fresh Catch

Fresh Fish Selected and Prepared by our Chef. Served with our Charleston Red Rice and Fresh Vegetable Medley.

Pesto Chicken

Chicken Breast Dusted with a Mixture of Basil, Parsley, Pine Nuts, Garlic and Parmesan Cheese then Pan Seared. Served with Pasta in a Pesto Cream Sauce.

Pork Chop

A Center Cut Pork Chop Butterflied and Stuffed with Feta Cheese, Spinach, and Roasted Red Peppers, Accompanied by a Buerre Blanc Sauce. Served with Horseradish Smashed Baby Red Potatoes and Fresh Vegetable Medley.

Carolina Crabcakes

A Delicious Blend of Succulent Crab Meat, Seasoned with our Freshest Ingredients and Sauteed Golden Brown. Served with a Dijon Cream Sauce, Charleston Red Rice and Fresh Vegetable Medley.

Lowcountry Special

Chef Introduces Visitors to Various Dishes that have made the South and Charleston Famous.

Fresh Bakery Rolls and Sweet Cream Butter
Coffee and Tea

Assorted Desserts Available

Spirit of Carolina
Dinner Cruise

CHARLESTON
205 King Street, Suite 204
Charleston, SC 29401
PHONE
(843) 722-2628
FAX
(843) 720-4263
HOURS
6:30 Boarding
7:00 pm-10:00 pm
MEALS SERVED
Dinner
CUISINE
American Southern with Lowcountry Flair
DINING INFORMATION
Vegetarian Meals
Seasonal Menus
LOUNGE BAR
Monday-Saturday
6:30 pm-10:00 pm
MUSIC/DANCING
Monday-Saturday
7:00 pm-10:00 pm
ADDITIONAL SERVICES
Private Parties
Banquet Facilities
Private Rooms

ATTIRE
Resort Casual
RESERVATIONS
Required
SMOKING
Outer Decks Only
CREDIT CARDS
American Express
Visa
Master Card
Discover Card
CHECKS
Accepted

Starfish Grille

Perched at the entrance of the Folly Beach Pier, this is the ultimate in ocean-front dining. With an eclectic, moderately priced menu, this unique restaurant serves the finest in fresh local and regional seafood, Angus steaks, appetizers, pastas, salads, sandwiches and great desserts. Enjoy the panoramic view of the ocean, beach and pier while dining inside and the sound of the waves while seated on our deck. Children's menu and full service bar.

Starters

Calamari $5.75
Hand breaded squid, lightly fried to perfection, dressed with a citrus vinaigrette and served with our own marinara.

Artichoke Hearts $4.95
Tossed with fresh tomatoes, basil and feta cheese, wrapped in puff pastry, baked golden brown and served over a shrimp cream sauce.

Coconut Shrimp $7.95
Fresh shrimp dipped in a batter, rolled in coconut, fried and served over a sweet and spicy mustard sauce. Delicious!

Crab Wontons $6.95
Fresh crab meat mixed with a medley of cream cheese, chive, pecans, and herbs served with an oriental cucumber toasted sesame seed salad drizzled with a wasabe glaze.

Quesadilla .... $5.95...add chicken...$7.95
Grilled soft shell flour tortilla with melted smoked gouda and cheddar cheese, served with sour cream and fresh salsa.

Clams and Mussels $6.95
Steamed and sauteed in an herb garlic parmesan cream sauce.

Peel & Eat Shrimp $8.95
One half pound steamed to perfection and served with drawn butter and lemon.

Shrimp & Grits $6.95
Grits served with cheese, sauteed shrimp and diced tomatoes with a cajun country sauce.

Grille's Pita Pizza $4.95
Baked pita bread topped with gouda and cheddar cheese along with our house marinara.
Each additional topping...$.50

Spicy Buffalo Wings $6.95

Salads

House Salad $2.25
Fresh garden greens served with choice of bleu cheese, vinaigrette, roasted garlic honey dijon, or ranch.
Caesar dressing available add $.50

Caesar Salad $5.95
Add: Chicken Breast $8.25
Fried Oysters $9.95
Fried Shrimp $9.95
Traditionally prepared with a large portion of crisp romaine and our own dressing tossed with parmesan and croutons.

Spinach and Fried Oyster Salad $9.95
Fried oysters served on a bed of spinach, tossed with a warm vinaigrette bacon dressing and topped with portabella mushrooms and julienne roasted peppers.

Shrimp Salad $6.95
Lightly poached baby shrimp tossed with pepper and onion, sprinkled with toasted pecans, accompanied with tomato and parmesan toast rounds.

Our Famous Greek Salad $5.95
Garden greens mixed with tomatoes, Greek olives, cucumbers, onions, feta cheese and Greek peppers on a bed of diced potatoes served with vinaigrette.

Starfish Grille

FOLLY BEACH
101 E. Arctic Ave.
Folly Beach, SC 29439
PHONE
(843) 588-2518
FAX
(843) 588-2523
E-MAIL
starfishgr@aol.com
HOURS
Sunday-Thursday
11:00 am-10:00 pm
Friday-Saturday
11:00 am-11:00 pm
(Nov.-March close
1 hour earlier)
MEALS SERVED
Lunch
Dinner
Sunday Brunch
CUISINE
Eclectic
Seafood
DINING INFORMATION
Terrace/Patio Dining
Heart Smart Meals
Vegetarian Meals
Take Out Meals
Childrens Menu
LOUNGE BAR

ATTIRE
Casual
RESERVATIONS
Not Required
SMOKING
Smoking Section
No Cigar or Pipe Smoking
HANDICAP FACILITIES
CREDIT CARDS
American Express
Visa
Master Card
Discover Card
Diners Club Card
CHECKS
Accepted

Pasta

Seafood Festival $13.95
Steamed clams, mussels, and sauteed shrimp tossed with toasted pecans, tomatoes, olives and fresh herbs deglazed with white wine and simmered in shrimp stock served over linguini and sprinkled with parmesan.

Pasta Marinanra $7.95
Add Chicken Parmesan.....$4.75 Sauteed fresh tomatoes, garlic, and fresh herbs tossed with our delicious marinara sauce over spaghetti.

Veggie Pasta $8.50
Seasonal sauteed vegetables tossed with fresh herbs and garlic over penne pasta, tossed either in a light white wine veggie broth or with a marinara sauce.

Blackened Chicken Breast $10.95
Boneless breast of chicken rubbed with cajun spices and blackened, served over spaghetti with julienne peppers, onions, mushrooms and tomatoes in a cajun bourbon cream sauce. (spicy)

Grilled Lemon Chicken $10.95
Grilled marinated chicken breast served over spaghetti tossed with calamata olives, tomatoes, pepperoncini and feta in a light white wine sauce.

Three Cheese Pasta $12.95
Steamed mussels, served over a bowtie pasta, tossed with sundried tomatoes, olives, spinach and prosciutto in a smoked gouda, feta, blue cheese cream sauce.

Chicken Marsala Pasta $10.95
Lightly breaded and pan fried chicken breast topped with sauteed mushrooms, capers and lemon Marsala cream sauce over linguini.

Specialities

Carolina Crab Cakes $12.95
Fresh crab meat mixed with chef's special ingredients, lightly sauteed, floated on a smoked gouda jalapeno relish cream sauce.

Salmon Filet $11.95
Dijon herb crusted filet, pan seared and topped on a roasted red pepper coulis.

Angus N.Y. Strip Steak $15.95
Add Sauteed Shrimp Scampi - $4.95
A 10 oz. portion of Certified Angus Beef, sprinkled with seasoning, grilled to your liking.

Baby Back Ribs $14.95
Tender smoked Baby Back pork ribs basted in an orange BBQ sauce, grilled to order.

Fresh Catch

Shrimp $12.95
Catfish $9.95
Oysters (Fried Only) **........................ $11.95**
Scallops $11.95
Flounder $10.95
Calamari (Fried Only) **........................ $9.95**
Any 2 .... $13.95
Any 3 .... $14.95
Any 4 .... $15.95

Sandwiches

Blackened Birdie (spicy) **.................. $7.95**
A tender boneless breast of chicken pressed in our blend of cajun spices and pan seared, topped with bacon, lettuce, tomato and melted cheddar cheese.

Gyro $5.75
Slices of gyro meat with tomatoes, onions, tsatziki sauce on a pita.

Souvlaki $5.75
Pork loin marinated with lemon, garlic, olive oil and herbs grilled and topped with onions, tomatoes and tsatziki sauce on a pita.

Hand Patted Angus Burger $5.95
Fresh lean ground Certified Angus Beef chargrilled to order with lettuce, tomato and onions.

Greek Style Burger $6.25
Fresh lean ground Certified Angus Beef blended with feta cheese, onions and spices, chargrilled to order.

Fried Flounder $6.95
Fresh filet lightly fried served on a kaiser roll with tartar sauce, lettuce and tomato.

Crab Cake Sandwich $7.75
Our in house crab patty, lightly fried, accompanied with a side of roasted red pepper aioli,

Portabella Grill $6.50
Marinated portabella mushroom grilled, served with marinara and topped with melted provolone and parmesan.

Club Sandwich $6.95
Toasted triple decker layered with fresh roasted turkey, bacon, swiss cheese, tomato and lettuce, served with mayonaise.

Folly Poor Boy $7.95
Choice of fresh oysters scallops or shrimp lightly breaded and fried, served with a side of cajun remoulade.

Tuna Salad Sandwich $5.95
Fresh tuna salad with tomato, lettuce and swiss on toasted bread.

Shrimp and Chicken Philly $7.95
A variation from the Philadelphia style, grilled with mushrooms, julienne pepper and onions with melted swiss cheese.

Heart healthy cooking begins with canola oil that contains no cholesterol and is low in saturated fat. We are proud to use canola oil when preparing fried foods.

Sticky Fingers Restaurant & Bar

CHARLESTON
235 Meeting Street
Charleston, SC 29401
PHONE
(843) 853-7427
MT. PLEASANT
341 Hwy 17N Bypass
Mt. Pleasant, SC 29464
PHONE
(843) 856-9840
SUMMERVILLE
1200 North Main Street
Summerville, SC 29483
PHONE
(843) 871-7427
HOURS
Daily
11:00 am-10:00 pm
MEALS SERVED
Lunch
Dinner
CUISINE
Rib House
DINING INFORMATION
Terrace/Patio Dining
Take Out Meals
Seasonal Menus
Childrens Menu
LOUNGE BAR
ADDITIONAL SERVICES
Full Service Catering
Private Parties
Banquet Facilities
Private Rooms
ATTIRE
Casual
RESERVATIONS
Accepted for Large Parties
SMOKING
Smoking Section
HANDICAP FACILITIES
CREDIT CARDS
American Express
Visa
Master Card
Discover Card
Diners Club Card
Carte Blanche
CHECKS
Not Accepted

"An unbelievable rib joint."
Asheville Citizen-Times

"Delicious."
Food & Wine Magazine
"Unbelievable Ribs."
Golf Magazine

"Make it a point to visit Sticky Fingers"
Chattanooga Free Press

Enjoy the ribs, chicken, and barbecue that locals , tourists, and critics rave about.
Featuring large banquet rooms at all three locations and full service catering.

starters

Onion Loaf **$4.99**
The house speciality. A mountain of onion rings deep-fried and served in the shape of a loaf with Sticky Fingers special dipping sauce.

Savannah Dip **$5.99**
Our own concoction of spinach, artichoke hearts, and melted mozzarella cheese. Served piping hot with tortilla chips and salsa.

Loaded Potato Skins **$4.99**
Two cheeses, real bacon, sour cream, and chives.

Sticky Skins **$5.99**
Chopped barbecue pork topped with melted cheddar cheese and a touch of dark sauce. Served with sour cream, and chives.

Chicken Fingers **$5.99**
Tender strips of chicken deep-fried to a golden brown. Served with our signature barbecue sauce and honey mustard for dipping.

salads

Pick-A-Chick Salad **$6.99**
Pick either a grilled breast of chicken or hickory smoked chicken on a bed of mixed salad greens with cheddar cheese, tomatoes, cucumbers, and croutons.

Chicken Finger Salad **$6.99**
Tender strips of chicken deep-fried and served atop a bed of mixed greens covered with cheddar cheese, tomatoes, cucumbers, and croutons.

Grilled Chicken Ceasar Salad **$6.99**
Slices of marinated or barbecue breast of chicken heaped atop our Ceasar Salad garnished with tomatoes, croutons, and fresh parmesan cheese.

Charleston Sunshine Salad **$7.99**
Slices of marinated chicken heaped atop a bed of mixed greens garnished with raisins, mandarin oranges, celery, and almonds.

ribs

All ribs served with Baked Beans and Homemade Cole Slaw. Add a house salad to any order for $1.99

Memphis Style Wet
Tender pork ribs slowly hickory smoked in our pits and covered with our dark barbecue sauce.
Lunch Special **$6.50**
Regular Order **$10.99**
Large Order **$14.99**

Memphis Style Dry
The choice of the true rib connoisseur. Just as tender as the wet ribs, but carefully seasoned with our mild blend of spices.
Lunch Special **$6.50**
Regular Order **$10.99**
Large Order **$14.99**

Carolina Sweet
Tender pork ribs basted with our Carolina Sweet sauce made with real honey. Nothing could be finer...
Lunch Special **$6.50** Regular **$10.99**
Large Order **$14.99**

Tennesse Whiskey
A unique blend of our dark sauce and Jack Daniels sippin' whiskey. A true Tennessee original.
Lunch Special **$6.50** Regular **$10.99**
Large Order **$14.99**

PORK RIB SAMPLER
Wet? Dry? Sweet? Whiskey? If you can't decide–try them all.
$12.99

RIB SAMPLER FOR TWO
Too much pork for just one fork. An enormous mound of pork ribs accompanied with baked beans and homemade cole slaw for two.
$24.99

combinations

Carolina Combo **$12.99**
Any style of pork ribs combined with either a marinated or barbecued chicken breast. Served with dirty rice, baked beans, and homemade cole slaw.

Tennessee Triple **$13.99**
Our three house specialities straight from the smoker. Ribs any style, chopped barbecue pork, and a 1/4 hickory-smoked chicken. Served with dirty rice, barbecue baked beans, and homemade cole slaw.

dinner specials

Barbecue Pork Dinner **$7.99**
We slowly smoke our pork overnight, pull it by hand, and top it with our mild sauce. Served with baked beans and homemade cole slaw.

Grilled Breast of Chicken **$8.99**
Boneless chicken breast marinated 36 hours and charbroiled over an open flame with or without our dark sauce. Served over dirty rice with a side of cinnamon baked apples.

Chicken Fingers Dinner **$7.50**
Tender strips of chicken, deep-fried until golden brown. Served with honey mustard, seasoned fries, and cole slaw.

Barbecue Beef Dinner **$8.99**
For the beef lover. Generous portions of our lean, tender barbecue beef, topped with our tomato based barbecue sauce. Served with barbecue baked beans and homemade cole slaw.

Rotisserie Half Chicken **$8.50**
The hickory wood we use in our pits turns this meat slightly pink but also makes it incredibly tender. Served over dirty rice with a side of cinnamon baked apples.

sandwiches

Barbecue Pork Sandwich **$5.99**
Our lean and tender barbecue pork piled high on a toasted bun and topped with our famous sauce. Served with seasoned fries or with baked beans and homemade cole slaw.

Sticky Fingers Burger **$5.99**
Half a pound of choice chopped sirloin topped with cheddar and mozzarella cheese, bacon, and barbecue sauce. Served with lettuce, tomato, onions and seasoned fries.

Grilled Breast of Chicken Sandwich **$6.50**
Tender chicken breast grilled to perfection. Served with or without our dark sauce and seasoned fries.

Cheesy Chicken Supreme Sandwich **$6.99**
A marinated chicken breast, charbroiled and topped with cheddar cheese, mozzarella cheese, and bacon. Served with seasoned fries.

Stono Cafe

JAMES ISLAND
1956 Maybank Highway
James Island, SC 29412

PHONE
(843) 762-4478

FAX
(843) 762-7667

HOURS
Lunch
Tuesday-Friday
11:30 am-2:30 pm
Dinner
Tuesday-Saturday
5:30 pm-10:30 pm
Sunday Brunch
10:00 am-2:00 pm

MEALS SERVED
Lunch
Dinner
Sunday Brunch

CUISINE
Lowcountry
Seafood
Southern

DINING INFORMATION
Terrace/Patio Dining
Vegetarian Meals
Take Out Meals
Seasonal Menus
Childrens Menu
Extensive Wine Menu

LOUNGE BAR
Tuesday-Saturday
5:30 pm-10:30 pm

ADDITIONAL SERVICES
Full Service Catering
Private Parties

ATTIRE
Casual

RESERVATIONS
Not Required

SMOKING
Smoking Section

HANDICAP FACILITIES

CREDIT CARDS
American Express
Visa
Master Card

CHECKS
Accepted

The Stono Cafe

◆ Good Service ◆ Good Food
◆ Warm Ambiance

When Barry Waldrop cooks, no one goes hungry.
The Stone Cafe provides generous portions with non-stop, Mediterranean flavor.
Stono can also cater your special event and help with all the details!

APPETIZERS

She Crab soup ...$2.95 cup ...$4.95 bowl
A Lowcountry Traditional favorite

Soup du jour ...$2.75 cup ...$3.95 bowl

Classic Ceasar Salad ...$4.95

Ceasar Salad with Mildly spiced Cajun fried oysters ...8.95

Wild mushroom salad and feta cheese with balsamic vinaigrette ...$6.95

California Greens with choice of dressing ...$3.95

Sauteed Oysters "Stono" with Lemon Beurre Blanc served on baguette croutons ...$6.95

Cajun Chicken Livers mildly spiced in cream sauce ...$6.95

Shrimp and Artichoke hearts in a Parmesan cream sauce ...$5.95

Prince Edward Mussels in a white wine and garlic broth ...$6.95

ENTREES

Crab and Crawfish Cake with lemon Beurre Blanc ...$10.95

Pecan encrusted Farm raised Catfish with orange soy glaze ...$10.95

Wild herb Breast of Chicken with green tomato relish ...$10.95

Almazzo Primavera sautéed red and yellow peppers and onions over angel hair pasta ...$11.95

Pasta Leda-Louise marinated chicken breast with shallots over angel hair pasta ...$14.95

Shrimp and Grits in Canadian Bacon cream sauce ...$15.95

Shrimp and Scallop Fettucine ...$16.95

Seared Atlantic Salmon and garlic roasted mashed potatoes ...$16.95

Grilled Rosemary Garlic Pork Tenderlion ...$16.95

Scallop and Crawfish in puff pastry ...$16.95

Tenderloin "Stono Cafe" 8 o.z. Filet with Shrimp and Béarnaise ...21.95

Sushi Kanpai

CHARLESTON
40 N. Market Street
Charleston, SC 29401
PHONE
(843) 723-7800
HOURS
Lunch
Monday-Friday
11:30 am-2:00 pm
Dinner
Monday-Thursday
5:00 pm-10:30 pm
Friday & Saturday
5:00 pm-11:00 pm
MEALS SERVED
Lunch
Dinner
CUISINE
Japanese
Seafood
Sushi
DINING INFORMATION
Vegetarian Meals
Take Out Meals
ATTIRE
Casual
RESERVATIONS
Suggested
SMOKING
Smoking Not Permitted
HANDICAP FACILITIES
CREDIT CARDS
American Express
Visa
Master Card
CHECKS
Not Accepted

Sushi Kanpai

Journey to the Historic Downtown Market and encounter Japan. Nestled in the Rainbow Market, Sushi Kanpai is a delight, not only for sushi lovers, but also for those desiring traditional Japanese dishes. Only the freshest fish and ingredients are used in our restaurant. With over fifteen appetizers and oh so many different entrees, it's hard not to find something to please everybody.

Choose from several different Japanese beers, and for the less adventuresome we carry several domestics. Or if it's sake you desire, we have the traditional hot sake and several Momokawa Premium chilled sakes. So please travel to our part of town and visit Japan.

Appetizers

Tempura-*Shrimp and Vegetables dipped in Tempura batters and lightly fried* ... $6.00
Calamari Tempura-*Squid and Vegetables fried to a golden brown* ... $5.50
Veggie Tempura-*A perfect set of Tempura for Vegetarian* $4.50
Yakitori-*Very tasty, Japanese favorite Chicken Shish Kebab* .. $4.00
Gyohza-*Moon shaped dumplings pan fried* ... $4.00
Shrimp Katsu-*Breaded shrimp fried to a golden crisp* $4.80
Chicken Katsu-*Breaded chicken fried to a golden crisp* $4.50
Chicken Karaage-*Japanese style fried chicken* ... $4.50
Agedashi Tofu-*Tofu fried and dipped in special sauce* $4.00
Muscles-*Green lip mussels grilled with special sauce* . $4.80
Soft Shell Crab-*Breaded and fried to a crispy served with special sauce* ... $8.00
Gyuu Negimaki-*Sliced beef rolls with scallion and baked with special sauce* ... $6.00
Sashimi-*Assorted thin sliced fresh raw fish for appetizer. Very delicate taste* ... $7.50
Tako-su-*Octopus, seaweed, and cucumber marinated in sweet vinegar sauce* ... $4.50
Edamame-*Lightly salted boiled soybeans in pod* ... $3.80
Hiyashi Wakame-*Marinated seaweed with sesame based sauce* ... $3.50
Hijiki-*Hijiki seaweed cooked with fried bean curd, and potato noodle in sweet sauce* ... $3.00

Soup and Salad

Miso Soup *traditional Japanese soup* ... $1.50
Soba Soup *buck wheat noodle soup with scallion and seaweed* ... $4.00
Seaweed Salad *wakame seaweed and fresh vegetables with sweet vinegar sauce* ... $4.00
Crab Salad *crab and fresh vegetables, choice of sweet vinegar or ginger dressing* ... $4.25

Sushi Bar Juubako-Special

Una-Juu-*Eels with sweet sauce over rice* ... $16.50
Tekka-Juu-*Fresh Tuna over sushi Rice* ... $15.00
Chirashi-Juu-*Tuna, Salmon, Whitefish, Shrimp, Crab, Egg, and Veggie over sushi rice* ... $15.00

Combination Plates

Tempura and Teriyaki Chicken Combo . $13.80
Tempura and Sushi Combo ... $15.80
Tempura and Sashimi Combo ... $16.80
Teriyaki Chicken and Sushi Combo ... $14.80
Teriyaki Ckicken and Sashimi Combo ... $15.80
Kanpai Combo *Tempura, Gyuu Negimaki, Tuna Roll, and Daily Suprise* ... $16.80
Veggie Combo *Veggie Ten, Agedashi Tofu, Veggie Roll, and Daily Suprise* ... $11.80

Dinner Entrees

Teriyaki Chicken Dinner ... $9.80
Chicken Katsu Dinner-*Breaded Chicken fried to a golden crisp* ... $10.80
Yakitori Dinner-*Very tasty, japanesese favorite Chicken Shish Kebab* ... $10.80
Teriyaki Beef Dinner-*Beef steak with teriyaki sauce* . $13.80
Gyuu Negimaki Dinner-*Beef rolls with scallion baked with special sauce* ... $13.80
Tempura Dinner-*Shrimp and veggie Tempura* .. $12.80
Salmon Steak Dinner-*Baked salmon steak with teriyaki sauce* ... $12.80
Poached Salmon Dinner-*Poached salmon steak with tartar sauce* ... $12.80
Kushiyaki Dinner-*Shrimp, scallop, beef, and chicken shish kebab* ... $16.50
Avo Maki Dinner-*Salmon, shrimp, and avacado wrapped w/seaweed paper and seared and sautéed with oyster sauce* .. $16.50

Sushi Bar Specials

Sushi Deluxe-*10 pcs of Nigiri Sushi and a california roll* ... $16.99
Nigiri sushi: Tuna (2), Salmon (2), Shrimp (2), Yellow Tail (1), White Fish (1), Smelt roe(1), and Eel (1)
Sushi Special-*8 pcs of Nigiri Sushi and a California roll* ... $14.99
Nigiri sushi: Tuna(2), Salmon(2), Shrimp(2), Yellow Tail (1), White Fish (1)
Sushi Sashimi Special-*(served with a bowl of rice)* ... $19.99
8 pcs of Nigiri sushi (as the same as Sushi special), and a california roll Assorted Sashimi: Tuna (3), Salmon (3), White Fish (2)

TBONZ Gill & Grill

TBONZ Gill and Grill has been voted "Best Steak in Charleston" every year since opening over ten years ago. Three area locations, including the TBONZ Brewery in Mount Pleasant, make TBONZ a favorite with visitors and locals alike. TBONZ Gill & Grill offers a unique steakhouse menu featuring choice aged beef, fresh local seafood and Lowcountry specialties in casual and friendly atmosphere. Be sure to sample one of the award-winning handcrafted TBONZ HomeGrown Ales - 1999 Great American Beer Festival Bronze Medal Winner.

TBONZ Gill & Grill's Downtown and Mt. Pleasant locations have the bonus of being right next door to Kaminsky's Most Excellent Cafe. These two eclectic dessert cafes offer the finest and most creative homemade desserts in Charleston along with an inventive martini menu and a full service bar. TBONZ Gill & Grill's West Ashley location serves a selection Kaminsky's desserts. Save room for dessert!

APPETIZERS & LIGHTER FARE

LOWCOUNTRY FLOWERING ONION **4.95**
Plump sweet onion, lightly battered & fried, served with our honey mustard dipping sauce

FRIED SHRIMP **reg. 5.95 large 9.95**
Spicy fried select shrimp served with a zesty cocktail sauce

BEER BOILED SHRIMP **reg. 5.95 large 9.95**
Peel & eat select shrimp boiled in Old Bay and our handcrafted Cooper River Red Ale. Served chilled

TOMMY'S TEXAS CHEESE FRIES DELUXE **5.95**
A generous portion of crispy potato fries smothered with ranch dressing, Monterey Jack and cheddar cheeses and covered with apple smoked bacon

STEAKS

PHIL'S FILET	**7 oz. (Petite)**	**12.95**
	9 oz.	**14.95**
	14 oz.	**18.95**
RIBEYE	**12 oz.**	**13.95**
TBONE	**16 oz.**	**15.95**
PORTERHOUSE (MR. TBONE)	**22 oz.**	**18.95**
NY STRIP	**11 oz.**	**12.95**
	14 oz.	**15.95**
PRIME RIB	**12 oz.**	**13.95**
	16 oz.	**16.95**
CHARGRILLED SIRLOIN	**12 oz.**	**12.50**
CHOPSTEAK with grilled mushrooms & onions	**12 oz.**	**9.95**
STEAK KABOB with mushrooms, onions & peppers		**11.95**

STEAK SPECIALTIES

DRUNKEN RIBEYE **14.95**
Our 12 oz. ribeye steak, marinated in a Kentucky Bourbon sauce

PEPPERCORN CRUSTED NEW YORK STRIP **16.95**
Our 11oz. N.Y. Strip steak rolled in crushed black peppercorns, grilled and topped with a Béarnaise sauce

This is just a small selection of the wonderful cuisine available at TBONZ

SEAFOOD

ATLANTIC GROUPER & SHRIMP DELUXE **14.95**
Fresh grilled grouper fillet topped with sautéed select shrimp, smothered with a creamy Chardonnay sauce

LOWCOUNTRY DEVILED CRABCAKES **14.95**
Two crabcakes from our Chef's famous Lowcountry recipe, sautéed to perfection and served with a homemade Béarnaise sauce

SEARED JUMBO SEA SCALLOPS **13.95**
Tender sea scallops lightly seared with a blend of garlic, ginger and white pepper spices. Served with stir fried veggies (instead of potato)

EDISTO FRIED SHRIMP **13.95**
Select shrimp lightly battered and fried. Served with a homemade cocktail sauce

BLACKENED "CENTER CUT" TUNA **12.95**
Served with our special citrus butter; zesty and delicious!

GRILLED NORWEGIAN SALMON **12.95**
Herb–crusted salmon fillet coated in a Lowcountry blend of herbs & spices served with a creamy cucumber–dill sauce

GRILLED JUMBO SHRIMP **15.95**
Select shrimp, grilled and served with our homemade cocktail sauce

GILL & GRILL

FILET AND GRILLED JUMBO SHRIMP **7 oz. 15.95 9 oz. 18.95**
Choice aged filet combined with an order of jumbo shrimp served with our homemade cocktail sauce

NY STRIP AND BLACKENED JUMBO SEA SCALLOPS **16.95**
11 oz of succulent New York Strip topped with 4 oz of blackened fresh sea scallops

RIBEYE AND LOWCOUNTRY DEVILED CRABCAKE **14.95**
7 oz of juicy ribeye topped w/our original Lowcountry crabcake

MARKET STREET CHICKEN & SHRIMP **12.95**
Grilled double breast of chicken topped with select shrimp and a spicy smoked jalapéno cream sauce

PRIME RIB AND EDISTO FRIED SHRIMP **8 oz. 14.95 12 oz. 17.95**
Tender prime rib combined with 4 oz of lightly battered and fried select shrimp

FILET AND MARKET STREET CHICKEN & SHRIMP **14.95**
Marinated chicken breast topped with shrimp and served with our 7 oz aged filet. Served with a spicy smoked jalapéno cream sauce.

TBONZ Gill & Grill

- **CHARLESTON**
80 N. Market Street
Charleston, SC 29401
PHONE
(843) 577-2511
WEST ASHLEY
1668 Old Towne Rd.
Charleston, SC 29407
PHONE
(843) 556-2478
- **MT. PLEASANT**
1028 Johnnie Dodds Blvd.
Mt. Pleasant, SC 29464
PHONE
(843) 971-7777

HOURS
11 am-Late

MEALS SERVED
Lunch
Dinner
Late Night Dining

CUISINE
American
Microbrewery
Steak House

DINING INFORMATION
Terrace/Patio Dining (Mt. Pleasant Only)
Vegetarian Meals
Take Out Meals
Childrens Menu

ADDITIONAL SERVICES
Full Service Catering
Private Parties
Banquet Facilities
Meeting Facilities

ATTIRE
Casual

RESERVATIONS
Not Required
Suggested for Parties of 8 or More

SMOKING
Smoking Section
No Cigar or Pipe Smoking

HANDICAP FACILITIES

CREDIT CARDS
American Express
Visa
Master Card

CHECKS
Accepted
(Local Only)

Bronze Medal
Great American Beer Festival 1999

Tommy Condon's

IRISH PUB & SEAFOOD RESTAURANT

Believe it or not, the East Coast's most authentic Irish pub is located in downtown Charleston, just off The Market...it's Tommy Condon's! Like all true Irish pubs, Tommy Condon's welcomes families, and offers great food at an affordable price. You'll also find live Irish music every Wednesday through Sunday night, and for the truly thirsty we serve up the fun until late at night. Imagine - fresh seafood and a pint of your favorite...does it get any better?

Starters

Church Street Crab Dip *A favorite local recipe of choice, blue claw crabmeat, a blend of cheeses and traditional crab spices served with captain wafers.* **$4.95**

Chicken Tenders *Tender fried chicken filets served with honey mustard dipping sauce.* **$3.95**

Spinach Dip *A delicious blend of spinach, cream cheese and vegetables. Served with corn tortilla chips.* **$3.95**

Buffalo Wings *Traditional Buffalo wings spiced with our own Firecracker Sauce served with homemade blue cheese and celery sticks.* **$4.95**

Irish Nachos *A terrific blend of cheddar cheese, chopped bacon, chives, jalapeno peppers, and ranch dressing over crispy fried potatoes.* **$4.95**

Crab Fritters *Lump crabmeat lightly breaded then deep fried, served with red pepper dijonnaise sauce.* **$5.95**

Stuffed Baked Potato *Stuffed with all your favorite cheddar cheese, butter, sour cream, bacon bits, and chives.* **$3.50**

Stout Steamed Shrimp *1/4 pound of fresh shrimp, steamed in Guinness and served chilled with zesty cocktail sauce.* **$4.95**

Salads & Sandwiches

Grilled Chicken Caesar Salad *Crisp Romaine lettuce tossed with fresh Bermuda onions and garlic croutons finished with our special Caesar dressing and shredded parmesan cheese then topped with grilled, marinated chicken breast.* **$6.50**

Grilled Shrimp Caesar Salad **$6.95**

House Salad *Fresh mixed greens with tomato wedges, cucumber slices, thinly sliced Bermuda onions and garlic croutons.* **$2.95**

With entree **$2.25**

Caesar Salad **$3.95**

The Original Tommy Burger *Charleston's best 1/2 pound chargrilled burger with lettuce, tomato, sliced onion and choice of cheeses.* **$5.50**

With cheddar & bacon **$5.95**

With Swiss & mushrooms **$5.95**

Market Street Chicken *Our six-ounce chargrilled marinated boneless chicken breast served on a deli roll with lettuce and tomato.* **$5.50**

With cheddar & bacon **$5.95**

With Swiss & mushroom

From The Kettle

Irish Potato Chowder *A 19th century Condon family recipe handed down through generations. Made with bacon, cheddar cheese, and scallions.* **Cup $2.75 Bowl $3.75**

Charleston She-Crab Soup *Savor the rich taste of fresh crabmeat and choice crab roe, which makes this soup a "local" favorite.* **Cup $2.95 Bowl $3.95**

Tommy Condon's

Irish & Lowcountry Specials

Fish 'N Chips *An ol' Irish favorite! Basket of french fries and lightly battered whitefish served with homemade cole slaw.* $7.95

Shepherd's Pie *An Old World casserole of tender choice beef and sweet root vegetables in a rich brown gravy, topped with mashed potatoes.* $8.95

Chicken Tender Platter *A plate full of chicken tenderloins deep fried until golden - served with french fries, cole slaw and a honey mustard dipping sauce.* $8.95

Award Winning Signatures

Shrimp & Grits *A lowcountry tradition of whole ground grits blended with cheddar cheese, topped with fresh sauteed creek shrimp, peppers, onions, bacon, celery, tomatoes, and black olives in a rich cream sauce.* $12.95

Lowcountry Jambalaya *Delicious creek shrimp, marinated chicken and smoked sausage sauteed with tomatoes, celery, onions, and peppers in a Lowcountry spiced brown sauce served over Carolina white rice.* $12.95

Meat, Poultry & Combos

Smothered Chicken *Grilled boneless breast of chicken smothered with sauteed peppers, mushrooms and onions, finished with melted cheddar cheese.* $10.95

Rib-eye Steak *12 ounces of choice rib-eye chargrilled to your liking.* $13.95

New York Strip *Our choice 12 oz. New York Strip chargrilled to order.* $13.95

Baby-Back Ribs *A full rack of the tenderest ribs in town, grilled to perfection and coated with our Irish gold bbq sauce.* $12.95

Steak & Crab Cake *Lump crabmeat lightly breaded and fried, served with a red pepper dijonnaise sauce and a petite N.Y. Strip.* $14.95

Shrimp & Chicken *A skewer of fresh grilled shrimp and a large tender chargrilled chicken breast.* $13.50

Steak & Shrimp *An 8 oz. choice New York Strip and a skewer of grilled succulent shrimp.* $14.95

Fresh Lowcountry Seafood

*All entrees are served with fresh seasonal vegetables and choice of baked potato, french fries, or Charleston red rice. *Except noted item.*

Fried Shrimp *Fresh succulent shrimp lightly battered and deep fried til golden.* $12.95

Lowcountry Oysters *Our delicious, select oysters are harvested right from regional creek beds.* $12.95

Sea Scallops *Plump and tender sea scallops from the cold Atlantic.* $12.95

Tommy's Seafood Platter *A delectable deep fried combination of fresh shrimp, sea scallops, oysters and filet of fish.* $14.95

Charleston Crab Cakes *Two crab cakes seasoned with Old Bay then deep fried. Served with a roasted red pepper dijon cream sauce.* $13.95

Seafood Alfredo *Fresh lowcountry shrimp and tender sea scallops sauteed in a creamy alfredo sauce, served over fettuccine*.* $11.95

Stuffed Salmon *Fresh N. Atlantic salmon grilled then served over a bed of crabmeat stuffing, topped with our chef's hollandaise.*

Dessert Selections

Bailey's Irish Cream Cheesecake *The smoothest of cheesecakes with the taste of Bailey's Irish Cream liqueur.* $14.95

Snickers® Pie *Chunks of Snickers "smooshed" with vanilla bean ice cream in a graham cracker crust topped with hot mocha fudge.* $3.95

Hot Fudge Sundae *Hot mocha fudge, whipped cream, and walnuts on top of two scoops of vanilla ice cream.* $3.95

Double Fudge Brownie *Our giant walnut cream cheese brownie and vanilla ice cream with hot mocha fudge and whipped cream. Enough for two.* $3.95

Southern Pecan Pie a la mode *A temptation for your sweet tooth. Served with vanilla ice cream.* $3.95

Try one of our delicious coffee drinks with your dessert.

CHARLESTON
160 Church Street
Charleston, SC

PHONE
(843) 577-3818

WEBSITE
www.charleston.net/com/tcondons

HOURS
7 Days A Week
11:00 am-1:00 am

MEALS SERVED
Lunch
Dinner

CUISINE
Irish
Seafood

DINING INFORMATION
Terrace/Patio Dining
Take Out Meals
Childrens Menu

LIVE MUSIC
Thursday-Saturday
9:00 pm-1:00 am

ADDITIONAL SERVICES
Full Service Catering
Private Parties
Banquet Facilities
Private Rooms
Meeting Facilities

ATTIRE
Casual

RESERVATIONS
Not Required

SMOKING
Smoking Section
Cigar & Pipe Friendly

HANDICAP FACILITIES

CREDIT CARDS
American Express
Visa
Master Card
Discover Card
Diners Club Card
Carte Blanche

CHECKS
Accepted

Vickery's Bar & Grill

CHARLESTON
15 Beaufain St.
Charleston, SC 29401
PHONE
(843) 577-5300
FAX
(843) 577-5020
MT. PLEASANT
1313 Shrimp Boat Lane
Mt. Pleasant, SC
PHONE
(843) 884-4440
FAX
(843) 849-8211
HOURS
11:30 am-2:00 am
MEALS SERVED
Lunch
Dinner
Sunday Brunch
Late Night Dining
CUISINE
American Fare with Cuban Influence
DINING INFORMATION
Terrace/Patio Dining
Heart Smart Meals
Childrens Menu
Extensive Wine Menu
LOUNGE BAR
11:30 am-2:00 am

ATTIRE
Casual
RESERVATIONS
Not Required
SMOKING
Smoking Section
VALET PARKING
Mt. Pleasant Only
HANDICAP FACILITIES
CREDIT CARDS
American Express
Visa
Master Card
Discover Card

Best Recipe
Oyster Festival '97
Best Patio
City Paper '97-'99
Best Bartender
City Paper '98-'99
Best Martini
City Paper '98
Best Happy Hour
City Paper '98

Downtown Charleston's favorite watering hole since 1993 now also serving Mt. Pleasant on Shem Creek. All day every day. Funky decor and a funky staff, creative bar and grill fare, big 16-ounce mugs of beer, late night bar, and two of the best outdoor dining experiencs in the Charleston area create an environment you won't want to miss.

APPETIZERS

Oyster Bisque First Place 1996 Charleston Oyster Festival! 5.95

Crispy Vegetable Spring Roll with zippy Thai dip 5.50

Southern Fried Squid with wasabi marmalade ... 4.75

Black Bean Cake with sauteed spinach, red onion and balsamic vinegar, garnished with salsa & sour cream 3.95

Mojo Wings (1/2 dozen) 4.75

Warm Artichoke Dip with parmesan cheese and scallions, served with warm pita wedges 5.95

SOUPS & SALADS

Black Bean Soup with sour cream and diced red onion and galletas .... cup...1.95 bowl....2.95

Gazpacho with sour cream and galletas .... cup...1.95 bowl....2.95

Crispy Fried Oyster Salad with gazpacho vinaigrette and parmesan cheese 8.25

Grilled Jerk Chicken Salad tomato, onion, roasted red peppers, jack & cheddar with tortilla straws and blue cheese vinaigrette 7.75

Grilled Salmon Caesar Salad 8.25

BURGERS & SANDWICHES

Vicksburger topped with broiled mushrooms and a side of classis bearnaise 6.25

Ranchburger ranch dressing, crumbled bacon and scallions 6.00

Black Bean Burger with salsa & sour cream (vegetarian) 5.50

"Classic" Cuban roasted pork, ham, swiss cheese, pickles and mustard, pressed in Cuban bread 6.50

Oyster Po'Boy crispy fried oysters, served on Cuban bread with lettuce and jalapeno tartar sauce 7.95

Crab Cake Sandwich southern style crab cake, pan fried, and served on a sesame seed bun with jalapeno tartar sauce 6.95

Grilled Salmon BLT 6 oz salmon filet, grilled and served with apple smoked bacon, lettuce, tomato, and cracked black pepper mayonnaise, on thick cut ciabatta 8.25

Veggie Pita sauteed seasonal vegetables with shredded jack & cheddar on pita bread 6.25

ENTREES

Shrimp, Sausage & Grits 1/2 dozen shrimp sauteed with sausage and garlic served over creamy cheese grits 12.95

Grilled Jerk Chicken Plate with raspberry sauce, served with black beans & rice, blue cheese cole slaw, and blackened pea fritters 11.95

Down South Pork Loin pan fried, breaded pork loin with pepper gravy, served with garlic mashed potatoes 12.95

Three Sauteed Crabcakes with corn relish, roasted red pepper hollandaise, and black eyed pea fritters 13.95

Lowcountry Saute shrimp, crabmeat and crawfish tails in bourbon butter served overy creamy grits and topped with crispy fried oysters 14.95

Seared Pork Tenderloin with sauteed spinach and apple smoked bacon over garlic mashed potatoes with nut brown ale sauce and feta cheese 13.50

Black Bean Cakes over sauteed spinach with red onion, balsamic vinegar, salsa & sour cream 7.95

Pecan Encrusted Grouper over mashed potatoes with a creamy bourbon & brown sugar sauce and greenbeans 14.95

Cuban Style Roasted Chicken 1/2 bird served with blue cheese cole slaw, black beans & rice and blackeyed pea fritters 11.25

Seared Shrimp & Scallops Over Penne Pasta with pesto, chopped tomato and parmesan cheese ... 11.95

Homemade Sausage & Black Beans over yellow rice topped with salsa and sour cream 8.50

Jumbo Three Cheese Ravioli tossed with crawfish & tasso ham in a garlic parmesan cream sauce 12.95

Fettucine with Fresh Spinach, Mushrooms and cherry tomatoes with an herb vegetable broth and parmesan cheese 8.50

Angus Center Cut Sirloin over demi-glace, topped with a white horseradish sauce, served with greenbeans and gratin potatoes 15.95

DESSERTS

Warm Bread Pudding 4.00

Old Fashioned Coconut Cream Pie 5.00

Crusted Orange Flan 3.50

Triple Layer Chocolate Cake 5.75

Wild Wing Cafe

One of Charleston's most popular spots for casual gourmet foods. Famous for 25 different chicken wing flavors. Homemade dressings and sauces, fresh cut onion rings and handpattied burgers topped hundreds of ways, baby back ribs in 7 flavors, homemade soups, huge salads, quesadillas, wrap sandwiches, appetizers. Over 40 beers in stock, 20 brews on tap...Home of the Original Bucket of Beer. Lots of fun housed in a charming 225 year old building on the vendors market Downtown. Mount Pleasant location offers great patio dining!

Wild Wings

"The Best Wings South of Buffalo"
25 flavors of plump, poultry perfection.
10 pc. $4.95 - 16 pc. $7.50
20 pc. $9.25 - 50 pc. $20.95
100 pc. - $38.50

Mild • Medium • Chernobyl • China Syndrome • Habeñero Hots • Ginger • Wild West • Italian • Thai • Honey Mustard • Flying Fajita • Lemon Pepper • Ragin Cajun • Island Wing • Bubba's BBQ • Gold Rush • Colorado Copper • Old Smokey • Ol' Yeller • Ranchilada • Garlic • Carolina Fireball • Jalapeno Cheddar

All of our wings are served with lots of crispy celery and our homemade blue cheese dip.

Sampler Platter

Choose up to five different styles in groups of five. - $10.95

Wild Things

SUPER SPINACH DIP $4.25
CHILI CON QUESO DIP $4.95
LOADED SKINS $5.25
JALEPENO POPPERS $4.95
SHRIMP POPPERS $5.95
BUFFALO BREATH CHILI $2.75/$3.95

BABY BACK RIBS

Try our Chargrilled Ribs in ANY of our Wild Wing flavors!

Full Rack **$13.95**
Half Rack **$8.95**
Served with Fries & slaw
Sampler **$13.95**
4 flavors - 3 bones each served w/ Fries
Wings & Ribs Combo **$12.95**
Half Rack & 10 wings served with Fries

CHICKEN feathers

Boneless, skinless chicken strips grilled in any of our marinades. Lowfat & light. Served with fries or celery & blue cheese.

4-piece $4.25 6-piece $5.95
(choose 2 marinades)
Sampler 12-piece $9.95
(choose 4 marinades)

Sensational Salads

THE INCREDIBLE CHARGRILLED CHICKEN SALAD
Strips of grilled marinated chicken breasts served hot over a bunch of cold, crisp greens & topped with shredded cheese, crumbled bacon & toasted almonds. You can have your choice of dressings, but we think our honey mustard is just right with this one...$6.95

THE TOTALLY TERRIFIC THAI CHICKEN
A generous portion of crisp, cold greens with cucumbers, tomatoes & shredded carrots topped with strips of chicken breast grilled in a nutty marinade & sprinkled with toasted almonds, shredded cheese & Chinese noodles. Served with our warm peanut sesame dressing...$6.95

Great Grillers

THE BASIC CHICKEN SANDWICH
Six ounces of moist, mouth watering chicken breast with shredded lettuce & our secret sauce on a toasted bun & a healthy portion of Big, Fat Fries...$4.95

THE BIG BEEFY BURGER
Eight ounces of lean ground beef grilled to your order & served on a toasted bun with lettuce, tomato, pickle, mustard, ketchup & mayonnaise. Served with Big, Fat Fries...$4.95

BUILD YOURSELF A BEAUTY
Pick A Marinade - Any one of the 23 different flavors...$.30
Choose a Cheese - Monterrey Jack, Cheddar, Crumbled Blue Cheese, Mozzerella, Queso Dip...$.50
Then add a Topper or Two - Choose from 12 items.

The Ultimate Chicken Sandwich (A WILD WING CAFE ORIGINAL)
A 8 ounce breast of grilled chicken brushed lightly with barbeque sauce, then topped with mounds of shaved ham & melted Monterrey Jack cheese. It's served open faced on a toasted bun. Served with Big, Fat Fries...$6.55

THE WILD WILLIE
The Wild Wings very special stacked sandwich. Start with piles of hot shaved ham, layered with sauteed mushrooms, then topped with melted cheese (your choice). We suggest Monterrey Jack. Served on a toasted bun with dijon mustard spread...$5.95

MUCHO MUNCHOS

THE WILD WING'S WONDERFUL QUESADILLAS
Soft flour tortilla stuffed with lots of cheese & other goodies then grilled til golden brown. Caramba! It's great with homemade salsa & sour cream. Guacamole on request.
Chicken - Chunks of marinated chicken, onions, peppers & two cheeses...$5.95
Shrimp - Spicy sauteed shrimp, onions, peppers & two cheeses...$6.95
Veggie 'Dilla - Onions peppers, mushrooms, scallions, mozzerella cheese & a dollop of spinach dip...$5.95

NOT'CHO ORDINARY NACHOS
A Mexican Mouthful! Mounds of golden brown chips topped with cheese and Jalapenos.
Cheese - $4.95 BBQ Chicken - $5.95
Chili Cheese - $5.95

WILD WRAPS

FAJITA FIESTA - Grilled fajita chicken breast, sauteed onions & peppers, rice and cheese in a grilled garlic herb tortilla. Served with southwest ranch for dipping...$5.95

BUFFARELLA - Fried chicken strips dipped in our famous buffalo hot sauce, lettuce, tomatoes, mozzarella & cheddar cheese with ranch dressing, stuffed in a jalapeno cheddar tortilla. Served with blue cheese dip & celery...$5.95

THE COOL CHICK - Hunky Chunky Chicken Salad, toasted almonds, crumbled bacon, crispy lettuce & diced tomatoes in a garlic herb tortilla. Served with potato salad...$5.95

Chargrilled Chicken Platters

ULTIMATE CHICKEN PLATTER $7.50
MEXICALI CHICKEN $7.25
TERIYAKI CHICKEN $7.25
SMOTHERED CHICKEN $7.25
THE FLYING FAJITA $7.25
LEMON PEPPER CHICKEN $7.25

CHARLESTON
36 North Market St.
Charleston, SC 29401
PHONE
(843) 722-WING
MT. PLEASANT
644 Coleman Blvd.
Mt. Pleasant, SC 29464
PHONE
(843) 971-9464
HOURS
Monday-Saturday
11:00 am-2:00 am
Sunday
12:00 pm-2:00 am
MEALS SERVED
Lunch
Dinner
Late Night Dining
CUISINE
American, Barbeque, Mexican
DINING INFORMATION
Terrace/Patio Dining
Heart Smart Meals
Vegetarian Meals
Take Out Meals
Seasonal Menus
Childrens Menu
LOUNGE BAR
Full Service Bar
LIVE MUSIC
5 Nights A Week At Both Locations
TEAM TRIVIA
Tuesday Night/Charleston
Wednesday Night/Mt. Pleasant
ADDITIONAL SERVICES
Full Service Catering
ATTIRE
Casual
RESERVATIONS
Not Taken
SMOKING
Section Available
VALET PARKING
HANDICAP FACILITIES
CREDIT CARDS
American Express
Visa
Master Card
Discover Card

Dining Room at Woodlands

For an exceptional dining experience, we invite you to visit this unique dining room located at Woodlands Resort & Inn a beautiful 1906 classic revival home. Meet our talented culinary team and enjoy the exuberant masterpieces that flow from the kitchen of the only AAA Five Diamond, award-winning dining room in South Carolina. The menus, according to Esquire Magazine, "blend modern concepts with traditional fare." John Mariani recently mentioned Woodlands as among the most acclaimed restaurants in the United States. Executive Chef, Ken Vedrinski has reached a new summit of excellence and creativity.

Gourmet Magazine praises Woodlands' kitchen for "innovative Lowcountry cooking with a sophisticated international accent." Chef Vedrinski has been featured at the James Beard House in New York and has shared the stage and kitchen with bright luminaries of the culinary world, such as Paul Bocouse, Jeremiah Tower, Todd English, Elizabeth Terry, Andre Jaeger, Joseph Matter and Lea Linster. *Wine Spectator* has awarded Woodlands' its Best of Award of Excellence.

With this unique combination of talent, ambiance and elegance, Woodlands' dining experience becomes unforgettable.

ADDITIONAL SERVICES
Full Service Catering
Private Parties
Banquet Facilities
Lodging
Private Rooms
Meeting Facilities
Spa Services
Leisure Activities

ATTIRE
Jacket Required (Dinner Only)

RESERVATIONS
Suggested

SMOKING
Available On Porches and Terrace

VALET PARKING

HANDICAP FACILITIES

CREDIT CARDS
American Express
Visa
Master Card
Discover Card
Diners Club Card
Carte Blanche

CHECKS
Accepted

AAA Five Diamond Award

1999 BEST OF AWARD OF EXCELLENCE
Wine Spectator

1999 GRAND AWARD WINNER
Andrew Harper Hideaway Report

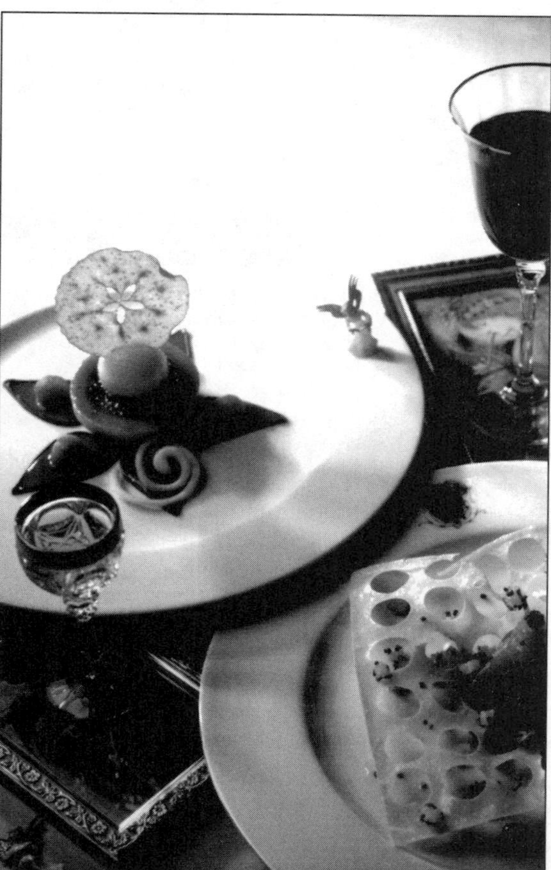

~Sample Tasting Menu~

Sashimi of Bluefin Tuna and Crispy Maine Calamari with Mint & Thai Chilis
"Sauvignon Blanc, Matanzas Creek, Sonoma Valley, 1996"

Seared Mignon of Foie Gras with a Salad of Smoked Duck, Fresh Figs, and Roasted Mushrooms
"Pinot Noir, Ph Leclerc, Bourgogne "les Bons Batons, 1993"

Roast Loin of Rabbit, Confit of Artichokes, Cerignola Olives and Blood Oranges
"Cabernet Sauvignon, Monticello, Napa Valley, 1995"

Warm Spiced Crepes, Roasted Winter Fruits, Pomegranate-Maple Ice Cream
"Moscato Bianco, Gato Selvaggio, California 1997"

Chef's Tasting...$89.00

The Dining Room at Woodlands is committed to using absolutely the best ingredients available. Our menu changes daily to utilize ingredients at their utmost peak.

Dining Room at Woodlands

SUMMERVILLE
125 Parsons Rd.
Summerville, SC 29483
PHONE
(843) 875-2600
FAX
(843) 875-2603
WEBSITE
www.woodlandsinn.com
HOURS
Breakfast
7:00 am-10:00 am
Lunch
11:00 am-2:00 pm
Dinner
6:00 pm-Until
MEALS SERVED
Breakfast
Lunch
Dinner
CUISINE
American, Contemporary
Regional, Asian
DINING INFORMATION
Terrace/Patio Dining
Vegetarian Meals
Seasonal Menus
Extensive Wine Menu
LOUNGE BAR
10:00 am-Until
LIVE MUSIC
Piano
Friday-Saturday
6:30 pm-11:00 pm
DANCING
During Special Event
(New Years Eve)

~First Course~

Trofie Noodles with Sweetbreads, Maine Cape Scallops and Zucchini

Chilled Butterbean Soup with Preserved Lemon, Truffle Oil and Warm Lobster Salad

Grilled Fresh Atlantic White Shrimp and Yukon Gold Potato Puree and Pinot Noir Sauce

Potato Crusted Lump Crab Cake with Confit of Fennel and Gewurztraminer Reduction

Smoked Carpaccio of Buffalo with Parmesan Tuile, Micro Arugula, and Intenso Olive Oil

Small Stack of Sour Cream Pancakes with Applewood Smoked Salmon, Osetra Caviar and Horseradish Citrus Syrup

Roasted Breast of Palmetto Quail with Organic White Grits, fresh Crepes and Salsify

Seared Foie Gras and Wild Game Spring Roll with Ginger Pink Peppercorn "Sweet and Sour"

~Salad and Intermezzo~

Green Apple Rosemary Granité

Caesar Salad with Hearts of Romaine and Truffled Boschetto Cheese

Goat Cheese "Cheese Cake" with Pecan Oil and Late Summer Lettuces

~Main Course~

Sauteed Local Black Bass in Duck Prosciutto with Shellfish Risotto, Artichokes and Fennel Broth

Roasted Rare Bluefin Tuna with Chinese Black Bean Sauce, Yellow Wax Beans and Long Life Noodles

Roasted Rack of Summerfield Farms Lamb with Whole Wheat Cous Cous, Asparagus and Zinfandel Reduction

Roasted Breast of Amish Poussin with Pearled Pasta, Wild Huckleberries and Pomegranate Jus

Grilled Medallion of Naturally Raised Veal Foi Gras Fingerling Home Fries

Asian Spiced Crispy Whole Maine Lobster with Stir Fry of Baby Vegetables

~Dessert~

Tahitian Vanilla Crème Brulee

Housemade Ice Creams or Sorbets

Caramelized Pear Napoleon, Fig Crisps, Sourwood Honey-Crème Fraiche Ice Cream

Milk Chocolate Peanut Butter Torte Caramelized Bananas and Banana Crunch Ice Cream

Bourbon Chocolate Torte, Candied Pecans and Dried Apricot Compote

Selection of Local Egg Farm Dairy Cheeses

$56.00 for Four Courses

Tasting Menu Available Each Evening
$89.00, Five Courses With Matching Wine

Chef's Table Available
Tuesday–Thursday $120.00

Recipes

Recipes

Appetizers

Chef Stephen Kish

McClellanville Crabcakes

Ingredients:

1 lb	Lump Crabmeat
1/2 C	Mayonnaise
2	Green Onions Chopped Fine
2 dashes	Tabasco
1dash	Worchestershire Sauce
1/2 C	Coarse Bread Crumbs
1/2 oz	Fresh Lemon Juice
1/2 t	Ground Thyme

Method:
- Combine above ingredients thoroughly, then form into desired cake size about 4 oz.
- Make egg wash of 2 eggs and 1/4 half and half.
- Dip cakes in egg mixture, then roll in more bread crumbs.
- Sauté in butter or olive oil until golden brown.

Chef Arthur Godinez

Charleston Crab House Crab Dip

Serves 20-25 people

Ingredients:

1 lb	Special Crab Meat (Lump)
8 oz	Machine Pick (Claw)
1 C	Minced Celery
5 C	Mayonnaise
1 C	Shredded Cheddar
2 C	Shredded Mozzarella
2 t	Onion Powder
2 t	White Pepper

Method:
- In a medium size mixing bowl add the special/machine pick crab meat (pick for shells).
- Remove any excess water
- Mince 2 celery stalks and strain. Add to crab meat.
- Add the cheese and seasonings to the crab meat.
- Add the mayonnaise and mix well.
- Refrigerate.

Presentation:
- Using a small oval, place a full piece of leaf lettuce covering on half of the tray.
- Using a 5 oz. disher (scoop) place the crab dip over the leaf lettuce.
- Place (8) salad crackers on the other half of the plate.
- Place a spread knife between the crab dip and crackers.
- Sprinkle Paprika over the crab dip.
- Serve cold.

Chef Jeff Lanzaro

Dry Cured Smoked Salmon Appetizer with Wasabi Cream

Yields: 15-20 hors d'oeuvres

Dry Cure Mix:

6 1/2 oz	Kosher Salt
3 oz	Brown Sugar
1/2 t	Garlic Powder
1/2 t	Onion Powder
1/2 t	Nutmeg
1/2 t	Ground Sage
1/8	Ground Thyme

Method:
- Mix Ingredients thoroughly.

Salmon:

4-5 lbs	Side - Skin On - Pin Bones Removed
1/4"	Dry Cure on Salmon

Method:
- Cure for 8 hours.
- Wash off salmon, let dry in cooler 4 hours or overnight (leave uncovered)
- Smoke at 100^{0} for approx. 2 hours or until salmon is medium (140 degrees internal temp.)

Wasabi Cream:

1 1/2 oz	Wasabi Powder
1/2 C	Heavy Cream
1 1/4 oz	Sour Cream
1/4 C	Rice Wine Vinegar
1/4 C	Water (to thin if necessary)

Serve With:
- Garnish plate with baby greens and fresh tomatoes and a few crackers.

Restaurant

Chef Peter Thomason

Artichoke and Parmesan Crusted Jumbo Prawns with Sweet Basil Tomato Caper Beurre Blanc

Yields: 4

Ingredients:

12	Jumbo Prawns peeled & deveined. (Marinate in basic garlic, olive oil, salt and pepper)

Ingredients for Artichoke Mix:

2	Small Cans Artichoke Hearts crushed fine.
1 C	Mayonnaise
1 C	Parmesan Cheese
2 t	Fresh Garlic
1 T	Fresh Parsley
1/2 C	Chopped Scallions
2 T	Extra Virgin Olive Oil

Method:

- Put in bowl and mix into paste and set aside.

Ingredients for Beurre Blanc:

2 C	White Chablis Wine
2 T	Shallots, minced
1 C	Heavy Cream
1 lb	Butter
1/4 C	Tomato, diced
1/4 C	Capers
1 T	Basic Chiffonade
1	Fresh lemon, juiced
1 T	Sugar
	Salt and Pepper to taste

Method:

- Slowly reduce wine with shallots until about evaporated.
- Top with cream and reduce slowly by 3/4. Be careful not to scorch.
- Cut butter into small cups and whisk into reduced cream, 3 squares at a time. Leave heat on low.
- After butter is whisked in add tomato, capers, chiffonade, lemon juice, sugar, salt and pepper to taste.
- Hold sauce in saucepan over warm oven.

Savannah Dip

Serves : 6

Ingredients:

6 Packs	Stouffers Creamed Spinach
3/4 lb	Shredded Mozzarella Cheese
1 can	Campbell's Cream of Mushroom Soup
2 C	Chopped Artichoke Hearts
1/2 t	Garlic Powder

Method:

- Thaw creamed spinach.
- Add all ingredients into 8'x12' casserole dish and mix.
- Heat at 250^0 for 15-20 minutes (or until hot).

S·A·R·A·C·E·N

Chef Charlie Farrell

Blue Cheese Fondue

Ingredients:

1/4 C	Port Wine
1 1/4 C	White Wine
2-4 T	Lemon Juice
1/4 C	Heavy Whipping Cream
1/2 C	Roasted Garlic
22 oz.	Blue Cheese
	Nutmeg and Pepper to Taste

Method:

- Reduce port & white wines to 3/4 cup.
- Add heavy cream.
- Add lemon juice and seasonings.
- Puree roasted garlic and add to above.
- Add blue cheese and refrigerate.

LOCKLEAR'S

Chef Lance Howard

Bulls Bay BBQ Corn Oysters

Serves 2 or Appetizers for 4

Ingredients:

1 C	Corn Fritter
1 T	Butter
1 C	BBQ Sauce
1 C	Confetti Sauce
1 C	Cajun Cream Sauce
1.5 C	Oyster (fresh shucked)

Ingredients For Corn Fritter:

1	Egg
3 T	Milk
2 T	Flour
1 dash	Tabasco
1/2 C	Corn (fresh stripped off the cob or frozen)
1 T	Red Bell Pepper (diced small)
1 T	Green Onion (sliced)
1	Jalapeno (diced small)

Method:

- In a mixing bowl combine egg and milk and whisk together.
- Fold in remaining ingredients.

Ingredients For BBQ Sauce:

3	Strips Bacon (chopped)
1 T	Red Onion (diced small)
1 T	Red Bell Pepper (diced small)
1 T	Green Bell Pepper (diced small)
3/4 C	Ketchup
1 t	Brown Sugar
	Salt and Pepper to taste

Method:

- In a skillet brown off bacon and add onion and bell pepper.
- Sauté until tender and add remaining ingredients.
- Correct seasoning to taste.

Ingredients For Cajun Cream Sauce:

1 T	Clarified Butter*
1	Shallots
1 T	Flour
1/2 C	White Wine
3/4 C	Heavy Cream
1 t	Dijon
	Blackened Spice, to taste
1 T	Sour Cream

Method:

* Clarified butter is produced by slowly heating whole butter and retaining the clear yellow liquid and discarding the rest. Using clarified butter will allow cooking at higher temperatures without burning.

- In medium size sauce pan heat clarified butter and shallots and cook until translucent.
- Add flour and stir until smooth.
- Add wine and stir until smooth then slowly incorporate the heavy cream.
- After sauce begins to thicken add dijon mustard and blackened spice.
- Cook until creamy and smooth to the taste and add sour cream.

Ingredients For Confetti Sauce:

This recipe should produce a light sauce with a multitude of shapes and color. Take time when dicing vegetables so as to attain a uniform cut.

1 T	Clarified Butter
1	Shallot
1 T	Carrot (diced small)
1 C	Chardonnay or other Preferred White Wine
1 T	Mushroom (cap only, diced small)
1 T	Red Bell Pepper (diced small)
1 C	Oyster Liquor*
1 T	Corn Starch
	Salt and Pepper to taste
1 T	Green Onion Sliced

Method:

- In a medium size sauce pan heat butter and add shallots and carrots.
- Sauté until carrots are tender without browning.
- Add wine and reduce by half, this will intensify flavor while it cooks out the alcohol in the wine.
- Add mushrooms, red bell pepper and oyster liquor and reduce by half again.
- The overall volume should be one cup and the consistency should be that of thin syrup.
- Season with salt and pepper and add sliced green onion last so a to retain the fresh green color.

*Oyster liquor is produced by the oyster itself after it is shucked. If you buy your oysters in a pint it will be the liquid surrounding them.

Method:

- Using a counter top griddle set temperature to 375^0 and allow to warm. In place of a griddle you can use a non-stick skillet.
- Pour your corn fritter mixture onto the buttered griddle forming four equal sized fritters.
- Allow to brown on both sides, remove and keep warm.
- Heat all three sauces separately and shuck the oysters.
- Add oysters to the BBQ sauce and allow to simmer, be careful not to overcook or the oyster will be tough and chewy.
- Take two heated dinner plates and divide the confetti sauce on each.
- Place one corn fritter on the center of each plate and spoon one fourth of the oysters on each fritter, place a second fritter over the oysters and place the remaining oysters on the top of each.
- Drizzle the tops with cajun cream sauce.
- I like to garnish with fried onions or fresh herbs and lemon.

Chef Ken Vedrinski

Butternut Squash Soup

Servings: 4-6

Ingredients:

1	Large Butternut Squash, peeled, seeded, diced and cubed (1 inch cubes)
1	Large, Sweet Onion, chopped
1	Leek (white), chopped
1 qt	Chicken Stock
1 C	Crème Fraiche or Whipping Cream
3	Strips of Smoked Bacon
	White Pepper to taste
	Salt to taste
2 T	Organic Honey
3	Stalks of Celery, peeled and chopped

Method:

- Sauté sweet onion, bacon, and celery.
- Add peeled and seeded butternut squash and chicken stock.
- Simmer until squash is soft; add heavy cream, salt, white pepper, and honey.
- Blend together and pass through strainer.
- Garnish with chives and pancetta or smoked duck.

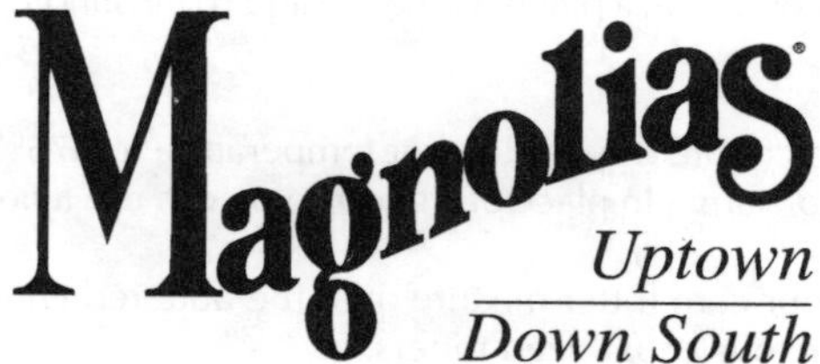

Chef Donald Barickman

Creamy Tomato Bisque with Lump Crabmeat and a Chiffonade of Fresh Basil

Yields: 8-10 oz. servings

Ingredients:

1/4 C + 1 t	Extra Virgin Oilive Oil
1/2 C	Chopped Yellow Onion
1 t	Chopped Garlic
1/2 C	Flour
3 C	Chicken Broth
1	Chicken Bouillon Cube
4 C	Homemade Tomato Sauce or 2 14 1/2 oz. Can of Tomato Juice
3/4 C	Thinly Sliced Fresh Basil loosley packed
1 C	Heavy Cream
1/2 t	Salt
	Dash of White Pepper
8 oz.	Fresh Lump Crabmeat picked clean of all shell

Method:

- Heat the olive oil over medium heat in a heavy-bottomed stockpot.
- Add the chopped onion and garlic.
- Sauté for 2 to 3 minutes, stirring until the onions are translucent.
- Reduce the heat and make a roux by adding in the flour and stirring until well combined.
- Continue to cook over low heat for 5 minutes stirring constantly.
- Turn heat up to medium and add 1 1/2 cups of the chicken broth, stirring vigorously.
- Keep stirring constantly until the broth begins to thicken and is smooth.
- Gradually add the remaining 1 1/2 cups of chicken broth and the bouillon cube, stirring constantly until the broth re-thickens.
- Reduce heat to low and simmer for 5 minutes to cook out the starchy flavor.
- Add the tomato sauce, tomato juice, chopped tomatoes and 1/2 cup sliced basil.
- Simmer for 10 minutes.
- Skim off any foam that may collect on the top.
- Add the heavy cream.
- Bring to a simmer and skim again if necessary.
- Taste and add the salt and pepper if desired.
- When ready to serve, warm the soup bowls.
- Divide the hot soup mixture between the eight bowls.
- Garnish by sprinkling the crabmeat and the remaining 1/4 cup basil over the soup.
- Serve at once.

Chef Donald Barickman

Horseradish Fried Oysters with a Salad of Baby Spring Greens and a Tomato Vinaigrette

Serves 4

Ingredients:

24	Select oysters
1 1/2 C	Flour
2	Eggs
8 T	Horseradish, Prepared, squeezed of all juices
1 1/2 C	Bread Crumbs

1/2 C	Parmesan Cheese
1 t	Black Pepper
1 t	Salt
48 oz	Peanut or Vegetable Oil
6 oz	Baby Spring Lettuces (Found in speciality grocery stores)

Method:

- Wash the oysters 2-3 times in cold water to remove all of the dirt from the shell.
- Shuck the oysters and drain them of all of their liquid, reserve.
- Assemble the breading for the oysters by placing the flour in a separate container.
- Squeeze the horseradish of all of its juice and mix together with the eggs, and keep in a separate container.
- Mix together the bread crumbs, parmesan, salt and black pepper for the final stage of the breading process and keep in a separate container.
- Wash and spin dry the lettuces. Reserve
- Bread the oysters by first placing 4 oysters in the flour until well coated. Shake off all of the excess.
- Then dip them in the horseradish and egg mixture.
- Finally dip them in the bread crumb mixture, toss around until all of the oysters are completely coated.
- Continue this process until all of the oysters are breaded.
- Toss the lettuce with half of the vinaigrette and place an equal amount in the center of four plates.
- Gently place the oysters in the hot oil one at a time up to 12 each. Fry for less than a minute until they are golden in color.
- Continue to do so until all of the oysters are cooked.
- Place them immediately on absorbent paper and keep warm.
- Place the oysters around the salad and drizzle some of the remaining vinaigrette around.
- Serve immediately.

Ingredients For Vinaigrette:

1 T	Dijon Mustard
2 oz	Cidar Vinegar
3 oz	Extra Virgin Oilive Oil
3 oz	Salad oil
1 T	Red Onion, minced
1 T	Red Pepper, minced
1 T	Parsley, minced
1 C	Tomatoes, peeled, seeded and diced
1/2 t	Garlic, minced
	Salt and pepper to taste

Method:

- In a small stainless steel or glass mixing bowl, mix together the mustard and the vinegar to combine.
- Mix the oils together and place in a pourable cup.
- Starting with a slow steady stream, whip the oil into the mustard and vinegar mixture using a wire whisk.
- Do not add the oil too fast or the emulsion will not take place.
- When all of the oil is incorporated, add the minced vegetables, herbs and spices.

To Serve:

- Pour the oil into a heavy bottomed pot and heat gradually to 350 degrees. A candy thermometer works well to see how hot your oil is.

Chef's Dan Keagan and Jim Barcelo

Vickery's Oyster Bisque Recipe

Servings: 1

Ingredients:

2 T	Scallions (chopped, green part only)
1 T	Tomato, diced
2 T	Whole Kernel Corn (Frozen is OK)
	Salt and Pepper to Taste
10 oz	Heavy Cream
Dash	Favorite Hot Sauce
6	Oysters
1 T	Oyster Liquor
1/2 t	Unsalted Butter

Method:

- Sauté scallions, tomato, corn and salt and pepper to taste.
- Sauté until corn is just turning in color to darker yellow.
- Add heavy cream and dash of your favorite hot sauce.
- Reduce by half.
- Add 6 oysters with tablespoon of oyster liquor.
- Bring to second boil and serve with 1/2 teaspoon of butter on top (optional).

Sermet's CORNER

Chef Sermet Aslan

Sermet's Calamari Salad

Yields 2 Servings

Ingredients:

5 oz	Cleaned and Sliced Calamari
6 oz	Spinach, picked and washed
3 T	Balsamic Vinegar
1 T	Fresh Chopped Mint
2 T	Capers
1 t	Lemon Zest
	Juice of 1 Lemon
3 T	Extra Virgin Olive Oil
1	Large Tomato, diced
2	Green Onions, sliced
1/4 bulb	Fennel, shaved thinly
	Salt and Pepper to taste

Method:

- Combine all ingredients (except calamari, spinach, and balsamic vinegar) in a mixing bowl.
- Heat skillet until olive oil just starts to smoke. Add calamari and sauté for 1-1/2 minutes or until just cooked through. Add to mixing bowl - toss.
- Reheat same skillet, add spinach and balsamic vinegar. Cook until spinach starts to wilt. Remove and arrange on serving plates. Top with ingredients in the mixing bowl.

Chef's Jassen Campbell and Chad Campbell

Bleu Cheese Oyster Stew in a Warm Bouli

Ingredients:

1 oz	Diced Onions, Fine
1 t	Chopped Garlic
1 t	Chopped Shallot
12 oz	Heavy Cream
1 oz	Bleu Cheese
6-7	Extra Select Oysters
1 Strip	Cooked, Crumbled Applewood Smoked Bacon
1 t	Parsley, chopped
1	Small Bread Bouli

Method:
- Cut off top of bouli, remove filling to create bowl, save top.
- Bake in 350 F oven for five minutes until crisp.

Presentation:
- Sauté onions, garlic, and shallots until translucent.
- Add heavy cream and bleu cheese, reduce by 1/3.
- Add oysters, cook for 30 seconds, season with salt and pepper.
- Pour stew in bouli, garnish with bacon, parsley, and crumbled bleu cheese; lay top halfway across bouli.

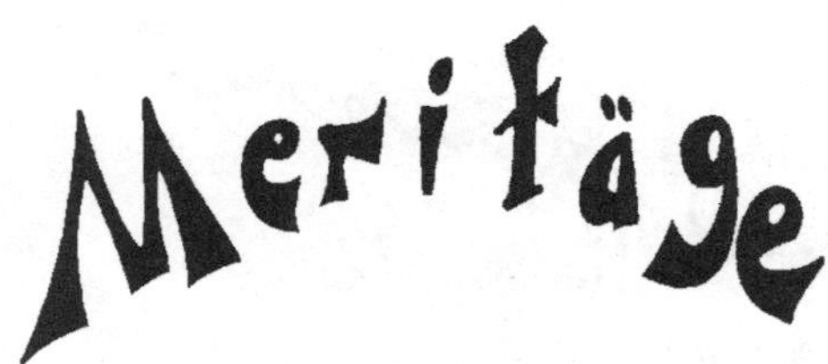

Chef John Olsson

Grilled Beef Salad

Ingredients:

2 lb	Sirloin butt cut into 2 inch thick slices
1/2 C	Soy Sauce
2 T	Fish Sauce
1 T	Sugar

Method:
- Combine all ingredients and marinade for several hours.

Ingredients:

1/2 C	Shallots
1/4	Bunches Cilantro
1/2 T	Coarsely Ground Dry Red Chili
1 Tbs C	Sugar
1/2 C	Fish Sauce
1/2 C	Lime Juice

Method:
- Chop the shallots and cilantro in the robot coupe.
- Mix all ingredients.
- Adjust the seasonings and reserve in a clean container.

Chef Andrew Cook

Parmesan Crusted Oysters Served Over Fresh Spinach with a Balsamic Vinaigrette

Ingredients for Spinach Salad:

2 C	Fresh Clean Spinach
4	Sliced Mushrooms
3	Pieces Diced Cooked Bacon
2 T	Sliced Red Onion (sauteed in bacon grease)
1 T	Diced Red Bell Pepper

Method:
- Toss all ingredients in mixing bowl with 3 oz vinaigrette

Balsamic Vinaigrette (Mix in order listed):

1/4 C	Balsamic Vinegar
1 T	Dijon Mustard
1 T	Worchestershire
1/3	Fresh Lemon
1 t	Fresh Ground Black Pepper
1 T	Fresh Chopped Garlic
2 t	Salt
1 T	Fresh Chopped Parsley
2 t	Fresh Chopped Oregano
	Lastly slowly incorporate 1 C Olive Oil
Dredge 8-10	Select Oysters per salad in Parmesan Mixture
1/2 C	Grated Parmesan Cheese
1/4 C	Flour seasoned with salt, white pepper, granulated garlic and old bay seasoning
1 T	Corn Meal

Method:
- Sauté in preheated non stick saute pan with 1 T of olive oil until brown on each side.
- Serve atop spinach with fresh grated parmesan cheese.

Chef Robert Carter

Wild Mushroom Grits with Lowcountry Oyster Stew

Serves 4

Ingredients for Wild Mushroom Grits:

2 C	Water
1 t	Garlic, minced
2 oz	Butter
1/2 t	Salt
3 oz	Grits
1 oz	Heavy Cream
1 oz	Asiago
4 oz	Cooked Wild Mushrooms

Method:
- In medium sauce pan, bring water, garlic, butter and salt to boil.
- Whisk in grits, return to boil, stiring constantly, reduce to

simmer.
- Simmer 10 minutes, until Grits are tender, stirring frequently.
- Fold in heavy cream, Asiago and wild mushrooms.
- Set aside in warm place.

Ingredients for Oyster Stew:

1 oz	Smoked Bacon, diced in 1/4 inch pieces
1 T	Vidalia Onion, diced
1 T	Garlic, minced
2 T	Sweet Corn Kernels
2 T	Tri-Colored Peppers, diced small
2 oz	Veal Stock
2 oz	Chicken Stock
2 oz	Heavy Cream
2 T	Fresh Basil, chopped
	Pinch Salt and Pepper
16	Oysters, with liquor

Method:
- In medium sauce pan, over medium high heat, saute bacon until crisp.
- Add onion and garlic, sauté until translucent.
- Add corn and peppers, sauté 1 minute.
- Add veal stock, chicken stock, heavy cream and basil, reduce until thick.
- Add oysters and simmer just until oysters are beginning to set and are slightly curled on edges (1 to 2 minutes).
- Season with salt and pepper.
- Scoop 2 ounces of grits into middle of warm bowl.
- Spoon stew around grits and place oysters in each bowl.

Chef's Ken Vedrinski

Chilled Yellow Tomato Soup With Truffle Oil & Crayfish

Ingredients:

1 t	Truffle Oil
1 C	Lobster Stock
4 each	Ripe Yellow Tomatoes (Cored)
2 each	Roasted & Peeled Red Pepper (Brunoise)
3 each	Celery Stalks (Peeled)
2 each	Cucumber (Peeled, Euro, Brunoise)
1/2 C	Cilantro (Chopped)
1 C	Olive Oil
3 T	Aged Sherry Vinegar
1/2 C	Radish
1/4 C	Red Onion (Peeled & Diced)
	Salt & Pepper to Taste
1 each	Jalapeno (Seeded & Diced)

Method:
- Puree yellow tomato in olive oil, add lobster stock and sherry vinegar.
- Strain through medium hole china cap.
- Add vegetables and cilantro. Season to taste.
- Chill for four hours.
- To serve, add fresh crayfish and truffle oil and a touch of Crème Fraiche.

Chef Bill Brodsky

John's Island Heirloom Tomato Gazpacho

Components:
- Yellow Gazpacho
- Red Gazpacho
- Sliced English Cucumbers
- Tri Pepper Salsa
- Cilantro Sprig

Ingredients For Red Tomato Gazpacho:

30	Heirloom Roma Tomatoes
1	Peeled Seedless Cucumber
1	Red Onion, diced
16 oz	Roasted Red Peppers
4 oz	Celery (de-veined)
1 oz	Garlic, minced
2 oz	Olive Oil
16 oz	Tomato Juice (V8)
1/2 C	Red Wine Vinegar
1 t	Chili Paste
1 oz	Sugar
	Salt and Pepper

Method:
- Combine all in a processor and blend until very smooth.
- Adjust seasonings with vinegar, sugar, salt and pepper.

Ingredients For Yellow Tomato Gazpacho:

15	Heirloom Yellow Tomatoes
2	Peeled Seedless Cucumber
1	Yellow Onion, diced
16 oz	Roasted Yellow Peppers
4 oz	Celery
1 t	Garlic, minced
2 oz	Olive Oil
16 oz	Ver Jus (White Grape Juice)
1/2 C	Champagne Vinegar
1 oz	Sugar
1 t	Chili Paste
	Salt and Pepper

Method:
- Combine all in a processor and blend until very smooth.
- Adjust seasonings with vinegar, sugar, salt and pepper.

Ingredients For Tri Pepper Salsa:

1	Yellow Pepper, small dice
1	Red Pepper, small dice
1	Poblano Pepper, small dice
1 T	Cilantro, chopped
1 oz	Lime Juice
1 t	Garlic, minced
	Salt and Pepper

Method:
- Combine all and adjust seasonings.

Chef Jason Scholz

High Cotton's Fried Abbey Egg Salad With Frisée, Pickled Beets and Sherry Vinaigrette

Serves 4

Ingredients:

1 lb	Frisée
4	Mepkin Abbey Eggs (or other extra large eggs)
3 T	Extra Virgin Olive Oil
6	Slices Bacon, (fried till crisp, crumbled and kept warm)
1/2 C	Pickled Beets, diced into small cubes
	Sherry Vinaigrette

Method:

- In a nonstick or well-seasoned cast iron skillet, heat olive oil over medium high heat.
- Fry eggs sunny side up until center of yolk is set, about 2 minutes.
- Remove to a plate and keep warm.
- Toss Frisée to coat with vinaigrette and divide onto four salad plates.
- Sprinkle with crumbled bacon and beets; place an egg atop each.

Sherry Vinaigrette:

9 T	Sherry Vinegar
1	Shallot, minced
1 T	Dijon Mustard
1 T	Sugar
	Salt & Pepper Freshly Milled Black Pepper
3 T	Extra Virgin Oilive Oil

Method:

- Whisk together all ingredients except olive oil.
- Drizzle oil in slowly until incorporated.

Chef's Wayne Simms, Charlie McAdams and Kerri McGill

Crawfish Chowder

Ingredients:

1 lb	Unsalted Butter
8 oz	Onion, Small dice
2 ribs	Celery, small dice
4 medium	Cloves Garlic, chopped
3 ears	Yellow Corn
3 oz	Flour
2	Russet Potatoes, peeled, small dice
1 pint	Shrimp Stock
1 pint	Heavy Cream
1 t	Chopped Basil
1/2 t	Thyme
1/2 t	Dried Oregano
	Salt and Pepper to Taste
	Hot Sauce to Taste
1 lb	Crawfish Tailmeat

Method:

- Melt butter in a 2 quart saucepan and sweat onions, celery, and garlic until tender.
- Cut kernels off corn and add to stockpot. Save cobs.
- Add flour and continue to cook, stirring constantly for five minutes.
- Add stock, potatoes, and heavy cream. Stir until thickened.
- Add corncobs and herbs and simmer until potatoes are tender.
- Season to taste.
- Add crawfish to chowder just before serving.

Chef George Odachowski

Deep Fried Oyster Salad with Tasso Ham and a Maple Cider Vinaigrette

Yield: 2 Servings

Ingredients:

4 C	Mixed Field Greens & Romaine Lettuce
1/2 C	Tasso Ham, sliced
1 T	Olive Oil
1 C	Cornmeal
1 t	Salt
1/8 t	Cayenne Pepper
16	Large Oysters, shucked

Vinaigrette Ingredients:

1	Shallot finely diced
2 T	Dijon Mustard
1/4 C	Cider Vinegar
1/4 C	Pure Maple Syrup
3/4 C	Canola Oil
	Salt and Pepper To Taste

Method:

- Place salad greens in a mixing bowl.
- Mix cornmeal with salt and cayenne pepper.
- Prepare vinaigrette by placing shallot, cider vinegar, mustard and maple syrup in a blender.
- Blend at medium speed, slowly add canola oil until it is emulsified.
- Thin out with water if dressing becomes too thick.
- Season with salt and pepper to taste.
- Sauté Tasso ham in olive oil until slightly brown.

- Toss oysters in the cornmeal mixture to coat.
- Deep-fry until golden brown.
- Add Tasso ham to the salad greens with enough vinaigrette to coat leaves.
- Season with salt and pepper and place on two large plates.
- Place 8 fried oysters atop each salad and serve.

Chef Frank Lee

Maverick Grits

Serves 4

Ingredients For Grits:

4 C	Water
1/2 t	Salt
1 T	Butter
1 - 1 1/2 C	Stone Ground Grits
1/4 C	Cream
1 T	Butter

Method:

- Bring water, salt and 1 tablespoon butter to a boil.
- Stir in grits.
- Reduce heat to low and cook, stirring occasionally, until grits are thick and creamy.
- Approx. 40 minutes.
- Remove from heat and finish by stirring in cream and remaining butter. Keep warm.

Topping Ingredients:

8	Sea Scallops
12	Shrimp, peeled and deveined
4 oz (4 T)	Country Ham, julienned
4 oz	Smoked Pork Sausage cut in circles (can be andouille or other spicy sausage if you prefer)
4 T	Fresh Tomato, seeded and diced
4 T	Green Onion
1/8 t	Minced Fresh Garlic
	Pinch of Cajun Spice
1 T	Water
1 T	Butter

Method:

- Sauté ham and sausage in 1 teaspoon butter.
- Add shrimp and scallops and saute for 1-2 minutes.
- Add garlic and Cajun spice.
- Sauté 30 seconds.
- Add green onion and tomato. Add water.
- Finish with remaining butter.

To Assemble:

- Spoon grits onto plates in equal portions.
- Place 2 scallops and 3 shrimp per person on grits and spoon equal parts of topping over each.

Sauces

SEAFOOD & STEAK HOUSE

Chef Trace Paradise

Steamed Asparagus with Chive Sauce and Roasted Red Pepper Puree

Ingredients:

2	Red Bell Peppers
1 T	Olive Oil
1	Small Shallot, minced
1	Bay leaf
3 T	Chicken Stock
1	Small Garlic Clove, minced
2 T	Minced Chives
2 T	Heavy Cream
1/2 lb	Butter (unsalted) cut into 1/2 inch cubes
24	Spears Fresh Asparagus cut into 4 inch lengths
1 1/2 C	Dry White Wine

Method:

- Preheat oven to 400° F.
- Rub the peppers lightly with olive oil.
- Place on baking sheet and roast until they begin to turn black.
- Remove from oven, place in a bowl, and cover tightly with plastic wrap.
- Sit for 15 minutes.
- Cut open the peppers and separate the skin and seeds from the flesh.
- Discard the skin and seeds.
- Remove the peppers and chicken stock to a food processor and puree.
- Set the puree aside, keeping it warm.
- Sauté the shallot, bay leaf, and garlic in the olive oil for 3 or 4 minutes.
- Add the wine and simmer until approximately 2 tablespoons remain.
- Add the cream, and bring the sauce back to a simmer.
- Add the butter, a few cubes at a time, and stir continuously until all the butter is incorporated.
- Strain, add chives, and season to taste with salt & pepper.
- Add roasted red pepper puree to sauce, add lemon juice to taste.
- Ladle sauce onto serving plate, add steamed asparagus spears and serve as entree.
- Serve sauce with seared Yellowfin Tuna Filet.

SpiritLine Dinner Cruise

Chef's Robert Short

Tasso Ham Cream Sauce

Yields: 10

Ingredients:

2 C	Diced Tasso Ham
3 qts	Heavy Cream
1 T	Old Bay Paprika to color

Method:

- Add roux until consistency desired.

Chef's David Bucks, Mark Campese, Robbie Little

TBONZ World Famous Salsa

Ingredients:

6 16 oz	Cans Crushed Tomatoes
1	Large Onion
1 1/2	Green Bell Pepper
2 8 oz	Jars Jalapeno-Pepper Rings
1 1/2 C	Fresh Parsley Leaves
1 1/2 C	Cilantro Leaves
1/2 t	Cayenne Pepper
1/4 t	Black Pepper
2 1/2 T	Chili Powder
1/4 t	Minced Garlic
1 T	Tabasco
4 1/2 T	Hot Sauce
1 1/2 t	Salt
3/4 C	Vinegar

Method:

- Dice onion and peppers.
- Chop parsley and cilantro
- Thoroughly mix all ingredients (in the order they are listed) in a glass, stonewear or plastic mixing bowl.
- Cover with plastic wrap and refrigerate for 2 hours.
- Serve with corn tortilla chips for dipping.

Note: Do not store in a metal container, the taste of product will be altered.

Chef Frank McMahon

Roast Grouper Sauteed Mushrooms, Garlic Sage Broth

Yields: 4

Ingredients:

4 each	7 oz. Filet of Black Grouper
1 qt	Fish Fume
2 T	Shallots Chopped
2 T	Leeks Chopped
8 oz	Mushroom Stems
2	Bunches Sage
2	Bunches Flat Leaf Parsley
8 oz	White Wine
2 Heads	Garlic, Roasted
4 oz	Butter

Method:

- Sweat shallots, leeks and mushroom stems in a little butter, add roasted garlic, sage and parsley.
- Sweat further, add white wine.
- Reduce by 1/2. Strain, place in blender.
- Add about 4 oz. of butter. Salt and pepper to taste.
- Blend and strain.
- Finish with chopped sage and parsley, place mushroom saute (oyster shiitake and button mushrooms) in center of bowl.
- Place fish on top. Surround with broth.

Chef Mark Gibson

Shrimp & Blue Crab Strudel

Serves 4

Ingredients:

2 T	Whole Butter
1/2 C	Minced Shallots
1 t	Minced Garlic
1 C	Sliced Mushrooms
1/2 lb	Peeled & Deveined Small Shrimp
1/2 C	Brandy
1 T	Flour
1 C	Half & Half

1/2 lb	Picked Blue Crab
Pinch	Leaf Thyme
To taste	Salt & Cayenne Pepper
12 sheets	Phyllo Dough

Method:

- Heat butter in a large sauté pan over medium high heat until it sizzles.
- Add shallots and garlic, stir.
- When shallots become translucent add mushrooms and shrimp, stir.
- When the shrimp and mushrooms are half cooked add brandy.
- When the liquid that has accumulated reduces by half, sprinkle flour over the mixture and stir thoroughly until all flour lumps have dissolved, add half and half, stir.
- Fold in the crabmeat trying not to break it up more than necessary. Season with thyme, salt and cayenne pepper.
- Reduce the liquid until it becomes a creamy sauce.
- Chill mixture. As the mixture cools it will become thicker and will be easier to work with.
- Stack and lay out 3 sheets of dough on to a work sruface, spoon 1/4 of the chilled seafood on to one end of the dough and roll up as you would an egg roll.
- Repeat this step for servings 2, 3 & 4.
- Lay the strudels in a greased baking dish.
- Bake at 350 for about 20 minutes or until the dough becomes golden brown.

(2% milk maybe substituted for half & half)

Shrimp and Grits

Yields: 1 serving

Ingredients:

1 oz	Butter
6 oz	Shrimp
1.5 oz	Green Peppers (chopped)
1.5 oz	Yellow Onions
1 oz	Celery (chopped)
1 t	Old Bay Seasoning
2 dashes	Worchestershire Sauce
1 dash	Tabasco
2 dashes	White pepper
1/2 oz	Black Olives (sliced)
1/2 ea	Bacon Bits (chopped)
3 oz	Alfredo Cream Sauce
2 oz	Tomatoes (diced)
6 oz	White Grits
1 oz	Sharp Cheddar Cheese (shredded)

Method:

- Sauté shrimp, peppers, onions, and celery in butter.
- Add bacon bits.
- When shrimp is cooked, add worchestershire, tabasco, white pepper and Old Bay.
- Throw in black olives and tomatoes.
- Stir in Alfredo Cream Sauce and finish cooking in two minutes.
- Follow directions on grits container (use stone ground grits if available).
- Grits should be slightly thick after cooking.
- When hot, stir in cheddar cheese.
- Pour sautéed shrimp sauce over cheddar grits.

Chef Brian Dunn

Grilled Salmon with Honey Dijon Glaze

Serves: 2

Ingredients:

1 lb	Salmon Fillets
	Honey Dijon Glaze
	Red Rice
	Sauté Vegetables

Method:

- Char-grill Salmon fillets for four minutes on each side to medium rare.
- For each serving, place 8 oz. Salmon fillets on a shingle and drizzle with glaze.
- On side place red rice & vegetables. Place fresh parsley sprig on top of salmon.

Ingredients for Honey Dijon Glace:

1/8 C	Heavy Cream
1/8 C	Creole Mustard
1/8 C	Dijon Mustard (Grey Poupon)
	Pinch Ground Cumin
	Salt and Pepper to Taste

Method:

- In a mixing bowl wisk all ingredients together.

Ingredients for Red Rice:

1 1/2 C	White Par Boiled Rice
8 oz	Tomato Sauce
1/2 lb	Smoked Sausage
1/2 lb	Diced White Onion
1/2 lb	Diced Green pepper
1/2 t	White Pepper
1/2 t	Salt
1 oz	Butter

Method:

- In a double boiler melt butter.
- Sauté onions & peppers.
- Add in all other ingredients except rice and bring to a boil.
- Add in rice. Cook till done.

Ingredients for Sautéed Broccoli & Mushrooms:

6 oz	Broccoli Spears
4 oz	Baby Mushroom Caps
2 oz	Butter, Sweet Cream
1 T	Chopped Garlic
1 t	Roasted Garlic Salt
1 t	White Pepper
2 oz	Dry White Table Wine

Method:

- Steam broccoli and mushroom for 3 minutes. Let cool.
- Heat butter in a sauté pan.
- Brown garlic in butter.
- Toss in broccoli and mushrooms.
- Deglace in white wine.
- Toss with salt and pepper.

Chef Charlie Giordano

Seared Yellowfin Tuna with Roasted Red Peppers and Wasabi Caviar

Yields: 2

Ingredients:

8 oz	Yellowfin Tuna
3 each	Roasted Red Peppers - Julienned
1-1/2 C	Teriyaki Sauce
1 t	Sesame Oil
1 T	Wasabi Powder
1 T	Honey
3	Fresh Basil Leaves - Chopped
1 pinch	Black Pepper
1/4 C	Cilantro Paste
1 t	Extra Virgin Olive Oil
1	Garlic Clove - Minced
1 T	Soy Sauce
1 oz	Wasabi Caviar
1 t	Black and White Sesame Seeds
	Salt and Pepper To Taste

Method:

- Combine Teriyaki sauce, sesame oil, Wasabi powder, honey, basil and black pepper and mix well.
- Marinate yellowfin tuna in mixture for 2-3 hours.
- Sear in smoking hot sauté pan with 1 tablespoon peanut oil for 1 minute a side. Let cool in refrigerator.
- Combine roasted red peppers, extra-virgin olive oil, minced garlic and sesame seeds in small bowl. Salt and pepper to taste.
- Remove tuna from refrigerator and slice thinly.
- Place roasted red peppers on serving plate and top with wasabi caviar. Arrange sliced tuna around roasted red peppers and garnish with cilantro paste and soy sauce.

Chef Jeff Lanzaro

Braised Sea Bass with Shallots, Tomatoes and Wild Mushrooms

Yields: 1

Ingredients:

8-8 1/2 oz	Sea Bass - Cleaned Filet
1 serving	Grits
4 oz	Saffron Stock
2 oz	Roma Tomatoes - diced
1 1/2 oz	Shallots - Sliced
1 oz	Cremini Mushrooms
1 oz	Shiitake Mushrooms
1/4 oz	Fresh Garlic - Minced
1 oz	Chardonnay
1 oz	Butter
1 oz	Herb Mix (parsley, chives, basil)

Grits Cake:

- Make your favorite grit recipe, put in 1/2″ deep pan and refrigerate when cool, cut out 1 square (approx. 4 oz).

Saffron Stock:

Yields 1 gallon

1 1/4 lbs	Flounder Bones
1/2 lb	Yellow Onions
1/4 lb	Celery
1 1/2 qts	Water
1 qt	Chardonnay
46 oz	Bottle Clam Juice
Pinch	Saffron

Method:

- Put all ingredients into a stock pot except saffron.
- Bring to a slight simmer, then leave on heat for 45 minutes.
- Strain and add saffron.

Procedure:

- Season sea bass filet and brown on both sides in olive oil.
- Add tomatoes, mushrooms, shallots and garlic and sauté.
- Deglaze with chardonnay and saffron stock.
- Place in oven at 400° for approximately 8 minutes or until fish is just done.
- Do not overcook. Heat grit cake in oven until hot in center.
- Place grit cake in large bowl with sea bass on top.
- Put sauté pan back on burner and reduce liquid.
- Add whole butter, fresh herbs, and season with salt and pepper.
- Put finished sauce on top of fish.

Chef Barry Waldrop

Shrimp & Grits

Serves 4

Ingredients:

1 C	Chopped Fresh Ripe Tomatoes
1/4 C	Chopped Cooked Crisp Bacon
3	Chopped Scallions
15	Medium Size Peeled & Deveined Shrimp
1/4 C	Heavy Cream
4 C	Cooked Prepared Grits

Method:

- Reduce cream until shrimp are fully cooked with remaining ingredients.
- Salt and pepper to taste.
- Serve over grits.

Poogan's Porch

Chefs Will Ratley

Leek-Wrapped Scallop Ceviche

Serves 4

Ingredients:

16 ea.	Large Sea Scallops
2	Leeks
2	Spaghetti Squash
2 C	Orange Juice
2 T	Lemon Juice
2 T	Pineapple Juice
1/2 C	White Wine
1 T	Chopped Garlic
1/2 C	Saga Blue Cheese
2 T	Brown Sugar
1/2 C	Melted Butter
1 C	Sour Cream
1/2 C	Heavy Whipping Cream
2 t	Wine Vinegar
	Salt & Pepper

Method:

- Cream fraiche - Make one day in advance.
- In bowl, whip together sour cream, Saga blue cheese, heavy cream & wine vinegar.
- Ceviche - Make one day in advance.
- Combine scallops, orange juice, lemon juice, pineapple juice, wine & garlic.
- Steam spaghetti squash for 12 minutes.
- Slice open, lengthwise.
- Hold with towel and scoop out insides with fork.
- Toss with brown sugar & butter.
- Slice leeks 1 inch wide and 4 inches long; wrap scallops individually and grill (just to add markings).
- Dust with salt and pepper.
- Tower spaghetti squash in center of plate; place 4 grilled scallops on top and around squash.
- Ladle cream fraiche over each scallop.
- Slice leeks thin and deep-fry and place on top.

Chef Michael Lata

Shrimp and Creamy Stone Ground Grits with Country Ham Gravy

Makes 4-6 servings

Ingredients For The Grits:

1 C	Stone-Ground White Corn Grits
	Water for soaking the grits
3 oz	Unsalted Butter
2 C	Water
1/2 C	Heavy Cream
	Salt and Pepper to Taste

Ingredients For The Shrimp:

2 T	Sweet Onion, Finely Chopped
2 T	Red Bell Pepper, Finely Chopped
2 oz	Country Ham, Diced
2 oz	Unsalted Butter
1 lb	Medium Local White Shrimp (raw)
1/4 C	White Wine
1/4 C	Shrimp Stock
1/2 C	Heavy Cream (Whipping Cream)
1 T	Chopped Chives
	Salt and Pepper to Taste

Ingredients:

2	Leeks, White Part Only
2 C	Vegetable Oil

Method To Make The Grits:

- Soak the grits with more than enough water to cover.
- Stir and let settle.
- Skim the top of the water to remove any of the hulls and impurities that might float to the top. Drain off water.
- In a heavy-bottomed pot, place the grits, butter and 2 cups water and cook over low heat until all the water is absorbed.
- If the grits are still tough, add water as needed until they become tender.
- To finish, add cream and continue to cook until desired consistency is achieved. Season with salt and pepper.

Method To Make The Shrimp and Gravy:

- In a large sauté pan over medium heat, cook the onion, peppers and ham in butter until onions are translucent and tender.
- Add shrimp and cook for one minute more.
- Add white wine and deglaze the pan, continuing to cook until the amount of the mixture is reduced by one-half.
- Add the stock and cook until mixture is reduced by one-half.
- Add cream and chives and continue to cook until reduced by one-half. Season with salt and pepper.

Method To Make The Fried Leeks:

- Split leeks in half and cut in julienne slices.
- Rinse under cold water to remove any dirt that might be inside the leeks. Drain and pat dry.
- In a small sauce pot, heat the oil to 300 degrees and fry the leeks until they are light brown and crispy.

To Assemble:

- Spoon grits onto the center of each plate and place some shrimp on and around grits.
- Spoon the gravy over the top and garnish with leeks and chives.

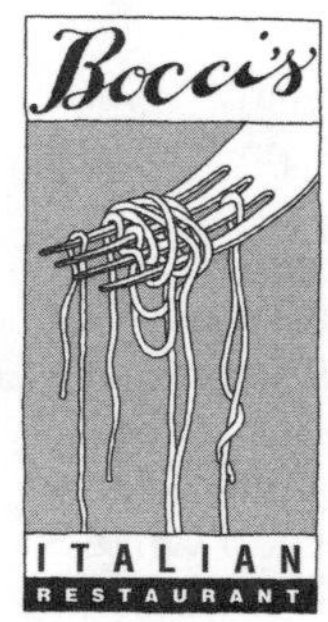

Chef Billy Noisette

Shrimp and Scallop Riso

Ingredients:

4 oz	Cooked Abario Rice
5	Large Sea Scallops
5	Jumbo Shrimp
2 oz	Julienne Red Onions
2 oz	Diced Scallions
3 oz	Diced Roma Tomatoes
1/2 T	Basil
1/2 T	Garlic
1/4 C	White Wine
2 T	Butter
	Salt and Pepper to Taste

Method:

- Sauté shrimp, scallops and red onions in butter.
- Add scallions and garlic.
- Deglaze with white wine.
- Cook for 1-2 minutes.
- Add remaining ingredients. Toss until all ingredients are warmed.
- Serve.

Chef Rose Durden

Carolina's Sweet Potato Crusted Filet of Flounder with Avocado Salsa & Blueberry Vinaigrette

Yields: 4 servings

Flounder Ingredients:

2 lb	Flounder (8 ounce filet per serving)
2 lb	Sweet Potatoes
6 C	Oil (for frying)
1/4 C	Flour
1 1/2 C	Heavy Cream
2 C	Corn Starch
	Salt & Pepper

Salsa Ingredients:

3	Avocados
2	Very Ripe Tomatoes
1/2	Red Onion
2	Cloves Garlic
3 t	Cilantro
1/4 C	Lime Juice
1/4 C	Olive Oil
	Salt & Pepper

Blueberry Vinaigrette Ingredients:

3	Cloves Garlic
1/4 C	Shallots
1/4 C	Lime Juice
1/2 C	Blueberries (may be frozen)
4 T	Dijon Mustard
1/2 C	Olive Oil
	Salt & Pepper

Method For Flounder:

- Heat oil in large heavy skillet.
- Peel and grate sweet potatoes.
- Sprinkle fish with salt, pepper and flour on both sides.
- Toss sweet potatoes with cornstarch.
- Dip fish in heavy cream; then lightly press sweet potatoes in the fish flesh.
- Deep fry fish for 15 minutes.
- Serve with avocado salsa and blueberry vinaigrette.

Method For Salsa:

- Peel and seed avocados; chop into large chunks.
- Wash, seed and chop tomatoes.
- Dice onions into small pieces.
- Chop garlic finely.
- Chop cilantro.
- In large bowl, mix all vegetables.
- Add lime juice and olive oil.
- Salt and pepper to taste.

Method For Vinaigrette:

- Peel garlic.
- In blender, puree garlic, shallots, lime juice and blueberries until smooth.
- Strain to remove seeds.
- Whisk in mustard and olive oil.
- Salt and Pepper to taste.

Chef Douglas Hepburn

Crab Crusted Grouper with Citrus Dijon

Serves 4

Ingredients:

4 ea.	6 oz. Grouper Fillets
	Crab Mix
3 oz	Fresh Crab Meat
5 T	Mayonnaise

2 T	Red Bell Pepper (fine dice)
2 T	Green Onions (sliced thin)
2 T	Celery (fine dice)
2 t	Parsley (chopped)

Method:
- Combine all ingredients and mix well.
- Refrigerate until ready to use.

Ingredients For Citrus Dijon Sauce:

1 C	Orange Juice
1 T	Shallots (minced)
3/4 t	Fresh Grated Ginger
1/2 C	White Wine
1/4 t	Whole Black Pepper
1/2 C	Heavy Cream
1/2 lb	Unsalted Butter
2 T	Dijon Mustard
	Salt and Pepper to Taste

Method For Batter:
- Combine orange juice, white wine, shallots, ginger and peppercorns in a stainless steel pot.
- Heat on medium and reduce until slightly syrupy.
- Add the heavy cream and reduce again until thick.
- Reduce heat and slowly add the butter a little at a time while stirring constantly.
- When butter has melted into sauce, remove from heat.
- Strain the sauce.
- Add the mustard and season with salt and pepper.
- Keep warm but do not let boil.
- Lay out Grouper filets and season with salt and pepper.
- Spread the crab mix evenly over the 4 fillets.
- Place the fish on a greased baking pan and place into a 350 degree oven for 8-10 minutes or until the fish is flaky.
- Serve over rice, pasta or potatoes.

Chef James Burns

Crispy Coconut Shrimp With A Spicy Pineapple Glaze

Yields: 4 servings

Ingredients:

20	Large Shrimp (peeled, de-veined and butterflied)
1 C	All Purpose Flour
1/3 C	Corn Starch
2	Eggs
	Salt, Pepper and Cayenne Pepper To Taste
2 C	Coconut Milk
4 C	Shredded Coconut Flakes
1 C	Japanese Style Bread Crumbs

Method For Batter:
- Combine flour, corn starch, seasoning and eggs. Mix well.
- Whisk in coconut milk to proper consistency. (Like pancake batter, may need to add water)
- Dip shrimp in batter.
- Press into coconut breadcrumbs mix.
- Repeat until all shrimp are coated.
- Fry in 350 degree oil until golden and crispy.

Ingredients For Spicy Pineapple Glaze:

1/4 C	Minced Garlic
1/4 C	Minced Ginger
1/4 C	Minced Shallots
2	Whole Pineapple (peeled and chopped)
2 C	Clam Juice
1/2 C	Rice Vinegar
	Salt, Pepper and Red Pepper Flakes to Taste
	Sugar as needed to sweeten

Method For Batter:
- Sweat garlic, ginger and shallots until tender.
- Add pineapple and cook for 5 minutes.
- Add juice, vinegar and seasoning.
- Cook for 10-15 minutes.
- Blend with hand mixer.
- Adjust seasoning.
- Let cool.
- Serve at room temperature.

Chef Eric Richards

Linguine with Shrimp, Artichoke, Tomato and Goat Cheese, White Wine Butter Sauce

Yields: 4-6

Ingredients:

1 #	21-25 Shrimp Peeled & DeVeined
8	Artichoke Hearts
1	Vine Ripe Tomato Diced
1/2 C	Sliced Shiitake Mushrooms
8	Large Leaves of Basil
	Pinch of Red Pepper
	Pinch Kosher Salt
4 T	Garlic Butter
4 oz	White Wine
3 oz	Chicken Stock
8 oz	Cooked Linguine
4 T	Real Butter
2 oz	Goat Cheese

Method:
- Heat garlic butter until melted.
- Add shrimp and cook until just pink.
- Add artichokes, tomato and shiitake mushrooms, cook for about one minute.
- Add white wine and chicken stock.
- Cook for one minute.
- Add butter, salt, red pepper & basil.
- Simmer, do not let come to a boil.
- Place over linguine and add goat cheese on top.

Chef Frank Lee

Pecan Crusted Black Grouper, Warm Green Tomato and Shiitake Mushroom Salad, Fried Sweet Potato Shoestring

Ingredients for Grouper:

2 oz	Pecan Chopped
1 oz	Breadcrumbs
1 C	Buttermilk
	Salt and Pepper
6 oz	Grouper Tranche

Method:

- Season Grouper with salt and pepper, flash sear in hot saute pan on both sides for two minutes. Remove from pan, place fish in buttermilk then in breading mix.
- Finish bake the fish in oven for 3-4 minutes.

Ingredients for Salad:

2 ea.	Green Tomatoes in Small Cubes
3 oz	Shiitake Mushroom in Small Cubes
1 T	Shallots, Diced
1 t	Garlic, Chopped
1/2 t	Chopped Rosemary
1 T	Sherry Wine Vinegar
1/2 T	Vegetable Oil
	Salt and Pepper

Method:

- Sweat shallots in oil until translucent, add garlic.
- Sweat 10 more seconds, add tomatoes and mushroom, rosemary, deglace with vinegar, season with salt and pepper

Ingredients for Garnish:

1 ea	Sweet Potato peeled cut in Shoestring
	Peanut Oil for Frying

To Assemble:

- Place salad in middle of plate, with vinaigrette as sauce Grouper on top and garnish with fried sweet potato stacked up.

LOUIS's

Restaurant

Chef Louis Osteen

McClellanville Lump Crab Cakes with Whole-Grain Mustard Sauce

Yields: 6 4-ounce dinner portion crab cakes

Ingredients For The Crab Cakes:

1 C	Best Quality Mayonnaise
1	Large Egg White
1/4 t	Cayenne Pepper
1/4 t	Seafood Seasoning
1/4 t	Dry Mustard
2 T	Fresh Lemon Juice
3 T	Extra Fine Cracker Meal
1 lb	Lump Crabmeat or 3/4 lb Crabmeat and 1/4 lb Lobster Meat (remove all shells)
1 1/2 C	Bread Crumbs
1/4 C	Peanut Oil
2 T	Unsalted Butter

Ingredients For The Whole-Grain Mustard Sauce:

1/4 C	Dry White Wine
2 T	Brandy
1 C	Heavy Cream
1/4 C	Whole-Grain Dijon Mustard
	Juice of 1/2 Lemon
	Scant 1/4 t Freshly Ground Black pepper

Method:

- To prepare the crab cakes, whisk the mayonnaise and egg white together in a small bowl until well blended.
- Add the cayenne pepper, seafood seasoning, dry mustard, lemon juice and cracker meal.
- Whisk until well blended.
- Carefully fold in the crabmeat (and lobster, if using it).
- Divide the mixture into 6 equal parts of 4 ounces each, and gently pat each portion into the round shape of crab cakes.
- Gently coat the cakes with the bread crumbs.
- Place on a platter lined with wax paper, cover with plastic wrap, and refrigerate for at least 1 1/2 hours, up to overnight.
- To prepare the sauce, combine the wine and brandy in a small nonreactive saucepan and boil over medium-high heat until there is only about 1 tablespoon of liquid left.
- Whisk in the cream.
- Reduce the heat to medium and briskly simmer for 6 to 8 minutes or until the mixture thickens slightly.
- Add the mustard and bring the mixture back to just a simmer.
- Do not boil it, or it will become bitter.
- Add the lemon juice, salt and pepper. Keep the sauce warm on the back of the stove until ready to serve.
- When ready to serve crab cakes, heat the oil and butter in a heavy-bottomed sauté pan over medium-high heat.
- Sauté for 1 minute and 45 seconds on each side, turning once.
- The cakes will be nicely browned on the outside but still very moist and creamy on the inside.
- When cooked, drain the cakes briefly on paper towels.
- Serve immediately with the mustard sauce or keep warm in a 200° F oven for up t0 15 minutes.
- If the crab cakes stay in the oven longer, they will dry out.

Chef John Hewson

Pan Seared Scallops with Lobster Mashed Potatoes and Creole Buerre Rouge

Yields: 4 servings

Ingredients:

1 C	Creole Buerre Rouge
20-24	Scallops (depending upon size)
4 C	Lobster Potatoes
	Sautéed Spinach

Creole Buerre Rouge:

1 T	Tasso Ham, minced
1	Shallot, minced
1/2 C	Red Wine
1/4 C	Red Wine Vinegar
1 T	Chopped Tomato
2 T	Heavy Cream
1/2 lb	Unsalted Butter, cubed and chilled
1 T	Minced Green Pepper
1 t	Minced Green Onion

Lobster Potatoes:

4	Large Gold Potatoes
1/2 C	Lobster Butter
1/2 C	Heavy Cream, warmed
1/4 C	Chopped Lobster Meat
1 t	Chopped Chives
	Salt and Pepper

Lobster Butter:

1	Small Lobster, steamed, meat removed
2	Stalks Celery, diced
1	Medium Onion, diced
1	Fennel Bulb, chopped
1 lb	Unsalted Butter
4-5	Thyme Sprigs
	Small Bunch Parsley Stems
1	Bay Leaf
1/2 C	Brandy
1/4 C	Dry Vermouth
3 qt	Water

Method for Creole Buerre Rouge:

- Place the wine, vinegar, Tasso and shallots in a shallow pan over high heat.
- Reduce the liquid to approximately 2 tbsp.
- Add the tomato, cream and green pepper, then warm.
- Slowly whisk in the cool butter a little at a time.
- Add green onion and season to taste. Keep warm.

Method for Lobster Potatoes:

- Peel potatoes. Cut them in large pieces and put in a pot of cold water.
- Bring to a boil, then simmer until potatoes are tender and drain them until dry.
- Mash potatoes with the lobster meat, chives, butter and cream and season to taste.
- Keep potatoes warm until serving.

Method for Lobster Butter:

- Lobster butter is obtained through the process of making lobster stock.
- Briefly steam the lobster, remove all the meat, and return the shells to the saucepot with butter and aromatic vegetables.
- The shells are sautéed until they turn bright red and the vegetables begin to sweat.
- Dry vermouth, a touch of brandy and water are added to the pot and simmered for one hour.
- The broth is strained and the shells and vegetables are discarded. As the broth cools, the lobster flavored butter rises to the surface and will harden.
- Scoop the hardened butter off the surface and keep refrigerated for up to one week.
- Use the broth for soups, sauces, risotto, or even add a little to the mashed potatoes for more flavor.

Method for Scallops:

- Preheat pan.
- Season the scallops and sauté until golden and crusty on one side.
- Turn and finish cooking on the other side.
- Serve with sautéed fresh spinach with garlic.

Chef Philip Corr

Thai Tuesday Shrimp & Mussels with Sweet Green Curry

Serves 4

Ingredients:

2 cans	Coconut Milk
2 T	Green Curry Paste
1/4 C	Sugar
1/4 C	Clam Juice
1/2 C	Pineapple Juice
1 T	Fish Sauce
24	Shrimp, peeled & deveined
24	Mussels

Method:

- In a medium saucepan simmer over low heat 1 1/2 cans of cocount milk to reduce by half its volume. Add curry paste and simmer for 15 minutes then add sugar, pineapple juice, clam juice and fish sauce.
- Set aside.
- In a large saute pan cook shrimp over medium heat until just turning pink.
- Add mussels and curry sauce and cook over medium-high heat until mussels begin to open.
- Serve over steamed jasmine rice.

Chef Ginny Regopoulos

Pasta Shrimp Dijonnaise

Yield: 2 Servings

Ingredients:

6 oz	Heavy Cream
1/2 T	Minced Shallots
1/8 C	White Wine
1 T	Dijon Mustard
2 T	Mayonnaise
	Pinch of Nutmeg
	Roux
1 doz.	Large Shrimp
	Prepared Angel Hair Pasta
	Salt and Pepper to taste

Method:

- Sauté shallots and deglaze with the white wine.
- Reduce heat a little.
- Add mustard and cream and thicken to a medium consistency.
- Season with salt and pepper.
- Strain sauce.
- Sauté six shrimp per person in butter and white wine.
- Add pasta and toss.
- Remove to plate and top with sauce and fresh parsley.

Chef Bill Brodsky

Potato Crusted Diver Scallops with Peekytoe Crab Salad

Components:

- Diver Scallops (3 ea.)
- Potato Basket
- Mushroom-Tomato Duxelles
- Lemon-Tarragon Emulsion
- Pea Tendrils
- Peekytoe Crab Salad
- Heirloom Currant Tomatoes

Ingredients For Lemon Tarragon Emulsion:

1/4 C	Lemon Juice
1 T	Dry Mustard
6 ea.	Egg Yolks
1/2 t	Turmeric
3 oz	Water
2 oz	White Vinegar
3-4 C	Salad Oil
2 T	Tarragon (Chopped)
	Salt and Pepper to taste

Method:

- Combine all but oil and tarragon and blend till frothy.
- Add in oil slowly till mayonnaise like consistency.
- Add tarragon and blend 30 seconds.
- Adjust seasoning and chill.

Ingredients For Peekytoe Crab Salad:

1/2 lb	Peekytoe Crab Meat
1 ea.	Lemon Juice
1 T	Mayonnaise
1 t	Chopped Herbs
	Salt and Pepper to taste

Method:

- Combine all and chill.

Ingredients For Mushroom-Tomato Duxelles:

3 ea.	Portabellas (grilled, diced)
3 ea.	Roma Tomatoes (diced)
1 T	Fresh Basil (chiffonnade)
1 T	Balsamic Vinegar
1 oz.	Olive Oil
	Salt and Pepper to taste

Method:

- Dice Portabellas after grilling and combine with all but the fresh basil.
- Cool, add basil and adjust seasonings.

Chef Brett McKee

French Cut Veal Chop, Cannellini Bean Fricasee, Oven Dried Tomatoes, Wild Mushrooms, & Creamy Parmesan Potatoes

Oven Dried Tomatoes
Ingredients:

12	Ripe Roma Tomatoes
2 t	Sugar
1 t	Salt
1 t	Fresh Thyme, Minced

Method:
- Preheat the oven to 200⁰.
- Cut out the stem end of each tomato, halve lengthwise & carefully scrape out seeds.
- Place the tomatoes half-cut side up on a wire rack on a baking pan.
- Season with the sugar, salt & thyme, then bake in preheated oven for about 4-5 hours.
- Let cool on rack.

Mushrooms
Ingredients:

6 T	Butter
1 C	Shiitake Mushrooms, Sliced
1/2 C	Cremini Mushrooms, Sliced
1/4 C	Heavy Cream
2 T	Chives, Minced
	Salt & Pepper

Method:
- Melt 2 tbsp. butter of the butter in a medium sauté pan over medium heat.
- Sauté mushrooms until golden brown, add cream and bring to a boil.
- Add remaining 4 tbsp. of butter and cook 1-2 minutes.
- Stir in chives and season with salt and pepper.

Veal
Ingredients:

1 tbsp.	Butter
4	12-14 oz. French Cut Veal Chops

Method:
- Meat butter in a medium skillet over medium-high heat.
- Sauté veal for about 7-8 minutes until golden brown on both sides.
- Be careful not to burn.

Chef Bob Waggoner

Slowly Grilled Veal Tenderloin Rolled in our Garden Herbs over Grits with Wild Mushrooms in a Light Truffle Jus

Serves 4

Ingredients:

24 oz	Fresh Veal Tenderloin
3 oz	Vegetable Oil
16	Baby Carrots, peeled and blanched
	Salt and Fresh Ground White Pepper to taste
1 oz	Butter
3 oz	Chopped Chives
2 oz	Chopped Chervil
2 oz	Chopped Parsley
2 C	Roasted Chicken Demi-Glaze
2 oz	Chopped Fresh Truffles

Method:
- Oil each veal tenderloin.
- Salt and pepper generously.
- Sear on all sides for one minute each on a hot grill.
- Then cook slowly on a warm side of the grill, turning frequently.
- Cook approximately five minutes for medium rare.
- Pull the hot veal from the grill and let it rest at room temperature for 3 to 4 minutes.
- Mix the 3 herbs together and roll the veal tenderloins across them.
- Slice 1/4 inch slices of veal, approximately 6 oz. per person.
- Spoon out 3 tablespoons of mushroom grits per person and layer the portions of veal over the grits.
- Heat the chicken demi-glaze.
- Add the truffles and spoon 2 to 3 tablespoons per person.
- Garnish with four baby carrots heated in a small amout of butter.

Chef's Gay and Joe Slough

Pork Tenderloin with Fresh Fig and Prosciutto Sauce

Serves 6

Ingredients:

30 slices	Pork Tenderloin
3 T	Olive Oil
1 T	Fresh Chopped Garlic
6-8	Fresh Figs, diced
1/2 C	Diced Prosciutto
1/4 C	Currants or Raisins
1 T	Butter
	Salt and Pepper to Taste

Method:

- Slice thirty pieces of pork tenderloin, pound thin and lightly dust with seasoned flour, patting most of the flour away.
- In a hot sauté pan add 3 tablespoons olive oil and 1 tablespoon fresh chopped garlic.
- Add fresh chopped figs and prosciutto ham, sautéing until a sauce develops.
- Add currants and butter.
- Salt and pepper to taste.
- Sauté the seasoned pork until white around the edges on one side, turn and sauté about another minute.
- Place on serving plate and dress with fig sauce.

Chef Peter Stone

Molasses Brine for Center Cut Pork Chops

Serves 8

Ingredients:

1/2 C	Granulated Sugar
1/2 C	Kosher Salt
3 C	Dark Molasses
2	Bay Leaves
2	Cloves of Garlic (smashed)
1 T	Black Peppercorns
2 Gallons	Tap Water
8	Center Cut Pork Chops

Method:

- In 3 gallon plastic container combine first 6 ingredients.
- Add water and stir until molasses, sugar and salt are dissolved.
- Brine pork chops for 24 hours.
- Grill pork chops and enjoy.

Chef John E. Cuff

Apple Chutney Pork Tenderloin

Serves 8

Ingredients:

8 ea.	Pork Tenderloin
2 C	Cider Vinegar
2 C	Sugar
6	Green Apples, Peel 4 and dice all 3/4 inch
1/4 C	Garlic, minced
1/2 T	Ground Ginger
	Salt to Taste
1 t	Crushed Red Pepper
1 1/2 C	Raisins
1 T	Dry Mustard

Method For The Apple Chutney:

- Boil the vinegar and sugar for 10 minutes.
- Toss in the apples and the rest of the ingredients.
- Simmer till slightly thick, but the apples still retaining form.

Method For The Pork Tenderloin:

- Clean off all fat and silver skin.
- Marinate in olive oil, garlic, rosemary, mint, salt and pepper.
- Marinate for 2 hours.
- Grill to desired doneness.

Lamb

Chef Ginny Regopoulos

Roasted Leg of Lamb over Pecan Wild Rice

Yield: 20 servings

Leg of Lamb Marinate

Ingredients:

8 to 10 lb	Leg of Lamb
1C	Red Wine
2	Bay Leaves
1/4 C	Virgin Olive Oil
10	Peppercorns
6	Garlic Clove Halves

Method:

- Marinate leg of lamb with 1 cup of red wine, 1/4 cup virgin olive oil, 10 peppercorns, 2 bayleaves and 6 garlic clove halves.
- Insert cloves - making 6 slits with a knife down the length of the meaty part of the lamb.
- Place lamb and marinate in a container with a cover.
- Refrigerate for 9 hours. Turn occasionally.
- Remove Lamb from container and discard marinate.
- Place marinated leg of lamb in an uncovered roasting pan and place in a preheated oven at 350 degrees.
- Roast to the desired temperature. Allow to cool 10 minutes before cutting.

Pecan Wild Rice

Ingredients:

8 C	Cooked Wild Rice
1/4 C	Virgin Olive Oil
2 C	Chopped Onions
2 C	Sliced Mushrooms (sautéed)
1 C	Celery
1 lb	Ground Sirloin
1 lb	Ground Lamb
1 C	Sliced Black Olives
1/2 t	Lavender
1 1/2 t	Thyme
1 1/2 t	Sage
16 oz	Fresh Pecan Halves
2 t	Worchester Sauce

Method:

- Combine the ground sirloin and ground lamb and pan fry in 1/8 cup of olive oil. Set aside.
- Sauté in remaining olive oil, sliced mushrooms, chopped onions and celery.
- Using same pan, sauté ground meats, (lamb & sirloin) adding all spices. Sage, thyme, lavender, salt, pepper and Worchester sauce.
- Combine meats and spices with cooked wild rice, sautéed mushrooms, cooked onions, celery, black olives, pecan and mix until blended.
- Bake covered until thoroughly heated at 350 degrees for 30 to 45 minutes.

Sauce

Ingredients:

	Defatted pan drippings of lamb
3 C	Chicken Stock
1 C	Red Wine
4 T	Flour
	Salt & Pepper to taste

Method:

- When lamb is roasted - reserve the pan drippings.
- Skim off fat and add 3 cups of chicken stock, wine, flour and salt and pepper to taste.

Presentation:

- Place pecan wild rice on plate, peaking rice in center.
- Slice 4 or 5 thin slices of lamb and lay around sides of the rice mound, horizontally.
- Ladle the sauce over the combination of lamb over rice and garnish with fresh mint leaves.

Chicken

"Life's Too Short to Eat Ordinary Food!"

Chef Herman McNeill

Chicken Melinda

Serves 4

Ingredients:

4	8 oz Skinless Boneless Chicken Breasts
1/2 C	All-Purpose Flour
7 T	Olive Oil
4 T	Grain Mustard
1 1/2 t	Dill Weed
1 1/2 C	Heavy Cream
	Salt and Pepper (to taste)

Method:

- Cut each chicken breast into 6 equal portions.
- In a large sauté pan, heat the olive oil.
- Dredge the chicken cutlets in flour, and add them to the hot oil.
- Sauté the chicken cutlets until they are golden brown and cooked through.
- Drain off any excess oil.
- Add mustard and dill, and sauté briefly.
- Add cream and simmer until the sauce reaches the consistency you desire.
- Season with salt and pepper.

Chef Jeffrey W. Mair

Black Molasses & Pecan Roasted Chicken

Serves 4

Ingredients:

2	Whole #3 Chicken
1/2 C	Dark Molasses
1/4 C	Pecan Pieces
1 T	Dark Brown Sugar
1/2 T	Dried Rosemary
1/2 T	Dried Thyme
2 T	Worchestershire
1 T	Kosher Salt
1 T	Coarse Ground Black Pepper
2	Lemons

Method:

- Preheat your oven to 425 degrees (convection). Place the chicken on a suitable roasting pan or sheet tray, tucking the wings under the back of the chicken.
- Mix the rest of the ingredients above in the order listed except lemons.
- This should produce a thick paste.
- Rub the chickens entirely with the paste covering all exposed areas with the seasoning, reserve the excess paste for later use.
- Cut the lemons in half and place one lemon per chicken in the cavity.
- Tie the legs of the chicken together before cooking.
- Place the chickens in the oven for a total time of 45-50 minutes checking every 15 minutes and basting with leftover seasoning paste.
- Remove the chickens from the oven when done let stand for 10 minutes and serve.

Preparation:

- Remove the string from the legs.
- Cut the breast and thigh from the chicken by cutting along the breast bone and down the rib cage leaving a semi-boneless breast and thigh still attached to each other.
- Remove the thigh bone and any rib bones that might still be attached. When you are finished, there should be a semi-boneless half chicken.
- Place your favorite starch and vegetable on the plate you are serving using one of the items to partial support the chicken half, breast side down, skin side up as too not lay flat on the plate. The chicken will be full of flavor and moist and is nicely accompanied by your favorite country potatoes and vegetables.

Beef

Chef Jeremy Butterfield

BBQ Beef Brisket with Smoked Bacon Mashed Potatoes

Serves 6

Ingredients:

5 lb	Beef Brisket
	Cayenne Pepper
4	Cloves Fresh Garlic
1 t	Cumin
2 lbs	Potatoes
6	Slices Smoked Bacon
2 T	Roasted Garlic
1/2 pint	Sour Cream
4 T	Butter
	Salt and Pepper

Method:

- Dry rub both sides of brisket with mix of cayenne pepper, crushed fresh garlic cloves, cumin, salt & pepper.
- Place brisket in smoker fatty side up & cook 12 hours at 200 degrees until tender.
- Peel and boil potatoes until soft.
- Mash together with roasted garlic, sour cream, cooked bacon slices, butter, salt and pepper to taste & serve with sliced brisket and vegetables.

Venison

Chef Massimiliano Sarrocchi

Venison Stew (Stufato di Daino)

Serves 6

Ingredients:

4 T	Butter
1	Red Onion
4 cloves	Garlic, minced
4 T	Dark Brown Sugar
3 C	Red Wine
4 T	Red Wine Vinegar
4 T	Tomato Paste
4 C	Chicken Stock
1 t	Cumin
1/2 t	Cayenne Pepper
2 T	Chopped Parsley
4 T	Extra Virgin Olive Oil
1 C	Diced Pancetta
2 lbs	Ground Venison
2 C	Cooked Pinto Beans
	Paprika and Salt to Taste

Method:

- In a large pot over medium heat, melt the butter and sauté the onion and garlic, stirring occasionally until soft, 3 to 4 minutes.
- Stir in the brown sugar and cook until onion and garlic brown.
- Stir in the red wine vinegar, tomato paste and chicken stock along with the cumin, cayenne, paprika, parsley and salt.
- Bring to a simmer and cook until reduced by half.
- Meanwhile, in a large fry pan over high heat, warm the oil and fry the pancetta until brown.
- Push the pancetta to the side and add the venison, season with salt and paprika.
- Brown the meat, stirring occasionally, until any liquid has evaporated, about 20 minutes.
- Add pinto beans and toss the mixture together.
- Transfer the meat and bean mixture to the sauce and stir.
- Simmer and cook until thickened.
- Check seasoning and adjust as needed.

Quail

Chef John E. Cuff

Southern Fried Quail with Black-Eyed Pea Chili

Serves 8

Ingredients:

1 1/4 lb	Black Eyed Peas, cooked tender
6 oz	Bacon, chopped
1 1/4 C	Onion, chopped
1/2 C	Red Bell Pepper, chopped
1/2 C	Green Bell Pepper, chopped
1 1/4 C	Celery, chopped
5 T	Garlic, minced
5 T	Shallots, minced
6 oz	Tomato, seed, chop
2 t	Cayenne
2 1/2 T	Cumin
6 oz	Tomato Paste
2 1/2 C	Cilantro
6 C	Chicken Stock
1/4 C	Roux
16	Quail

Method:

- Render the bacon and add the celery, bell peppers, and onion.
- Sauté for three minutes.
- Add the garlic and shallots and sauté two minutes.
- Add everything else but the Roux and peas, and bring to a simmer.
- Salt and pepper to taste, and add the peas - simmer ten minutes.
- Add the Roux and bring to a simmer for five minutes.
- Finish with the cilantro.

For Quail:

- Dredge in seasoned flour - buttermilk and then in flour again.
- Fry 325 degrees for three to four minutes.

Chef Jessica Cosner

Croissant Bread Pudding with Roasted Pecans and Bourbon Drunken Raisins in a Warm Coconut Caramel

For The Sauce:

1 C	Heavy Cream
1-13.5 oz	Can Coconut Milk
1-15 oz	Can Coco Lopez Cream of Coconut
2 C	Brown Sugar
4 C	Sweetened Shredded Coconut

For The Bread Pudding:

5	Whole Eggs
5	Egg Yolks
1 C	Brown Sugar
1/2 C	Granulated sugar
1 T	Vanilla Bean, scraped
2 t	Cinnamon
2 C	Heavy Cream
2 C	Jim Beam
1-1/4 C	Raisins
1 C	Pecans
2 T	Dark Caramel or 1 T Caramel Extract
8	Large Day Old Croissants

Method For The Sauce:

- Place all ingredients in heavy saucepan.
- Bring to a boil and boil for 25 minutes or until thick.
- Set aside and let cool.

Method For The Bread Pudding:

- In a small bowl, combine raisins and Jim Beam and let plump for 15-30 minutes.
- In a large bowl, whisk together eggs, yolks, and sugars and set aside.
- In a small saucepan, heat heavy cream, cinnamon and vanilla bean (scraped). Bring to a boil and pour into egg mixture while whisking constantly.
- Whisk in raisins, pecans and caramel.
- Slice croissants into 2″ cubes and stir into the egg mixture.
- Let soak for 15 minutes.
- Spoon into oven-proof bowls and bake at 350⁰ for 45 minutes or until golden.

Chef Simon Andrews

Italian Ricotta Cheesecake

Yield: 1 x 10 in cake

Ingredients:

20 oz	Ricotta Cheese
6 oz	Sugar
3/4 T	Flour
6 ea	Eggs (separated at room temperature)
3 oz	Cream
8 oz	Sour Cream
1/2 T	Vanilla Extract
1 oz	Orange Flower Water
1/2 oz	Lemon Extract
1/3 t	Salt
4 ea	Oranges (Grated for zest)

Method:

- Chill one prepared orange ricotta dough in a springform pan.
- Separate eggs and zest oranges.
- Blend ricotta cheese in a food processor until smooth and remove to a bowl.
- Add sugar, yolks, flour, cream, sour cream and extracts.
- Stir until blended and fold in zest.
- Beat egg whites separately with salt and add to ricotta mix.
- Pour filling into mould and bake at 350⁰ for approx. 45 minutes.
- Allow to cool before refrigerating.
- Serve at room temperature with fresh fruit and whipped cream.

Chef Molly Anderson

John's Island Berry Torte

Ingredients:

1/2 lb	Butter
2 C	All Purpose Flour
2 C	Sugar
1 t	Pure Vanilla Extract
2 t	Baking Powder
	Pinch of Salt
4	Large Eggs
1/2 C	Blueberries
1/2 C	Blackberries
1/2 C	Raspberries
1/2 C	Strawberries (slices)

Method:

- Preheat over to 325^0 and butter a 10″ springform pan.
- Cream butter and sugar with electric mixer (using whisk implement) until light and fluffy.
- In a separate bowl combine: flour, baking powder and salt.
- Combine the dry ingredients in the butter/sugar mixture.
- Add the eggs, one at a time, incorporating after each and scraping the sides of the bowl.
- Pour batter into springform pan.
- Place berries on top of batter.
- Place pan on a cookie sheet or jelly roll pan and bake for 50 minutes - 1 hour until cake pulls away from sides of the pan and is firm to the touch.
- Cool cake and remove from springform.

Chef Ginny Regopoulos

Lemon Silk

Ingredients:

1 T	Unflavored Gelatin
	Rind
5	Eggs
3T	White Wine
2 T	Powdered Sugar
1/2 C	Fresh Lemon Juice
2 C	Heavy Cream
	Dash of Nutmeg
3 T	Grated Lemons
1 1/2 C	Pound Cake Pieces

Method:

- Dissolve gelatin in the white wine using a double boiler for about 5 minutes.
- Heat over boiling water until hot.
- Cool until only partially set.
- Beat 5 egg yolks and 1/2 cup powdered sugar until creamy.
- In a separate bowl, beat 5 egg whites until stiff and then add the powdered sugar that is remaining.
- Whip the cream in another bowl and reserve 1/2 cup of whipping cream for garnish.
- Combine the lemon and yolk mixture and fold in the cream and egg whites.
- Place in six dessert glasses the pound cake pieces until about 1/2 full.
- Add Lemon Silk mixture and refrigerate until set (4 hours).

Presentation:

- Remove from refrigerator and garnish the Lemon Silk with the reserved whipped cream.
- Add a large fresh strawberry on top of the whipped cream.

Beaumont's Chocolate Supreme

Yeilds 8 to 10 Servings

Ingredients:

2 C	Unsweetened chocolate
1 C	Dark sweet chocolate
3/4 C	Unsalted butter
1 C	Espresso
5	Egg yolks
1 C	Heavy cream
	Lady fingers
	Grand Marnier

Method:

- Place chocolate with butter in double boiler and heat until melted. Add espresso, heavy cream and egg yolks.
- Remove from heat, place casserole in ice bath and mix by hand for 15 minutes.
- Mold pie pan with lady fingers drizzled with Grand Marnier.
- Pour chocolate mix into pan and chill overnight. Slice into wedges and serve upright on plate with vanilla cream and raspberry sauce.
- Garnish with strawberries.

Chef Jeff Gibbs

Montrechat Cheese Cake

Serves 36

Ingredients:

3 lb	Cream Cheese, whipped
2 lb	Montrechat Goat Cheese, whipped
2 Boxes	Confectioner's Sugar
2 oz	Vanilla
25	Egg Yolks
1 qt	Heavy Cream
2 C	Sour Cream

Method:

- Whip cheeses with sugar until smooth.
- Add remaining ingredients.
- Pour into greased 10" spring form.
- Bake at 275⁰ for approximately 1.5 hours.
- Cool to room temperature and refrigerate.

Chef Ginny Regopoulos

Carrot Soufflé

Yield: 6 to 8

Ingredients:

8	Large Whole Carrots, washed and cut in half
1/2 C	Sugar
2 T	Flour
1 t	Orange Zest
1 t	Vanilla
1/2 C	Heavy Cream
3	Whole Eggs, beaten
1/4 C	Confectionery Sugar
	Coconut Flakes for Garnish

Method:

- Cook carrots in water until tender.
- Drain-cool and then mash until smooth.
- Add in sugar, flour, zest, vanilla, cream, beaten and beaten eggs.
- Place in soufflé cups or small Ramekins and bake at 350 degrees for 30 minutes or until inserted knife comes out clean.
- Top with powered confectionery sugar and garnish with coconut if desired.

Chef's Molly Anderson and Stephanie Carr

Caramel Banana Buttercream Cake

Yield: 2-9 inch layers

Ingredients:

10 oz	Butter
1 lb	Brown Sugar
1 1/2 C	Sugar
6	Eggs
2/3 C	Safflower Oil
2 T	Vanilla
2 C	Mashed Bananas (about 6 very ripe bananas)
2 1/2 C	Buttermilk
5 1/2 C	Flour
1 T	Baking Soda
1 t	Salt
2	More Bananas sliced for cake filling

Method:

- Cream butter and sugars.
- Add eggs one at a time and oil.
- Add dry ingredients alternately with buttermilk.
- Fold in bananas with vanilla.
- Bake at 325⁰ 45-50 minutes until toothpick comes out clean.

Ingredients for Caramel:

3 C	Sugar
1 1/2 C	Water

Method:

- Boil until amber.
- Wisk in three tablespoons butter and add two cups heavy cream.
- Cool for six hours.

Ingredients for Buttercream:

2 1/2 lb	Butter, softened
1/2 lb	Shortening (Crisco only)
2 1/2 lb	10x Sugar
2 T	Vanilla

Method:

- Mix until well blended.

Method For Assembly After Layers Cool On Racks:

- Ice bottom layer in buttercream, pipe a circle of buttercream around perimeter of layer.
- Fill with 1/4 of caramel and sliced bananas.
- Top with second layer, ice with buttercream.
- Pipe border and top with 1/2 of caramel.
- Pipe a crisscross design on top of caramel and reserve the other 1/4 of caramel for plates.
- Enjoy.

Glossary

Glossary

Abalone
A mollusk found along the coastlines of California, Mexico and Japan in which the edible portion is the adductor muscle.

Aceto
The Italian term for vinegar.

Achiote
Paste made from ground annato seed, vinegar, salt and spices.

Aïoli
A strongly flavored garlic mayonnaise from the Provence region of southern France; the name is formed from ail (garlic) and oli (provencal dialect for oil).

A la carte
Each course is served and priced individually.

Albacore
A small tuna fish of the Atlantic and Tropical seas, which can measure up to five feet but is usually less than three feet long. Also called "white tuna" because of its rather pale flesh. It is the finest and most expensive of preserved tuna fish. Raw, it is highly prized in sushi and sashimi.

Al dente
An Italian expression (meaning literally "to the tooth") indicating the correct degree of cooking for pasta, which is still firm enough to offer a slight resistance when bitten into. The expression may also be applied to certain vegetables, such as green beans, which are served while retaining their crunchiness.

Amaretto di Saronno
An Italian liqueur flavored with almonds, apricots, and aromatic extracts. It may be used to flavor fruit, whipped cream, or consumed as an apéritif.

Amazu Shoga
Thinly sliced or shredded fresh ginger pickled in a sweet vinegar marinade and used as a garnish for many Japanese dishes, particularly sushi.

Anaheim Chile
A dark green chile about 7 inches long, mild in flavor and spice.

Ancho Chile
A broad dried and reddish brown chile about 3 to 4 inches long, ranging in flavor from mild to pungent. In its fresh, green state, the ancho is referred to as a poblano chile.

Antipasto
An Italian term for cold hors d'oeuvres, literally meaning "before the pasta".

Apéritif
A French term for an alcoholic beverage served before a meal to stimulate the appetite.

Arborio Rice
Short, fat-grained Italian rice that is high in starch and is used in risotto and other moist rice dishes.

Arrowroot
The starch extract from rhizomes (underground stems) of several tropical plants. It is so called because of the therapeutic qualities attributed to it by American Indians in the treatment of arrow wounds. Used as a thickening agent in puddings, sauces and other cooked foods, arrowroot is absolutely tasteless and more easily digested than wheat flour.

Arugula
A bitter, aromatic salad green with a peppery mustard flavor.

Asiago
A scalded curd cheese usually made from skimmed cow's milk and aged up to two years.

Aspic
A gelatin made from clarified meat, fish or vegetable stock used to coat cold dishes of meat, poultry, fish or eggs or to form a molded dish.

Au Gratin
Sauced food topped with buttered bread crumbs or grated cheese and baked or broiled until brown.

Bacalao
A Spanish term for dried salted cod. Also called bacala (Italian term).

Béarnaise
A type of hollandaise, flavored with shallots, wine, vinegar and tarragon usually served with meat, fish and egg dishes.

Béchamel
Invented in France under the reign of Louis XIV, this basic white sauce is obtained by stirring milk into a slowly cooked mixture of butter and flour called roux.

Beignet
A French doughnut, sprinkled with powdered sugar.

Belgian Endive
A specially cultivated chicory whose leaves are cut off and shielded from light, so the new pale yellow leaves grow back in their characteristic cigar shape.

Bel Paese
An Italian term for "beautiful country", this cheese is manufactured in Lombardy from cow's milk, is mild and creamy with a washed crust.

Belon Oyster
Originally from France and now aquacultured in California, Maine and Washington, this oyster is small (1-1/2 to 3-1/2 inches across) and considered superior when eaten raw.

Benedictine
A sweet liqueur named after the Benedictine monks of the Abbey of Fecamp in Normandy.

Beni Shoga
Gingerroot that has been pickled in sweet vinegar and colored bright red, used as a garnish for many Japanese dishes.

Bisque
A thick cream soup usually made from pureed fish, fowl or vegetable.

Blackened
A cooking technique made famous by New Orleans's chef Paul Prudhomme by which Cajun spice coated meat or fish is cooked in a cast-iron skillet that's been heated until almost red.

Blini
A small, thick, savory pancake made with a leavened batter that contains both wheat and buckwheat flour. In Russian cuisine, blinis are served with sour cream and melted butter as an hors d'oeuvre with caviar or smoked fish.

Bluepoint Oyster
Originally from Blue Point, Long Island, the "bluepoint" term refers to any of many small Atlantic oysters from 2 to 4 inches long. They are considered the best for eating on the half shell.

Bok Choy
Also called pak choy and white mustard cabbage, this oriental vegetable is dark green and leafy at the top and very white, crunchy and like a thick stem at the bottom. The flavor is very mild.

Bouillabaisse
A celebrated seafood stew from Provence, made with fish, shellfish, onions, tomatoes, white wine, olive oil, garlic, saffron and herbs.

Bouquet Garni
A small bundle of herbs, tied or wrapped in a

cheese cloth and added during cooking to enhance the flavor, removed before serving.

Bourguignon
Cuts of red meat prepared with red wine sauce, small mushrooms and white onions.

Braising
A method of cooking food in a closed vessel with very little liquid at a low temperature and for a long period of time.

Bresaola
Originating in Lombardy, Italy, air-dried salted beef filet has been aged for at least 2 months. Served thinly sliced with a drizzle of olive oil and lemon juice as an antipasto.

Brioche
A soft loaf or roll made from a yeast dough enriched with butter and eggs.

Brochette
A French term referring to food cooked and served on a skewer.

Bruschetta
Toasted bread rubbed with garlic and drizzled with olive oil. Served warm.

Bulghur wheat (bulgar)
Wheat kernels that have been steamed, dried and crushed. Bulghur is a nutritious staple in the Middle East.

Cafe au Lait
Strong chicory coffee, poured together with hot milk.

Cajun Spice
Generally a mixture of spices such as but not limited to garlic powder, onion powder, paprika, dry leaf thyme, salt, black and cayenne pepper and representative of Cajun Cooking.

Caldo Verde
Traditional Portuguese soup with shredded kale, sliced potatoes, linguica sausage and olive oil.

Canapé
Small decorative pieces of bread (toasted or not), crackers or pastry topped with a savory garnish and usually served as an appetizer.

Cannoli
Pastry tubes filled with cheese, chocolate or candied fruit.

Caper
This condiment is made from the flower bud of a bush native to the Mediterranean and parts of Asia. Generally pickled in a vinegar brine, capers can also be found salted and sold in bulk.

Carambola
(Starfruit) Thick-skinned, glossy fruit that forms golden star shapes when sliced. The flavor is complex, bitter sweet with hints of artichoke heart.

Caramelize
To turn sugar into caramel by slowly heating it. Alternatively it can mean coating a mould with caramel, flavoring a pudding or glazing sugar coated fruits, choux, pastry, etc. Certain vegetables, such as small onions, carrots, or turnips are "glazed" or lightly caramelized by being heated with sugar and a small quantity of water or butter in a saucepan.

Carpaccio
An Italian first course consisting of very thin slices of raw beef served cold, originally with a creamy vinaigrette sauce made with olive oil. The dish, named in honor of the Renaissance Venetian painter, originates from Harry's Bar in Venice.

Caviar
Sturgeons eggs that have been salted and allowed to mature. The three main types of caviar are Beluga, Osetra and Sevruga. The term caviar is also used to refer to other, less expensive fish roe (or eggs) such as lumpsfish caviar, whitefish caviar (also called American Golden), salmon or red caviar.

Cellophane noodles
Also called bean threads, Chinese vermicelli or glass noodles, these gossamer, translucent threads are not really noodles but are made from the starch of green mung beans.

Chayote
An avocado shaped squash.

Chicory
This relative of the endive has curly, bitter-tasting leaves that are often used as part of a salad or cooked as greens. Also used to flavor Louisiana coffee.

Chipotle Chile
Dried, smoked Jalapeño generally found dried, pickled and canned in adobo sauce.

Chorizo
A long, dry Spanish sausage, commonly made of pork and flavored with red peppers (either spicy or sweet) and garlic.

Cioppino
A dish originating in San Francisco, consisting of a stew of white fish, shrimp, clams, and mussels, with garlic, tomato and white wine base.

Clarified Butter
(also called drawn butter)
Butter which has been heated to separate the fat solids from the milk solids.

Concassé
Coarsely chopped or ground vegetables or fruit such as a tomato concassé.

Confit
A method of preserving meat such as goose, duck or pork by slowly cooking it in its own fat and keeping it in this fat which acts as a seal.

Consommé
Meat or fish stock that has been fortified and clarified.

Coulis
A thick puree or sauce usually made with vegetable or fruit.

Crawfish
Edible crustacean common to fresh water.

Créme Anglaise
A light egg yolk, sugar and milk custard sauce used in fruit or pastry desserts.

Crêpe
A paper thin egg and flour pancake served as a main course or dessert usually filled and covered with sauce.

Croissant
A light flaky pastry made of buttery dough formed in the shape of a crescent before baking.

Croustade
Pastry, hollowed-out bread loaf or pasta that is generally deep-fried or toasted and contains a thick stew, creamed meat or vegetable mixture.

Croûte (en)
Describes a food such as meat or pâté wrapped in pastry and baked.

Crustacean
Main classification of shellfish including barnacles, crabs, crayfish, lobster, prawns and shrimp.

Curaçao
A liqueur based on sweet and bitter oranges (originally it was made from the dried peel of bitter oranges from the island of Curaçao, off the west coast of Venezuela). It is now made by many liqueur houses and often sold as "triple sec".

Daikon
Japanese for "large root", this vegetable is a large Asian radish generally used raw in salads, shredded as a garnish or cooked in stir-fry and has a sweet flavor.

Dolmades
Arabic for "something stuffed", these are grapes leaves, vegetables or fruits stuffed with a filling, usually grape leaves filled with lamb, rice and seasonings.

Drawn Butter
See clarified butter.

Eclair
A light, oblong shape made of choux pastry split, filled with cream and topped with a sweet icing.

Egg Foo Young
A pancake made of bean sprouts, mushrooms and eggs with shellfish, chicken or meat, served with stock sauce.

Emmental
A Swiss cow's-milk cheese containing 45% fat, named after the Emme Valley in the canton of Bern where it was first made. It is a hard ivory-colored cheese with a good many holes and a golden-yellow to brown rind. Emmental is matured for 6-12 months in a cool cellar.

Entrée
The main dish served with a sauce and garnish. In a formal meal, it is third course following fish course.

Escabèche
Of Spanish origin, escabèche is a dish of poached or fried fish, covered with a spicy marinade and served cold as an appetizer.

Espagnole
A brown base sauce used for many other more elaborate sauces.

Farina
Flour of wheat, nuts and potatoes, very fine in texture.

Feta
Greek cheese made from goat's milk, salty.

Finocchio
The Italian word for fennel.

Flambé
Brandy or liquor added to food and then set alight.

Flan
A fruit or custard filled pastry shell.

Florentine
Dishes presented on a bed of spinach, or spinach used as a ring or topping.

Foie Gras
A goose or duck liver which is grossly enlarged by methodically fattening the bird. The top American producers of fresh duck foie gras are "Hudson Valley Foie Gras" and "Sonoma Foie Gras".

Fricadelle
Meat balls of pork and veal or beef with spices and bread crumbs, usually shallow-fried.

Fricassée
Stew made of pieces of chicken or veal cooked with vegetables and often flavored with wine.

Fritter
A small quantity of batter mixture deep-fried until crisp. The food is either chopped and mixed with the batter or dipped into it.

Fruits de Mer
A French term referring to a combination of seafood, very often crustaceans.

Fumet
A concentrated stock (usually of fish or mushrooms) that is added to a sauce or a cooking stock to enhance its flavor or give it extra body.

Galantine
A cold dish of boned and stuffed poultry or meat glazed with aspic.

Ganache
A flavored cream made with chocolate, butter and fresh cream, used to decorate desserts, fill cakes and make petits fours. It was created in Paris about 1850 at the Patisserie Siraudin.

Gazpacho
A Spanish soup, originally made with cucumber, tomato, onion, red pepper and bread crumbs, seasoned with olive oil and garlic, served ice-cold. Its name, of Arabic origin, means "soaked bread".

Génoise
Rich and light cake made with flour, sugar, eggs, butter and vanilla and used for many presentations such as petits fours, cake rolls, etc.

Giblets
Edible internal organs and trimmings of poultry and game.

Gnocchi
Small dumplings made from semolina, potatoes or choux pastry.

Goma
Japanese for "sesame seeds".

Gravlax (Gravlox)
Raw salmon cured in a salt-sugar-dill mixture.

Grenadine
Pomegranate-flavored syrup used as a flavoring, a sauce or for drinks.

Gumbo
In the Creole cuisine, thick soup or stew made with meat, poultry, fish or vegetables.

Habanero Chile
The world's hottest chile, orange in color when ripe and used in sauce, jerk spice, chile and barbecue spice.

Haggis
Scottish pudding made from sweet onions, oatmeal and a minced mixture of the sheep's organs, then stuffed into a sheep's stomach lining and boiled.

Hamman's Hats, Hammantaschen
Small triangular pastries filled with honey-poppy seed, prune or apricot and traditional sweets of Purim. A festive Jewish Holiday treat.

Hangtown Fry
Fried breaded oysters cooked together with eggs and fried bacon.

Harusame
Japanese noodles made from soybean, rice or potato flour.

Hollandaise
Egg yolks, butter and lemon juice made into a creamy sauce, served with fish or vegetables.

Hors d'oeuvre
Foods served as appetizers with a cocktail or "apéritif", as a first course, hot or cold.

Humus
A thick Middle Eastern sauce made from mashed chickpeas seasoned with lemon juice, garlic and olive or sesame oil.

Ile Flottante
French for "Floating Island", this is a liqueur-sprinkled sponge cake spread with jam,

sprinkled with nuts, topped with whipped cream and surrounded by a pool of custard.

Jambalaya
A specialty of New Orleans, inspired by Spanish paella and made of highly spiced rice, chicken and ham. Various ingredients can be added: for example, sausage, peppers, tomatoes, shrimp or oysters.

Jardinière
A French term meaning garnished with fresh vegetables, diced and cooked and arranged in separate groups.

Jubilée (Cherries)
A dessert of black cherries and ice cream, flamed with cognac.

Julienne
Food (usually vegetables or meat) cut into thin matchstick strips.

Jus
The French word for juice from fruits, vegetables or roasts (usually refers to the juices created from roasting meat and used as gravy).

Kasha
Roasted buckweat groats that have a toasty and nutty flavor.

Kedgeree
Originally from East India, this dish is made of cooked fish or meat, rice and eggs, served at breakfast or lunch.

Ketjap Manis
A thick, dark brown Indonesian sauce used for marinade or as a condiment.

Kibbeh
A Middle-Eastern dish that usually combines ground meat (lamb), bulghur wheat and various spices.

Kimchee
A hot and spicy condiment made of fermented vegetables, used in Korean cooking.

King Cake
During the carnival season in New Orleans, a special cake is decorated in Mardi Gras colors. A small bean or a tiny doll is hidden inside. When the cake is cut and served, the person who gets the special piece is then declared "King" for the evening and must host the next King Cake party.

Kumquat
A citrus fruit, yellow-orange in color with a tart orange flavor.

Langouste
A French term meaning crawfish.

Langoustine
A French term meaning prawn.

Langues de chat
A flat, crisp biscuit, finger-shaped, served with cold dessert.

Leaven
A yeast-like substance which causes dough to rise.

Legumes
Vegetables with seed pods, peas, or beans.

Lentils
Seeds of legumes soaked and used in soups, stews and in salads.

Limu
The Hawaiian word for seaweed.

Loquat
Yellow-orange pitted fruit, juicy, small and sour.

Lumpia
Philippine version of the egg roll, it consists of a filling wrapped and usually fried.

Macédoine
A colorful dish of either fruits or vegetables that are cut in small, uniform cubes and served either raw or cooked.

Mâche
Highly tender salad greens with a tangy, nutlike flavor.

Marsala
Sweet Italian wine occasionally used in cooking.

Médaillons
Small circular cuts of meat, fish or pâté.

Melba
The name of various dishes dedicated to Dame Nellie Melba, the famous 19th Century Opera singer. The best known is "Peach Melba", created in 1892 by Escoffier, when he was Chef at the Savoy in London at the time when Melba was starring in the opera *Lohengrin*. Peach Melba consists of poached peach halves on a bed of vanilla ice cream topped with a raspberry puree.

Mesclun
From a south of France dialect word meaning mixture, it is a mix of greens consisting of arugula, dandelion, mâché, radicchio, oak leaf lettuce and other greens.

Meunière (à la)
A method of cooking that can be used for all types of fish (whole fillets or steaks). The fish is always lightly floured (hence the name of the dish-meunière meaning "miller's wife") and sautéed in butter or oil. It is arranged on a long dish and sprinkled with lemon juice, then butter which has been cooked in a pan until it has turned golden brown, and garnished with finely chopped parsley.

Minestrone
Italian for "big soup", it is a thick vegetable soup containing pasta or rice. The Minestrina (Italian for little soup) is a lighter soup.

Mirabelle
A small golden yellow plum used for making preserves, tarts or liquor.

Mirepoix
A mixture of diced carrots, onions and celery used to enhance the flavor of meat, game, fish and broth or sauces.

Mirin
A low alcohol, sweet golden wine made from glutinous rice.

Miso
A Japanese condiment dressing consisting of fermented soya, made from cooked soya(soy) beans mixed with rice, barley or wheat grains and salt. Miso varies in color from a dark red to white.

Mocha
A variety of Arabian coffee bean grown on the boarders of the Red Sea, named after the Yeminite port from which they were traditionally exported. Mocha is a strong coffee with a distinctive aroma, but some people find it bitter, with a musky flavor. It is normally served very strong and sweet in small cups. Mocha is used as a flavoring for cakes, cookies, ice cream and various confections. The word is also used to describe various cakes with a coffee flavor, particularly a large genoese sponge cake with layers of coffee or chocolate butter cream (hence the association today of the word "mocha" with coffee and chocolate).

Mollusk
Shellfish such as clams and oysters.

Montmorency
"A la Montmorency" means made or served with cherries. Also the name of a popular sour cherry.

Moo shu (moo shi or moo shoo)
A Chinese dish made from shredded pork, vegetables and seasonings that are mixed and rolled in a small thin pancake.

Mousse
1.A cold dessert made with whipped cream/ egg whites, very light and sweet. 2. Savory mousses are made from meat, fish, shellfish, foie gras or vegetables by adding whipped cream, eggs and beaten egg whites and are baked in a water bath at a low temperature.

Muffaletta
A very large, round sandwich, containing a combination of thinly sliced meats, melted cheese and Italian "olive salad".

Mustard
A herbaceous plant, originating from the Mediterranean region, whose seeds are used to prepare the yellow condiment of the same name. There are three varieties: black, brown and white. Mustard has been known and used since ancient times.

N

Nan (Naan)
From East India, this little white flour bread in the shape of a leaf is traditionally baked in a tandoor oven.

Napoleon
Pastry layer cake with alternating layers of cream.

Navarin
Traditionally refers to lamb stew with vegetables, now used with many other meats or seafood.

Neapolitan
Different colored and flavored ice creams and sweet cakes in layers.

Newburg
A dish of shellfish (usually lobster) served with a cream and sherry sauce.

Niçoise (á la)
The name given to various dishes typical of the cuisine of the region of Nice, France, in which the most common ingredients are garlic, olives, anchovies, tomatoes and French (green) beans.

Nopales
Cactus paddles, which can be cooked like a vegetable and used as is, or in salsas. They are soft but crunchy, with a flavor similar to bell pepper and asparagus combined.

Nori
Paper-thin sheets of dried seaweed used for wrapping sushi and rice balls.

Normande (á la)
From the region of Normandy in France: 1. Refers to a fish dish garnished with shellfish, mushrooms and truffles and usually served with a Normande sauce (fish-stock velouté enriched with butter, egg yolks and cream). 2. Refers to traditional dishes from Normandy made with cream, butter, apples, apple cider and Calvados.

Nuoc Nam
Vietnamese for fish sauce.

Offal
Edible internal organs of meat, poultry and game.

Osso Bucco
An Italian dish of braised veal shanks with tomatoes, white wine and onions, served usually with risotto.

Paella
A saffron-flavored rice dish with chicken, vegetables, chorizo and shellfish and named for the large shallow pan in which it is traditionally cooked.

Parfait
Frozen dessert made of whipped cream and fruit puree.

Parmigiano-Reggiano:
The best Parmesan cheese, aged over 24 months and imported from the Italian regions of Bologna, Modena, Mantua or Parma.

Pâté
Refers to well-seasoned ground meat preparations that can be either smooth and spreadable or coarsly textured, served cold or hot.

Paupiette
A thin slice of meat (veal or beef) rolled around a filling.

Pavé
A large sponge cake filled with butter and cream, and coated with icing.

Pavlova
Named after the Russian ballerina Anna Pavlova, this Australian dessert consists of a crisp meringue base topped with whipped cream and fruit such as strawberries, kiwi or passion fruit.

Périgueux Sauce
Rich brown sauce flavored with Madeira and truffles and named after the City of Périgueux in Périgord, France.

Petit Four
Bite-size iced cakes or small fancy cookies that are finely decorated and highly elaborate.

Pilaf
An Eastern dish of spiced, cooked rice mixed with meat, chicken or fish.

Pine Nut
Sometimes refered to by its foreign name, (pignon *French*, pignoli *Italian*, piñon *Spanish*) these nuts are from the seeds of the cones of pine trees.

Pirogi or Piroshki
Russian turnovers.

Pith
White lining covering the flesh of citrus fruit.

Plat du jour
Dish of the day.

Poblano Chile
A large, dark green chile with a mild flavor (also called pusilliu chile).

Po-boy
A Sandwich served on long loaves of French Bread. Originally very inexpensive and filling fare, which explains the name.

Polenta
A cornmeal porridge that is the traditional basic dish of Northern Italy (both Lombardy and Venice claim to have invented it). The Greeks used to eat various cereal porridges called poltos, but corn did not arrive from America until the beginning of the 16th century. Polenta is made with cornmeal and water, cooked slowly in a large pot using a wooden spoon. In Italy the large-grained varieties of corn, which take a long time to cook, are preferred.

Poussin
The French word for a very young small chicken.

Praline
A brittle confection made of crushed almonds or hazelnuts that has been coated with caramelized sugar.

Prawn
Species from the lobster family, also called Italian scampi, langoustines (French), Dublin Bay prawns, they look like tiny "Maine lobster". The term is also used broadly to describe any large shrimp.

Prickly Pear
Also known as cactus fruit. An edible cactus with a spiny exterior and soft interior flesh. The fruit has the shape of a kiwi fruit with a melon like flavor.

Printanier
A garnish of spring vegetables, also referred to by its Italian name, "alla Primavera".

Proscuitto
Italian for ham, this term is broadly used to describe a ham that has been seasoned, salt cured and air-dried.

Provenéale (á la):
Refers to dishes prepared in the style of this French region, usually with garlic, tomatoes and olive oil.

Purée
Raw or cooked food sieved with a thick and smooth consistency.

Quenelle
A light dumpling made of ground meat or fish, used as a garnish with a rich sauce.

Quesadilla
A flour or corn tortilla folded around fillings including cheese, cooked meat, refried beans or other combinations.

Quetsch
A variety of plum used primarily to make liqueurs and can be used in desserts.

Quiche
An open tart filled with a mixture of beaten eggs, fresh cream and pieces of bacon for Quiche Lorraine but also with other ingredients such as onions, mushrooms, ham, shellfish or herbs. Its origin in Lorraine goes back to the 16th century in Nancy, France where it was a specialty.

Quinoa
Bead-shaped grain, with a delicate flavor that can be used in any way suitable for rice.

Ragoût
A thick stew of meat, poultry or fish with or without vegetables.

Ratatouille
A traditional dish from Provence, it combines eggplant, onions, bell peppers, tomatoes, zucchini, garlic and herbs, all simmered in olive oil.

Remoulade
A cold sauce made by adding mustard, gherkins, capers, and chopped herbs to mayonnaise.

Restaurant
The word appeared in the 16th century and meant at first "a food that restores" (from restaure, to restore) and then was used more specifically for a rich, highly flavored soup, capable of restoring lost strength. The 18th century gastronome Brillat-Savarin referred to chocolate, red meat and consommé as restaurants. From this sense, which survived the 19th century, the word developed the meaning of "an establishment specializing in the sale of restorative foods". Until the late 19th century, the only places for ordinary people to eat out were inns and taverns. In about 1765 a Parisian "bouillon seller" named Boulanger wrote on his sign, "Boulanger sells restorative foods fit for the Gods", with the motto in dog Latin: Venite ad me omnes qui stomacho laboretis, et ego resturabo vos (come unto me, all you whose stomachs are aching, and I will restore you). This was the first restaurant in the modern sense of the word.

Rice Paper
An edible thin white paper made from the pith of an Asian shrub called the rice-paper tree.

Rillettes
Meat, usually pork, slowly cooked in seasoned fat and then pounded or pulverized into a paste. Like a pâté, it is served cold, spread on toast or bread.

Ris
The French word for "sweetbreads".

Risotto
An Italian specialty made usually from arborio rice, that has first been sauteed in butter and then cooked by adding stock to it gradually. Risotto can be flavored with saffron and other various ingredients.

Rissole
A roll or patty of cooked minced meat or potatoes.

Roquette
The French word for arugula.

Rossini
Used to describe dishes including foie gras, truffles and a demi-glace sauce.

Rouille
Meaning rust in French because of its rust color, this spicy sauce is made of hot chiles, garlic and olive oil and generally diluted with fish stock and served as a garnish for fish and fish stews such as bouillabaisse.

Roulade
A French term for roll of meat, vegetable, chocolate cake, etc.

Roux
A mixture of fat and flour used as a sauce base.

Sabayon
The French word for Zabaglione.

Saffron
A spice consisting of dried stigmas of the saffron crocus, a bulbous plant originating in the East, introduced into Spain by the Arabs, and cultivated in Mediterranean regions. It takes between 70,000 and 80,000 stigmas- which must be picked by hand- to make approximately one pound of saffron.

Saganaki
A Greek appetizer made from kasseri cheese, fried, sprinkled with lemon juice and served with pita bread.

Saignant
Meat underdone.

Saint-Honoré
Traditional French cake consisting of cream puff pastry dipped in caramel, liquor flavored custard and whipped cream.

Salsifi
A root vegetable with a white flesh and a flavor that resembles an oyster.

Saltimbocca
Italian literally meaning "jump mouth", this Roman dish is made of finely sliced veal sprinkled with sage and proscuitto slices that is sautéed in butter and then braised in white wine.

Sashimi
Raw slices of fish served with daikon radish, gingerroot, wasabi and soy sauce.

Sauté
To cook food in a small amount of very hot oil until brown.

Scampi
The Italian term for a type of large prawn.

Sear
To brown meat rapidly with high heat to seal in juices.

Shish Kebab
Pieces of marinated meat and vegetables grilled or broiled on a skewer.

Shoga
The Japanese word for ginger.

Smorgasbord
A Swedish word referring to a wide range of cold or hot hors-d'oeuvre, salads, and various dishes served on a buffet.

Glossary

Sorbet
A type of flavored water ice (fruit and/or syrup and aromatic substances) that does not contain any fat, milk or egg yolks .

Soufflé
A baked dish made with egg whites beaten and thickened with egg yolk.

Souvlaki
A Greek specialty, skewers of marinated lamb.

Sousing
Pickling food in brine or vinegar.

Spanakopita
Greek phyllo-dough crusts filled with spinach, onions and feta cheese.

Spumoni
Flavored and colored ice cream made with whipped cream/egg.

Strudel
Pastry dough made into thin leaves and filled with various mixtures, then rolled and baked.

Sundae
A dessert originating in the United States, consisting of ice cream and fruit coated with jam or syrup. Originally, it was served for the family meal on Sundays: at the end of the 19th century, North America was fairly puritanical and the consumption of sweets was still frowned upon. But the fashion for ice cream, encouraged by the first manually operated ice cream freezers, was increasing and gradually the nickname "Sunday" was given to the traditional ice which could be served on Sundays without offending God.

Sushi
Rice molded and topped with raw fish.

Table d'hôte
Meal at a fixed price, usually three or more courses.

Tahiti
A thick paste made of ground sesame seed, used in Middle Eastern cooking.

Tamarind
The pod or fruit of a large tropical tree native to India. When fresh, its pulp is white, crisp and has a sweet/sour flavor. When dried, it turns brown and very sour.

Tapenade
From the south of France, this thick paste is made from olives, anchovies, capers, olive oil and seasonings and used as a condiment or as a spread.

Tempura
A Japanese specialty dish of small pieces of fish, poultry or vegetables that have been dipped into a batter and then fried.

Terrine
Meat, fowl and/or vegetables baked in a dish called a "terrine" and served cold.

Timbale
A hot pie filled with meats or vegetables, cooked in a dish called a timbale; cup shaped earthenware or metal mold.

Tobikko
Refers to flying fish roe. There are at least four different tobikko: orange (natural color), black (colored with squid ink), wasabi (flavored with Japanese horseradish-bright green color) and red (red colorant added). These various colored tobikko are used as a garnish for canapés, fish and shellfish dishes.

Tofu
Bean curd.

Tomatillo
A relative of the tomato, this fruit is used when still green and is covered with a brown paper like husk.

Tournedo
A thick cut of beef from the tenderloin, usually wrapped in pork fat or bacon prior to grilling and broiling.

Truffle
A subterranean fungus which lives in symbiosis with certain trees, mainly the oak, but also the chestnut, hazel and beech. A highly esteemed food item, the truffle can have various sizes and is divided in two main groups: winter black truffles or white truffles (most expensive and most intense in flavor).

Tuile
A crisp cookie topped with crushed almonds and rounded in shape (hence its name, meaning roof tile in French).

Turmeric
A spice obtained from the dried and powdered rhizome of an Indian plant. In the Middle Ages its color made it a substitute for saffron.

Velouté
White sauce made with chicken, veal or fish stock, very creamy.

Verjus
An acidic, sour liquid made from unripe fruit, primarily grapes, and used to flavor sauces.

Vichyssoise
Potato and leek soup, creamy and served cold.

Vol-au-vent
A puff pastry shell that is filled traditionally with chicken, fish, shellfish, meat or vegetables in a rich creamy sauce.

Wasabi
This green condiment is the Japanese version of horseradish and has a sharp and pungent flavor.

Won Ton
Bite-size pockets of paper thin dough filled with a mixture of meat, seafood and/or vegetables.

Yakitori
Chicken marinated in soy sauce, ginger and sake, skewered and broiled.

Yokan
A Japanese cake made with agar, adzuki beans and sugar.

Zabaglione
A rich dessert made of egg yolk, Marsala wine and sugar, usually served warm as a sauce for a cake, pastry, fruit or ice cream.

Zuppa Inglese
Meaning "English soup" in Italian, this dessert consists of layers of sponge cake moistened with rum, and alternate layers of whipped cream and candied fruits or almonds.

Aroma
The fragrance the wine acquires from the grapes themselves and from the fermentation process.

Barbera
A red grape grown in Piedmont, Italy.

Beaujolais
Red Burgandy wine from the Beaujolais region, with a light and fruity taste.

Blanc de Blancs
White wine made solely from white grapes.

Blanc de Noirs
White wine made solely from black (i.e. red) grapes.

Blush Wine
The term used to describe the pale rose-colored wines made from red grape varieties including Zinfandel, Cabernet Sauvignon, or Pinot Noir.

Body
The weight of the wine in the mouth, usually manifested by a richness, fullness or viscosity.

Bouquet
The fragrance or scent of a wine that develops from the aging process. It tastes and smells more pronounced in a bottle of mature wine.

Cabernet Franc
Less intense in color and in flavor than Cabernet Sauvignon, this red grape grows in cooler climates and ripens early.

Cabernet Sauvignon
A red grape which brings us several of the great wines of Bordeaux, said to be the most rewarding grape for wine in the world.

Chablis
A wine that is made from Chardonnay grapes.

Chardonnay
A grape used in the making of all Chardonnay wines, very exclusive grapes.

Chenin Blanc
A white grape common to California and the Loire Valley in France.

Chianti
A fine red wine from Italy.

Demi-sec
A French term meaning "half dry", used to describe wine that is sweet (up to 5% sugar).

Fermentation
The making of wine from grapes.

Grenache
A red grape grown in warmer climates (southern Rhone Region) and also used for rosés and blushes.

Macon Blanc
A simple white wine (French).

Malvasie
An Italian white grape.

Merlot
A red grape grown in the Bordeaux region, California, and the Pacific Northwest.

Mousseux (vin)
A French sparkling wine produced outside of the Champagne region.

Muscadet
A dry light wine.

Nebbiolo
A red grape used in Italy's Barolo and Barbaresco wines.

Palomino
The main grape used in the making of Sherry.

Pinot Blanc
A white grape from the Alsace region of France.

Pinot Gris
A white grape grown in Italy and California.

Pinot Meunier
A red grape from the Champagne region in France.

Pinot Noir
A red grape producing some of the most renowned wines in Burgundy.

Riesling
A white wine grape grown in Alsace, in Germany and in California.

Rippling
The annual turning of the bottles in the process of Champagne making, allowing the sediment to finally settle in the neck.

Sanglovese
A red grape used for Italy's Chianti.

Sauvignon Blanc
A white grape from the Loire Valley.

Semillon
A white grape found mostly in the Bordeaux region, used to produce dessert wines because of its susceptibility to Noble Rot.

Sherry
A fortified wine originally produced in Andalucia, Spain. These wines are obtained by topping off older wines with newer ones and by a complex aging process in barrels.

Spumante
A sparkling Italian wine.

Veneto
A large red and white wine producing region of Italy.

Vintage
The year the grapes were picked and the wine was produced.

Viognier
A white grape from the Rhone Valley region in France.

Zinfandel
A red grape grown exclusively in California.

Please send me my own cuisine publication.

Pricing on large quantities, call Feeding Frenzy, Inc. at (843) 851-1380

Ship To

Name ______________________________

Address ______________________ Apt # ________

City ______________ State ________ Zip ________

Pricing

☐	**New Orleans**	_____ books @ $7.95	$ __________
☐	**Las Vegas**	_____ books @ $6.95	$ __________
☐	**Charleston**	_____ books @ $7.95	$ __________
☐	**Phoenix**	_____ books @ $8.95	$ __________

Shipping & Handling *$4.00*

Total __________

You may charge your purchase on your American Express Card.

Name on Account ______________________________

Card Number ______________________________

Expiration Date ______________________________

Payment

Make checks and money orders payable to Feeding Frenzy, Inc.

Feeding Frenzy, Inc.
320 Club View Rd.
Summerville, SC 29485

Please send me my own cuisine publication.

Pricing on large quantities, call Feeding Frenzy, Inc. at (843) 851-1380

Ship To

Name ______________________________

Address ______________________ Apt # ________

City ______________ State ________ Zip ________

Pricing

☐	**New Orleans**	_____ books @ $7.95	$ __________
☐	**Las Vegas**	_____ books @ $6.95	$ __________
☐	**Charleston**	_____ books @ $7.95	$ __________
☐	**Phoenix**	_____ books @ $8.95	$ __________

Shipping & Handling *$4.00*

Total __________

You may charge your purchase on your American Express Card.

Name on Account ______________________________

Card Number ______________________________

Expiration Date ______________________________

Payment

Make checks and money orders payable to Feeding Frenzy, Inc.

Feeding Frenzy, Inc.
320 Club View Rd.
Summerville, SC 29485

CHARLESTON RIVERDOGS

2000 BASEBALL SEASON

"HOST OF THE 2000 SAL ALL-STAR GAME"

RIVERDOGS

CALL 577-DOGS FOR TICKETS

APRIL

SUN	MON	TUE	WED	THU	FRI	SAT
						1
2	3	4	5	6 CAP	7 CAP	8 CAP
9 CAP	10 7:05 AUG	11 7:05 AUG	12 TBA AUG	13 7:05 AUG	14 7:05 CLB	15 7:05 CLB
16 2:05 CLB	17 7:05 CLB	18 7:00 ASH	19 7:00 ASH	20 7:00 ASH	21 7:00 ASH	22 DEL
23 DEL	24 DEL	25 DEL	26 OFF	27 7:05 ASH	28 7:05 ASH	29 7:05 ASH
30 2:05 ASH						

MAY

SUN	MON	TUE	WED	THU	FRI	SAT
	1 7:05 HAG	2 TBA HAG	3 TBA HAG	4 7:05 HAG	5 6:35 PDT	6 6:35 PDT
7 2:05 PDT	8 12:05 PDT	9 7:05 MAC	10 11:00 MAC	11 7:05 MAC	12 7:05 MAC	13 HIK
14 HIK	15 HIK	16 HIK	17 7:00 MAC	18 7:00 MAC	19 7:00 MAC	20 7:00 MAC
21 OFF	22 7:05 CFC	23 7:05 CFC	24 7:05 CFC	25 7:05 CFC	26 CLB	27 CLB
28 CLB	29 CLB	30 7:05 GRE	31 7:05 GRE			

JUNE

SUN	MON	TUE	WED	THU	FRI	SAT
				1 7:05 GRE	2 7:05 GRE	3 7:05 SAV
4 5:05 SAV	5 SAV	6 7:05 CAP	7 7:05 CAP	8 7:05 CAP	9 7:05 CAP	10 7:15 CWV
11 2:15 CWV	12 7:15 CWV	13 7:15 CWV	14 OFF	15 7:05 SAV	16 7:05 SAV	17 2:00 SAV
18 2:05 SAV	19 OFF	20 ALL-STAR GAME	21 OFF	22 7:05 HAG	23 7:05 HAG	24 7:05 HAG
25 2:05 HAG	26 7:00 GRE	27 7:00 GRE	28 7:00 GRE	29 7:00 GRE	30 7:05 MAC	

JULY

SUN	MON	TUE	WED	THU	FRI	SAT
						1 6:05 MAC
2 5:05 MAC	3 7:15 SAV	4 7:15 SAV	5 7:15 SAV	6 7:15 SAV	7 7:05 DEL	8 7:05 DEL
9 5:05 DEL	10 7:05 DEL	11 OFF	12 7:05 SAV	13 7:05 SAV	14 7:05 AUG	15 7:05 AUG
16 5:05 AUG	17 12:00 AUG	18 CAP	19 CAP	20 CAP	21 CAP	22 CLB
23 CLB	24 CLB	25 5:05 CLB	26 OFF	27 7:05 HIK	28 7:05 HIK	29 7:05 HIK
30 5:05 HIK	31 AUG					

AUGUST

SUN	MON	TUE	WED	THU	FRI	SAT
		1 AUG	2 AUG	3 AUG	4 7:05 PDT	5 7:05 PDT
6 5:05 PDT	7 7:05 PDT	8 CFC	9 CFC	10 CFC	11 CFC	12 7:05 SAV
13 5:05 SAV	14 OFF	15 5:05 CWV	16 5:05 CWV	17 5:05 CWV	18 5:05 CWV	19 5:05 CAP
20 5:05 CAP	21 5:05 CAP	22 5:05 CAP	23 OFF	24 ASH	25 ASH	26 ASH
27 ASH	28 5:05 CLB	29 5:05 CLB	30 5:05 CLB	31 5:05 CLB		

SEPTEMBER

SUN	MON	TUE	WED	THU	FRI	SAT
					1 7:00 MAC	2 7:00 MAC
3 2:00 MAC	4 7:00 MAC	5	6	7	8	9
10	11	12	13	14	15	16
17	18	19	20	21	22	23
24	25	26	27	28	29	30

HOME

AWAY

ALL-STAR GAME

South Atlantic League

ASH	Asheville	Gre	Greensboro
AUG	Augusta	HAG	Hagerstown
CAP	Capital City	HIK	Hickory
CLB	Columbus	MAC	Macon
CWV	Charleston, WV	PDT	Piedmont
DEL	Delmarva	SAV	Savannah
CFC	Cape Fear		

The Post and Courier
InfoLine